The Sultan's Spymaster

Peera Dewjee of Z

D1578875

By
JUDY ALDRICK

Published by Old Africa Books
A division of Kifaru Educational and Editorial Consultants LTD
PO Box 2338, Naivasha, 20117, Kenya

A ny one visiting Sir John Kirk at home at the British Consulate will hardly have set foot in the door without remarking the arrival of an Indian gentleman in a suit of white clothes of half Asiatic half European cut with a magnificent gold embroidered turban, a watch chain and a ring and an umbrella. This is Peera Dewjee incorrectly known on board the mail steamers as 'The Prime Minister of Zanzibar' he is really an astute Indian trader who by his capacity for business and exceptional talents as a raconteur has known how to obtain a very large share of the Sultan's confidence and esteem.

'Sir John Kirk at Home'
from an article in *The Graphic* by HH Johnston, May 1885

Contents

Maps, Illustrations and Plates

Maps
1. Map of the Indian Ocean showing direction of Monsoon Winds
2. A Sketch Map of Zanzibar, based on Captain Charles Guillain's, map of 1846: Zanzibar a Plan for the historic Stone Town, The Aga Khan Trust for Culture (1996) p 16
3. Twentieth Century Map of Zanzibar Town: from G H Shelswell-White: *A Guide book to Zanzibar*, Government Printer, Zanzibar, 1939

Illustrations within the Text
1. Title page, Peera Dewjee with signature
2. A View of Zanzibar, c.1860: Cambridge University Library
3. 'The Very Intelligent Oriental': Cambridge University Library
4. 'Banyan Contemplating his Account-book': John Hanning Speke, *Journal of the discovery of the source of the Nile*, 1863, p 9
5. 'Reception at the Sultan's Court' engraving from a watercolour: *Illustrated London News*, March 9, 1889
6. The British Agency, Zanzibar: *Illustrated London News*, June 1, 1872
7. The Effects of the Hurricane of 1872, *Illustrated London News*, June 1, 1872
8. Sultan Barghash: Cambridge University Library
9. The Sultan in the Lift: *Illustrated London News*, July 17, 1875
10. The Sultan at Ascot: *Illustrated London News*, June 19, 1875
11. Lady Frere's Garden Party: *Illustrated London News*, June 19, 1875
12. Cartoon 'More Slaveries than One': *Punch*, June 26, 1875
13. The Sultan's ship, *Glasgow*
14. German Battlecruiser, *Gneisenau*
15. Sultan Khalifa
16. Abdulhussein Peera in the Cricket Team: courtesy Brentwood School, Essex

17. Pottery marks

18. Advertisement for Abdool Hoossein & Bros & Co: Zanzibar Gazette, October 27, 1897

Plates

1. Khojas (Bombay): Johnson, William (1863) The Oriental Races & Tribes, Residents and Visitors of Bombay (vol 1) plate 24, India Office Select Materials, British Library

2. Portrait of Sir Charles Napier: National Portrait Gallery, London

3. View of the Waterfront of Zanzibar: University of Cambridge

4. Princess Salme in Arab dress

5. Sir Bartle Frere: National Portrait Gallery, London

6. Major Charles Bean Euan-Smith: Royal Collection Trust, Her Majesty Queen Elizabeth II, 2014

7. Sir John Kirk: National Library of Scotland

8. Carte de Visite for Seyyid Barghash: the Sultan of Zanzibar, National Portrait Gallery London.

9. Staff of the British Agency, Dr Kirk, Mrs Kirk and daughter with Tharia Topan: National Library of Scotland

10. Group Portrait of Sultan Barghash and Entourage: National Library of Scotland,

11. Interior of the British Agency: 1884: National Library of Scotland

12. View of the Waterfront showing the clock tower and the Beit al-Ajaib under construction: image courtesy of the Melville J Herskovits Library of African Studies, Winterton Collection, Northwestern University

13. View of the Beit al Hukm with the Sultan's troops parading in the palace square: image courtesy of the Melville J Herskovits Library of African Studies, Winterton Collection, Northwestern University

14. View of the Beit al-Ajaib pre-1896, Melville J Herskovits Library of African Studies, Winterton Collection, Northwestern University

15. Sultan Ali: private collection

16. Sir William MacKinnon: National Portrait Gallery London

17. The Sultan's Customs officers, Mombasa, c.1895: private collection

18. The Custom House Door in Zanzibar: private collection
19. Slave Porters carrying package: image courtesy of the Melville J Herskovits Library of African Studies, Winterton Collection, Northwestern University
20. Busy Zanzibar Beachfront: image courtesy of the Melville J Herskovits Library of African Studies, Winterton Collection, Northwestern University
21. View of Celebratory Arch with family of Peera Dewjee in the foreground 1887: image courtesy of the Melville J Herskovits Library of African Studies, Winterton Collection, Northwestern University
22. Group portrait of Sultan Hamed, Arthur Hardinge and General Mathews, taken in 1895
23. Destruction of the Sultan's palace in 1896: image courtesy of the Melville J Herskovits Library of African Studies, Winterton Collection, Northwestern University
24. Brilliant Star of Zanzibar, medal awarded to Peera Dewjee: Courtesy of Nurdin Vasenji Jiwa
25. Sultan Hamoud disembarking from the Royal Barge: National Archives, Kew
26. Group of Prominent Citizens of Zanzibar: Zanzibar Archives
27. 1897 Diamond Jubilee Celebrations: The Marquee in Victoria Gardens: National Archives, Kew
28. Garden Party in the Victoria Gardens: image courtesy of the Melville J Herskovits Library of African Studies, Winterton Collection, Northwestern University
29. Portrait of Sewa Haji Paroo: private collection
30. Sultan Hamoud: Zanzibar Archives
31. Women of Zanzibar with water pots: courtesy of the Melville J Herskovits Library of African Studies, Winterton Collection, Northwestern University
32. African Woman, wearing turban and kanga taken in Zanzibar: image courtesy of the Melville J Herskovits Library of African Studies, Winterton Collection, Northwestern University
33. Lamu interior with plates taken in 1884: National Library of Scotland

34. Plate imported by Peera Dewjee, which now hangs on the wall in the Zanzibar Serena Hotel: courtesy Dewjee family
35. Zanzibar Plate: private collection
36. Aga Khan III, HH Sir Sultan Mohammed Shah: National Portrait Gallery, London
37. View of the new British Residency overlooking Victoria Gardens: courtesy of the Melville J Herskovits Library of African Studies, Winterton Collection, Northwestern University

Acknowledgements

Writing this book has been a labour of love. Zanzibar and the role of the Indian merchants in the development of 19th century East Africa are both subjects which interest me greatly and the opportunity to combine the two has been a rare privilege. For this my chief gratitude goes to Hussein and Audrey Dewjee who first suggested I write about their ancestor Peera Dewjee, an influential but forgotten figure in the era of the Sultans. Audrey's extraordinary and detailed preliminary research gave me a base from which to work, while my own further researches filled out the narrative of the story. And what an astonishing and surprising story it turned out to be!

There are many debts to acknowledge. I would particularly like to thank Vazir Amirali H Rashid, now aged over ninety and living in Canada, great-nephew of Peera Dewjee, for his recollections of the family; also Mumtaz Akberali, for her memories of her grandmother, Peera Dewjee's only daughter. Thank you to Professor Abdul Sheriff for taking me on a walk through Zanzibar Stone Town, showing me the area where the Indian merchants lived and the houses once owned by Dewjee family members. A special note of thanks goes to Dr Harshad Topiwala, who alerted me to Dr Christie's book and letters, and also to Alastair Hazel, whose book *The Last Slave Market*, gave insight into Sir John Kirk's correspondence and was to prove a valuable resource. I am grateful to Kevin Patience for his detailed knowledge of East African medals, ships and railways.

Thank you to the librarians of the British Library, Cambridge University Library, London University's School of Oriental Studies, the National Library of Scotland, The Royal Geographical Society, Manchester University Library, Manchester Museum of Science and Industry, the Zanzibar Archives, Durham University Library and the National Archives in Kew for their unstinting help with accessing information; also thanks go to the Headmaster's Secretary and Archivist of Brentwood School Essex. The Boston Spa branch of the British Library with its holdings of newspapers and periodicals deserves a special mention as a most helpful and fruitful research venue.

Thank you also to all those who have helped with translations from German and French; Dr Erich Meffert, David Paisey, Margaret Marks, Sister Evelyn Thompson and Marie-Paule Nicholson.

I am grateful to my husband Clive, for his patience and support and thank everyone who has given answers to specific questions and helped in various ways; Dr S A Hull, Nuruddeen Somji, Rozina Visram, Shariffa Keshavji, Abdulrazak Fazal, Sherali Champsi, Torrence Royer, Tim Jeal and Michael Sweeney. This list appears in no particular order and I have tried to acknowledge you all both here and in footnotes, where appropriate, to show my sincere appreciation and I apologise in advance for any inadvertent omissions.

I doubt this biography could have seen the light of day without the convenience of the internet, which has made worldwide communication so much quicker and easier. Countless numbers of emails have winged their way backwards and forwards over the two years I have spent writing and researching this book. Audrey Dewjee and I have corresponded almost daily sending pictures, snippets of information and new ideas on how to progress with the research. Information can now appear at the press of a key. Rare books, university theses and manuscripts can be downloaded, even translated, and read within the comfort of one's home, a priceless boon to the would-be researcher and writer.

In writing these acknowledgements I cannot fail to mention my late friend and colleague Cynthia Salvadori, who first inspired my interest in the Indian communities of East Africa and led me to realise how important and integral they are to the history of the region. Her research work recording family histories and describing the different communities lies behind much of the current interest in re-examining the Indian contribution to East Africa and recovering memories of pioneering settlers, before they are lost.

I would like to thank Shel Arensen chief editor of Old Africa books for his agreement once more to act as my publisher and Blake Arensen for the layout and design. Finally to you the reader I hope you will enjoy a new take on an old subject and agree that this is a life lived in Africa that needs to be told.

Judy Aldrick
Kent, 2015

Foreword

by Audrey Dewjee

*A people without the knowledge of their past history,
origin and culture is like a tree without roots.*

- Marcus Garvey

Imet my husband in the early months of 1968 and learned he had
been born in Zanzibar. Though at first we were just friends and
work colleagues, by the time we had agreed to marry, I had found out
all he knew about his ancestors – which was very little.

Of course he knew the names of his parents, grandfather and
great grandfather. According to traditional Muslim naming patterns,
there is no regular surname – a person's given name is followed by the
given name of his father and these two names are used for everyday
purposes. However, a person's full name lists as many ancestors' names
as can be remembered, thus Hussein's passport, when I first met him,
was made out for 'Hussein Gulamali Abdulrasul Peera, alias Hussein
Gulamali Abdulrasul Peera Dewjee,' and his status before he got his
naturalisation certificate was a 'British Protected Person of Kutch.'

Hussein's great grandfather was known as Peera Dewjee and his
grandfather as Abdulrasul Peera. Western influences and, no doubt,
British bureaucracy in Zanzibar resulted in changes to this pattern,
and subsequently this caused a good deal of confusion. Hussein's
father would have been known at some point as Gulamali Abdulrasul,
or Gulamali Abdulrasul Peera. When 'Dewjee' became accepted as the
family's official surname isn't remembered with certainty, but by the
time they left Africa, two of Gulamali's children were using Dewjee/
Dewji and a third used Peera.

Hussein told me four snippets of information about Peera Dewjee:
- that he was the 'right-hand-man' of Seyyid Barghash

- that he was known as 'the Prime Minister of Zanzibar'
- that he came to London with the Sultan to attend a coronation and that a large, thick book about Zanzibar, printed in English, contained details about him.

These 'facts' were all we had to go on in our search for Peera's story, and we had no idea whether or not they were true. Hussein had tried to bring the book with him to England, but had to leave it behind because he would have had to pay an excess baggage charge for it. Elderly friends and relatives added the information that Peera was a *jassus* – a spy, and that he was a very devout Ismaili, personally pulling the rickshaw of HH Sir Sultan Mohammed Shah, Aga Khan III, when he visited Zanzibar in 1899.

Apart from his brother and three sisters and their children, Hussein knew of few other Dewjee relatives and, in any case, contact with them had been lost. Splits between Ismaili and Ithna'asheri Khojas in the earliest years of the twentieth century had sundered many families apart, so we presumed that many more relatives existed somewhere in the world. Political upheavals and many migrations had further impacted the family structure. It was from this very meagre base that we started to search for more information, shortly after our marriage.

At that time there was no internet to help us and progress was slow. Zanzibar itself was pretty much out of bounds – partly from our lack of funds and partly because the island was not a very enticing holiday destination. The communist-inspired regime which then prevailed resulted in a poor tourist infrastructure in Zanzibar and shortages for the islanders of commodities of all kinds, such as foodstuffs, soap, and other necessities.

The first breakthrough in our search came in the old circular reading room of the British Library, which was then located within the British Museum. I was doing research for an exhibition of British Black History and at the same time looking through the catalogues to see if I could find a copy of the book Hussein had tried to bring to England. For a long time I had no success until I remembered that the British Library catalogue gave dimensions for all books, as well as details of title, author and publisher. I asked Hussein to demonstrate the rough size of the book and, armed with these measurements, I went through the catalogue again. This time I located the book relatively easily. It turned out to be a sort of upmarket trade directory, which gave brief histories of the many firms trading in East Africa in 1908. To my amazement, there, under the heading of Abdool Hoosein Brothers & Co., was a photograph of Peera Dewjee. We were thrilled to see what he looked like as there were very few old pictures in our Dewjee family album. Hussein often described with sadness the photographs they had had at home in Zanzibar showing his parents, himself and his siblings when young, dressed in their best – the boys wearing suits and ties. All had been lost in family migrations from Zanzibar to mainland Tanzania and, later on, to the United Kingdom and Canada.

Our second major breakthrough came on a trip to Paris. We went to see the new Pompidou Centre with its strange architecture. Hussein accompanied me into the Library in my quest for yet more British Black History. I was surprised to find a good proportion of the books on the shelves were in English and on a sudden whim I went to the section on East Africa and was electrified when I saw the title, *A History of the Arab State of Zanzibar*, by Norman R. Bennett. I had never seen this volume in a library or bookshop in England. We turned to the index and there, in black and white, was 'Pira Dewji' (Peera Dewjee's name is spelled by different writers in a huge variety of ways). There were two or three references to Peera in the book and these confirmed that he had indeed been the right-hand-man of Seyyid Barghash.

We are deeply grateful to Professor Bennett for his many informative publications on East Africa in which he makes a number of mentions of Peera, and also for his personal help and encouragement to us, both in the 1980s and in recent years. Once we knew we were on the right track, we started to find other references to Peera in nineteenth century books, just small snippets of information, which we carefully collected together.

In 2004 we visited Zanzibar and we returned for a second visit two years later. While there, we spent a day at the Zanzibar Archives and visited the museums in the Sultan's Palace and House of Wonders noting down everything that might be of relevance. We received help and information from Professor Abdul Sheriff who was then Senior Curator of Zanzibar Museums and also from Sherali Champsi, who had been a playmate of Hussein's when they were children.

The third and greatest breakthrough in our desire to research and record Peera's life story came after the rise of the internet. Online we found details of an article, 'The Painted Plates of Zanzibar,' by Judy Aldrick, in which she mentioned Peera Dewjee and Abdool Hoosein Brothers & Co. We contacted Judy via the Friends of Fort Jesus in Mombasa, an organisation which she helped to found when she lived in Kenya.

Now back in England, Judy invited us to her home so we could look through her archive of East African history and personalities. She also showed us her published books. One was a collaboration with Cynthia Salvadori –*Two Indian Travellers: East Africa, 1902-1905*. Judy had also written *The Fannin Papers*, a biography of Katharine Fannin, an intrepid British woman who crossed Ethiopia on holiday just before the Second World War, spying on the Italians as she went. By the time Hussein and I left Judy's home, we had decided to ask her if she would consider writing a biography of Peera and his times in Zanzibar. A year later we were overjoyed when she said 'Yes.'

The result is the book in your hands. We hope it adds to the record of history of Zanzibar, which was such an incredibly important place in the mid- to late-nineteenth century, an importance which few would realise who visit the island on holiday today. Even though Zanzibar is still remembered for the slave trade, the rest of its trading history, especially that conducted by Zanzibaris of Indian ancestry, is largely being lost. The island's heritage today is a blend of all who played a part in its amazing rise and tragic fall – Arab, Indian, American, European and African.

Research on the internet led to another bonus for us – the discovery of Peera's father's name – Dewjee Parpia. It was Dewjee Parpia who brought the family to Zanzibar somewhere around 1850. Internet research and contacts helped us find more relatives and allowed us to build up a much larger family tree. Descendants of Peera Dewjee – a number of them the children of inter-racial marriages – now live in many parts of the world including Canada, England, Kenya, Pakistan, Tanzania and the USA.

Although he may have been surprised, I am sure Peera would have approved of this dispersal of his genes. Having migrated as a child from his birthplace in India and having travelled a great deal during his life, as well as making his career in the heady world of international relations amidst a great mix of cultures and nationalities, he would, I think, be happy at his influence in the world.

Our family owes an immense debt of gratitude to Judy Aldrick for doing something we were unable to do. She has taken snippets of information and moulded them with a great deal of additional research into a coherent and lively narrative, which has brought Peera Dewjee back to life. We trust this book will not only connect Peera's descendants with the founders of their family, but that it will also be of value to all who have their 'roots' in the beautiful island of Zanzibar.

Author's Preface

On April 9, 1889, an Indian trader was put on board a ship of the British India Steam Navigation line in Zanzibar harbour and deported to Bombay. This man was Peera Dewjee, the sultan's prime minister and most trusted adviser. He was deported because he was seriously impeding British intentions to take over the Arab State of Zanzibar.

The life of Peera Dewjee (1841-1904) covers the period when European nations begin to take an interest in East Africa, first to trade and then to colonise. It is a time of momentous change as the traditional Arab domination of the region crumbles away before the onslaught from Europe. Foreign interference in Zanzibar increases with the opening of the Suez Canal and the arrival of the telegraph, which dramatically improves communications. Westernisation, bringing modern technology and Christianity in its wake, sweeps through the region, an unstoppable force, challenging old Arab ways and Islam itself. Slavery is abolished, steamships replace dhows, and muskets fall silent before the Maxim gun. As an adviser to the sultans, Peera Dewjee plays an important role in the history of Zanzibar. He sits at the centre of events as the social and geo-political map of East Africa is radically redrawn.

He comes into the spotlight in the 1880s just when the scramble for Africa, or the steeplechase as the Europeans like to call it, gets off the starting blocks. It is a far from edifying period, when old friends and allies are discarded, promises broken and weaknesses exploited. The Sultan of Zanzibar's East African territories are broken up and parcelled out amongst the European powers. He is helpless. In a few short years the Sultanate of Zanzibar is destroyed, the post of sultan remaining, in name only, a face-saving exercise for British convenience.

History, so they say, is written by the winning side and that is certainly the case in Zanzibar. The European invaders claimed the moral high ground and painted the Arabs as lazy and immoral, slave traders who were not fit to rule, while their Indian friends were no better; they were portrayed as mean and greedy only interested in personal gain. The Europeans were doing the world a favour, by stamping out slavery, and bringing the benefits of Christianity and Westernization to the heathens in Africa, and those back home believed what they were told. But on the ground reality was different as the European colonisers bulldozed their way into Africa destroying all opposition with their weaponry and superior technology, showing themselves as ruthless as the Arab slavers and their Indian financiers they supplanted.

The Indian merchants of Zanzibar could only stand and watch in dismay from the side lines as their formerly powerful friends the Arabs were brought low and their sources of revenue removed. Their status as 'British protected persons' made the Indian position particularly awkward. Most kept their heads down and concentrated on reorganising their business models, avoiding politics and trouble as a new world order emerged

This biography tells the extraordinary story of one Indian merchant, Peera Dewjee, who lived in Zanzibar and worked for the sultans. It records a period of history when the Indians of East Africa were at their most powerful and influential and helped shape the modern Africa of today. Foremost among them were the Khojas from Kutch, followers of the Aga Khan, who settled in large numbers from the early nineteenth century. Their talents and dedicated business ethic lay behind much of the success of Zanzibar as it quickly became the commercial hub of East Africa.

In this book I trace the life of Peera Dewjee from humble lamp cleaner, to palace messenger, spy, chief steward, ambassador and adviser to the sultans, his downfall and banishment, then return and rise again. He emerges from the shadows to provide a connecting thread throughout the dramatic twists and turns of nineteenth century Zanzibar and demonstrates the central part the Indian traders had to play, not only in the economic advance of the region, but also later in the ending of slavery and in facilitating European colonisation. Peera's irrepressible, intelligent and determined character shines through the fog of history and portrays a man doing his best to adapt to ever-changing circumstances and ensure a future both for Zanzibar and his family in challenging times.

Chapter One

Early life of Peera Dewjee

Very little is known for certain about the early life of Peera Dewjee, except that he was born in 1841 and came from Kera, a farming village in central Kutch. Nowadays Kutch forms a part of Gujarat, the large northwestern province of India, but when Peera was born a Maharao ruled the princely state of Kutch from his capital at Bhuj. Kera lies to the south of Bhuj not far from the old highway, which connected Bhuj to the main seaport at Mandvi. Peera was born during the reign of Rao Desalji Bharmalji II, known as Daishalji. He had been placed on the throne in 1819, at the age of three by the British, who ruled Kutch in all but name. The former Maratha fort at Bhuj was garrisoned by British soldiers, while the port of Mandvi, which in earlier days had a fleet of 400 vessels trading with East Africa and the Persian Gulf, was much diminished and the cloth and edible oil trade in the doldrums. But the young Rao, under the steadying hand of the British, proved to be a progressive leader and by 1840 Kutch's economic situation had stabilised and trade from Mandvi to Zanzibar improved.

Caste and religion defined life in India in those days. Peera Dewjee was a Nizari Ismaili by religion. Around the end of the fourteenth century, the great Nizari Ismaili missionary, Pir Sadruddin, had travelled from Persia (present-day Iran) to India where he converted many Hindus to Islam. Taking a Hindu name, Sahadev, he adapted existing Hindu beliefs in order to further his conversion aims. His Indian converts called themselves Khojas and organised themselves into a close-knit community. Kera, Peera's ancestral home, was an Ismaili centre. It had been the base of an important female Ismaili missionary, called Begum Sayeda, who lived from 1785-1866. She helped popularise the Nizari Ismaili branch of Islam in Kera by including many of the Indian/Hindu customs and rituals. This made the Muslim religion more attractive to the inhabitants, especially the women, and many more converted in the early nineteenth century. According to a British report of 1818, the more recent converts from Kutch were mainly 'cultivators,' peasant farmers from the rural areas. But the earliest Ismaili converts in India, dating back to the time of Pir Sadruddin, had been Lohanas coming from the merchant, *banyan*, Hindu caste.[1]

Both merchants and agriculturists were low down in the pecking order of the Hindu caste system. The priestly Brahmin families came at the top, followed by the warriors, the Kshatriyas. Nineteenth century Hindu society was rigidly stratified and bound by ancient customs, traditions, rules and restrictions based on caste. For instance, a high caste Hindu was not supposed to travel outside of India and low caste Hindus were not expected to read and write; learning was reserved for the priestly Brahmin caste. Becoming a Muslim, in theory, meant caste no longer applied, but old habits die hard and the converted Khojas did not discard their Hindu way of life entirely. Many Kutchi converts kept their Hindu names and even passed themselves off as Hindus when a tricky situation demanded it. The Ismaili practise of concealment, known as *takkiya, (taqiya)* allowed them to do this, as it protected them from persecution, and this gave rise to a reputation for secrecy and deception.

The Khojas followed the Shia branch of Islam, but they differed from other Shias in that they acknowledged an Ismaili Imam, later known as the Aga Khan, as their supreme spiritual leader. The Aga Khan, who first took this title in 1818, claimed direct hereditary descent from the prophet Mohammed. He traced his descent through Ali, who married the Prophet Mohammed's daughter Fatima, and after the seventh Imam, when there was a split in the line, to Ismail, and then when another dispute came in the line of inheritance, through Nizar – hence the name Nizari Ismaili.

Family tradition relates that Peera's grandfather, Parpia, was a *Rais* – an official messenger who delivered the tithe or *zacat* on behalf of the community. The coin or treasure was carried in special leather bags called *jowlies* and transporting it safely to Persia was an important and dangerous task. Parpia is said to have taken the offerings from Kera to the 45th Ismaili Imam when he lived at Yazd in Southern Persia. This Imam was Shah Khalil Allah, who died in 1817, so the journey must have taken place before that date. To this day devout Ismailis give a percentage of their earnings to the Aga Khan, which goes into a central fund for the Ismaili community, but in the early days the tithe went straight to the Imam who could spend it as he wished. It was a voluntary offering made out of reverence for their spiritual leader, but though not compulsory, a donation of some sort was expected on a yearly basis. Famously, when Bombay[2] failed to remit tithe in 1829, the Aga Khan sent his formidable grandmother to demand it.

Parpia's journey to Yazd was a perilous and risky undertaking. Long distance travel in India was slow and difficult at the best of times, but the Maratha wars were in full swing and Kutch swarmed with bands of armed marauders, looting and laying waste to land and property. The unrest affected the economy badly and the inhabitants of Kera suffered, but still the loyal Khoja community of Kera sent their offerings. In recognition for his services Parpia was given the honorific title of *Daras*.[3]

According to family memory, Peera's father, Dewjee Parpia, also travelled to Persia, possibly on pilgrimage. Khojas commonly made pilgrimages to Persia to pay homage to the Aga Khan. Bartle Frere describes a pilgrimage made in 1836-7 to Kerman from Bombay, which may have been similar to the one the Parpias made from Kutch. Entire families travelled together in a party of about 100 and sailed first to Bandar Abbas and then joined up with more pilgrims to walk in a caravan for 21 days across the mountains to reach Kerman. On arrival, the group now totalling more than 500 persons, lodged at the expense of the Aga Khan and stayed for about four weeks, during which time, having first made their offerings, they were admitted ten or twelve times to the presence of the Imam where they 'beheld his face [and] kissed his hand.' Bartle Frere was surprised that these ordinary traders and shopkeepers, not rich folk, travelled so far to see their religious leader.[4] The fact that Peera's ancestors went on this type of pilgrimage shows the family had converted relatively early and they were well respected in the community.

By a quirk of fate the leader of the Ismailis came to live amongst his followers in India and the formerly obscure and small community of Khoja Muslims grew in numbers and consequence as a result. Hassan Ali Shah Mahallati, (1804-1881) the 46th Ismaili Imam, who took the title Aga Khan I after the death of his father, was Governor of Kerman in southern Persia until 1840, when a quarrel with the ruler of Persia caused him to flee the country. He took refuge first in Kandahar in Afghanistan, from where he sent a letter to the British Envoy at Kabul and offered his services. Britain was involved in the first disastrous Anglo-Afghan war and welcomed his help. The Aga Khan with his 300 horsemen joined the British army. They proved a useful addition and held the rearguard when the British retreated from Afghanistan in 1842.

The Aga Khan followed the British forces in their retreat. Sir Charles Napier, appointed Major General in command of the Indian army in 1842, gave the Aga Khan a letter of recommendation and asked the Aga Khan to help in quelling an insurrection of Muslim rulers in Sindh. The Aga Khan with his cavalry fought under the command of General Napier in the battles of Miani and Dubba in 1843, after which Sindh was annexed to the British-ruled territories in India. The Aga Khan's comradeship in arms with the British Army cemented the ties of friendship.

General Napier valued his support and in a letter to Lord Ellenborough, the Governor General of India, praised him as a clever brave man. [5]

After leaving the employ of the British Army, the Aga Khan travelled to Kutch via the port of Karachi in 1844 and the Rao of Kutch feted him at Mandvi and took him to Bhuj and gave him a state bungalow to live in. But in 1845 he moved on and travelled to Surat and then to Bombay, where he was well received by the whole

Khoja population there. Under the protection of and with the aid of the British, Aga Khan I established his religious authority over the small Muslim Khoja community of converted Hindus living on the west coast of India.

During the 1840s a series of severe famines devastated Kutch, leaving it like a dust bowl, and many of the inhabitants starved and died. Kera, a centre for rice and cotton cultivation, was affected badly. In 1845 General Napier, now Governor of Sindh Province and the Aga Khan's friend, gave special permission for Khoja refugees to settle in Sindh. About 10,000 Khojas emigrated from Kutch at that time and many settled in the coastal towns, starting new businesses and finding alternative occupations.

It is likely Peera's family left Kutch during the famine years and possibly followed the Aga Khan to Bombay, where they had relatives. There are a number of Parpias, both Hindu and Khoja, listed as general merchants in the Bombay handbooks dating back to the 1850s. There was also a small community of Khoja Muslims, who had been settled there since the middle of the eighteenth century. The Bombay *jamat* was first established in 1740. A group of wealthy merchants called *shetias* controlled this Khoja community. The Khoja community of Bombay expanded greatly during the first half of the nineteenth century and by 1860 was estimated at around 6,000 persons.[6] They lived together in a Khoja quarter or *moholla* in the town, just north of the Fort behind the docks in the area called Masjid Bunder.[7]

By the 1850s some of the Khojas from the community who had been living in Bombay before the arrival of the Aga Khan began to feel dissatisfied about his presence amongst them. They revered him still, but opposed his presence in the community because he demanded payments and sought to control all affairs. They formed a separate group called the 'reform party' and matters came to a head in 1866 when they filed a lawsuit against the Aga Khan. They questioned his claim to be a god or *Pir* or saint. They said it was just a title used by an ambitious person for his own purposes, and accused him of wanting to control the *jamat* and the money of the community for his own benefit.

The English judge, Sir Joseph Arnould, came down on the side of the Aga Khan and ruled that the Aga Khan had the legal right to call himself Imam, spiritual leader of the Shia Ismaili sect and have control over its affairs and finances. This landmark ruling redefined the Khoja's religious identity and formally recognised the Ismailis as a distinct religious group within Islam. After this court case the Khoja Ismailis began to discard their Hindu names, and move away from their old Hindu and Sunni practices towards more traditional Shia teaching and liturgy. A small group remained outside, continuing with their former beliefs.

Luck always plays a part in life and Peera was born at a particularly fortunate time. Brought out of the rural backwater of Kera at a young age, he spent his formative years during a period in British India when Victorian ideals replaced old ideas and policies. It was a particularly vibrant time when western culture and industrialisation were just beginning to catch on in India. Much of India, at this point, was still ruled by the East India Company, a private chartered company of merchants chiefly interested in profit and trade. But as the Company expanded and took control of more land in India, its resources became overstretched and increasingly the British Government became involved in its administration and direction. The British port of Bombay emerged as the chief emporium for the west coast of India and controlled most of the Indian Ocean trade, superseding the old Gujarati ports of Cambay and Surat. Cambay had silted up in the sixteenth century, while Surat had suffered with the decline of the Mughals. Mandvi, the Maratha port and ship building centre of Kutch, had been resurgent in the eighteenth century, but decades of fierce infighting followed by a British takeover had taken its toll and it was a pale shadow of its former self. Kutch's traditional trade in cotton cloth was hit by punitive export duties and their shipping restricted by British monopoly laws on carriage. Big business centred on Bombay and it became the most populous city in India.

Successive ambitious British governors indulged in major engineering works, building causeways to link the formerly separate islands of the archipelago and had filled in former salt flats for housing and factories. They built railways and grand public buildings and churches, founded schools and sponsored libraries, museums and learned societies and supported religious freedom. Bombay by 1850 was the wealthiest and most forward thinking city in India and challenged the more conservative and senior British administrative capital of Calcutta. Famous British Bombay Governors such as Mountstuart Elphinstone, and Lord Canning set up a legal system and a framework of administration. Bombay grew larger and more prosperous. Its population more than doubled between 1830 and 1870.[8]

According to family tradition, Peera Dewjee was well educated and could speak English and read and write. This was fairly uncommon for the time and is in contrast to his younger brothers, born later in Zanzibar. No evidence survives on where he received his education, but Bombay is the most likely place. The earliest school to give Indians an English education was the famous Elphinstone College in Bombay. Elphinstone was an elite establishment, but following its foundation many other schools were set up in Bombay along similar lines. Wilson College, opened by an erudite Scottish missionary the Reverend John Wilson in 1832, was another early school, which taught English to all-comers regardless of religion or caste. These schools taught an English curriculum tailored for Indians. English, the language of the rulers, became in great demand as proficiency gave access to good jobs in government as well as the business world. In the handbooks for Bombay in the mid 1800s there are many advertisements for English language schools.

There is no record of which school Peera attended, or how he learnt to speak English and read and write, but the timing of his upbringing was a crucial factor. Although Ismailis today have a keen interest in education, the first two Aga Khans did not encourage education in their followers. In fact, Aga Khan I expressly forbade Ismailis to attend public schools and was strongly opposed to the teaching of English to Khoja children. This discouragement of education in the community was one of the major complaints of the reformist group of the 1850s and they established an English school near Masjid Bunder called the Goculdas Tejpal Anglo Vernacular School, and tried to encourage the attendance of Khoja children.[9] It is possible Peera Dewjee attended classes here. But once the Aga Khan gained overall control of the Ismailis, no schools were set up and no attempts were made to educate the community until much later in the century. Peera was unusual in that he received an education and had the opportunity to develop an inquiring mind and a thirst for knowledge unlike most of his fellow Khojas, who were expected to do no more than keep account of their businesses, enter numbers in ledgers and perhaps sign their name.

One of Peera's Bombay relatives was Nansi Parpia, an uncle, or cousin uncle. He was sympathetic to the reformist movement and was perhaps the guiding influence behind Peera's education. He had a large shop in Medows Street.[10] In the nineteenth century Medows street was the main commercial street in central Bombay, situated just behind the docks and the grand customs house, which dominated the harbour. Besides general merchandise, Nansi Parpia also sold furniture and leather shoes. He had wood working factories at Byculla, just to the north, where the fishermen and local dhows congregated. Nansi Parpia is featured in Johnson's book on the peoples of Bombay, printed in 1863, where he appears in the centre of the photograph on the page entitled Khojas.[11] His shop according to Johnson was much frequented by young British customers and Nansi Parpia was affectionately known to them as 'Old Nancy.' We are told he was exceedingly kind to those young men, who were just starting their careers in India. Presumably he helped them set up in lodgings and gave them generous credit, when they were short of money. These British youngsters were either new employees (factors) of the East India Company, or perhaps young officers in the Army or Navy or possibly representatives for British businesses (*box wallahs*).

It is not hard to imagine Peera as a cheeky and lively small boy frequenting his uncle's shop and meeting and helping to serve these young men, who were often not much more than boys themselves, set adrift in a foreign land far from home. Peera would have observed their manners and speech and perhaps copied from them. They were expected to learn Hindustani and Urdu, the language of business, as well as the laws and customs of India before being fully employed in their chosen line of work. Language proficiency and good examination results meant a more interesting posting, more money and better promotion prospects. There was a 'school for young gentlemen' close to Nansi's shop as well as a printing press down the road. Maybe one of the teachers at the school took an interest in young Peera Dewjee recognising his quick intelligence, or one of the printers at the printing press taught him his letters. Children with small deft fingers were often employed to set the letters for the printing presses. The truth will never be known, but Peera learnt to read and write and speak English.

During the period of the British East India Company communication between the races was relatively relaxed. The influences of childhood shape the character of the adult and Peera's early experiences of the lively atmosphere and interracial mix in British India of the late 1840s and early 1850s were evident in his later personality. He grew up confident, outgoing, inquisitive and socially adept and was always eager to speak English and to be in the company of foreigners. He had a strong religious belief and deep reverence for the Aga Khan, but he was also aware of British rule in India and understood the power it wielded over all aspects of his life. Even the Aga Khan could not escape the reach of the British. He owed his comfortable life in India and his secure position to them. The British, through their legal system, had enshrined the Ismailis as a recognised religious group and given them refuge. In return the Aga Khan was a good friend and loyal ally to the British in India and the Khoja community, following the example set by their leader, lent their support to British rule.

------

1 There is some controversy about the origin of the term Khoja. Some claim it is a derivative of the word Thakkar, an alternative name for Lohana, while others say it comes from Kwaja, a Persian honorific meaning lord. In Bartle

Frere's article 'The Khojas: The Disciples of the Old Man of the Mountain,' *Macmillan's Magazine,* Vol 34, 1876, p 431, he wrote that the Khojas were originally Hindus of the trading class and suggests that the term Khoja should be properly translated as 'the honourable or worshipful converts.' He pointed out that the Persian word *'Kwaja'* has two meanings: an honourable or worshipful person or a disciple. Bartle Frere was a notable linguist so his explanation seems plausible.

2 Bombay, now known as Mumbai.

3 Information from Amir Rashid, great-nephew of Peera Dewjee.

4 Frere, 'The Khojas,' p 432. This two-part article by Bartle Frere *(Macmillan's Magazine,* Vol 34, 1876, p 342-350 and 430-438) is interesting, being one of the earliest accounts of Khoja Muslims written in the English language.

5 Teena Purohit, *The Aga Khan Case: Religion and Identity in Colonial India,* Cambridge, Mass: Harvard University Press, 2012, p 18

6 William Johnson, *The Oriental Races and Tribes, Residents and Visitors of Bombay,* London: 1863, p 24

7 In 1820 the population of Khoja families living in Bombay was estimated to be 150 families; this had risen to 600 families by 1847. Carissa Hickling, *Disinheriting Daughters: Applying Hindu Laws of Inheritance to the Khoja Muslim Community in Western India, 1847-1937,* MA thesis, University of Manitoba, Winnipeg, 1998, p 11

8 George Smith, *The Life of John Wilson, D.D., F.R.S. For Fifty Years Philanthropist and Scholar in the East,* London: J. Murray, 1878, p 39. Estimated at 250,000 in 1830, the population had risen to 650,000 in 1870.

9 Christine Dobbin, *Urban Leadership in Western India: Politics and Communities in Bombay city 1840-1855,* London: Oxford University Press, 1972, p 116

10 Named after General Sir William Medows who had been governor of Bombay 1788-90, this street is now called Nagindas Master Road and is in the Kala Ghoda area.

11 Johnson, *The Oriental Races and Tribes,* plate 24

Chapter Two

To Zanzibar

Family tradition says Peera Dewjee's father, Dewjee Parpia, settled in Zanzibar in the early 1850s taking his wife and family with him. Three younger sons, Rashid in 1853, Hasham and Allaya, were born in Zanzibar, so he would have settled in 1853 at the very latest, when Peera was eleven or twelve. It is possible he left his eldest son in India with a relative to continue his schooling, but twelve was the normal age at this period for a boy to start his apprenticeship in business. Burton, writing in 1857,[1] tells us how Hindu merchants sent their children out to Zanzibar before puberty so they could learn the business of trade from the bottom up. They often worked for a relative doing the most menial tasks and receiving no more than a basic living allowance. They lived very frugally, often sleeping on the shop floor. They saved every rupee and gradually did a little trading on their own account. After nine or ten years training they would return to India, start in business themselves and find a wife.

Unlike Hindus, who did not bring their women or their families to Zanzibar until much later in the century, Khojas brought their wives and families out once their business was established. In a

Khoja household the wife played an essential part in the business. Traditionally the wife worked inside managing the shop, while the husband did the outside business, meeting customers and wheeling and dealing. Dr Christie in his famous book *Cholera Epidemics in East Africa* described how the Khoja families suffered badly in the cholera epidemic of 1869-70, when more than 100 died in Zanzibar. According to him, this was because the women were so busy with the work of the family business they did not have time to oversee domestic arrangements. He said that as a result, their children tended to be sickly and they left the cooking and washing unsupervised, allowing the spread of infection.[2] In contrast Christie noticed that the Hindus and Europeans, who were scrupulously careful about the water they drank and how their food was prepared, were the least affected of the population.

It is likely that Peera's father, Dewjee Parpia, started as a pedlar or general trader selling 'piece goods' and small manufactured items. Indian dyed or patterned cottons cut up into short lengths suitable for making a single garment, had long been the most popular traded item to East Africa and were known as 'piece goods.'[3] Other traditional Indian exports to East Africa included foodstuffs, particularly cooking oil, rice and ghee, and manufactured goods such as beads, metalware and earthenware pots. There was also a market for a variety of small luxury items such as hand mirrors, oil lamps and perfumes – indeed anything which could easily be transported from India and exchanged in Zanzibar and along the African coast and bring a profit to the trader.

In earlier times the dhows stopped along the East African coast at arranged points to meet caravans from the interior who gathered when they knew the arrival of the dhows was imminent. There was the famous annual Berbera fair on the Benadir coast, when ivory, hides, salt and slaves were traded for cloth, iron, rice, cooking oil and luxury goods. Huge trading caravans consisting of over a thousand persons with twice that number of cattle travelled down from inland centres such as Harar in Ethiopia, every year, for the fair. The wealthy overseas merchants stayed comfortably on board their ships, surrounded by

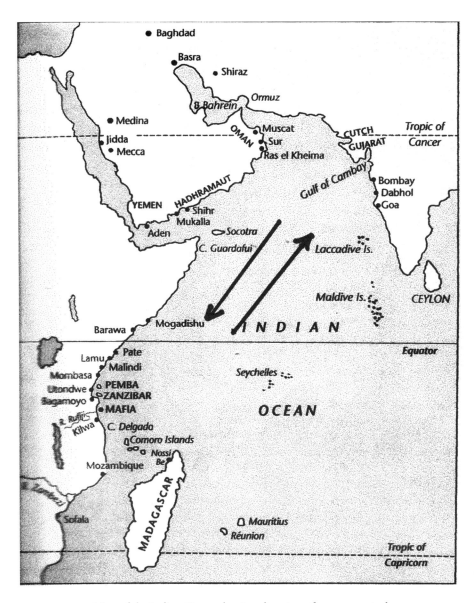

Map of the Indian Ocean showing direction of monsoon winds

bales of cloth, carpets and other goods, waiting for business to come to them. Smaller traders set up temporary stalls along the waterfront, spreading out their trinkets to attract custom. This bustling colourful event lasted for a few weeks before the dhows sailed on south and the caravans returned to the hinterland. Similar fairs were repeated on a smaller scale all along the African coast. But with the rise of Zanzibar as a central collection point, and its establishment as the main market for slaves and ivory, more and more dhows headed straight to Zanzibar.

There are a few documented mentions of a general merchant named Parpia, who could possibly be Peera's father or another relative. Spelling of Indian names at this period is notoriously erratic and the gradual discarding of Hindu names in favour of Muslim ones by the Khoja community only adds to the confusion, when checking archives. Even later on in the century spelling of Indian names is by no means standardised and Peera Dewjee appears spelt in at least twenty different ways ranging from Dautschi to Daudji to Deuzee to Deoji – according to how it was pronounced in, for example, English, German or French. Another added difficulty is that Muslims do not use surnames, but take the name of the father, therefore Peera's father's first name was Dewjee, while his grandfather's name was Parpia and Peera's son was called Abdulhussein Peera. Using just two names makes tracing descent especially difficult, which in the case of the Khojas may have been deliberate. Many Khoja families re-invented themselves when they came to Zanzibar, started a fresh dynasty and forgot who their ancestors had been.

A certain Dewchand Parpia turns up listed as a general merchant in the Bombay Calendar for 1868, but in the next year 1869 appears in the Bombay notices for the *London Gazette*, filing for relief of insolvency. His address is given as Masjid Bunder, which was the Khoja district of Bombay, although the government writer has him down as a Hindu. Some years later in the *London Gazette* for 1887, there is a Bombay bankruptcy notice for a Gulam Hossein Parpia, who 'formerly traded jointly with Dhunji Parpia Khoja, now deceased, and Manek Haji Khoja, and lately by himself, but is now unemployed.' This same

Dhunji Parpia is mentioned posthumously in a complicated court case of 1908 concerning a mortgaged house in Bhaji Pala Street, Bombay. The name of his wife is also given – Meenabhai, who inherited a share of the property on the death of her husband. She died before 1885 and her husband before that. Could this be Peera's father, and was Meenabhai his mother? Does Peera, coming from a later generation, style himself more elegantly as Dewjee, moving away from his father and his Hindu origins? The dates fit, so it is possible there is a connection. One further bankruptcy notice from Bombay, dated 1893, for 'Gulam Husein Parpia Cutchi' places the origin of these not very successful traders – from Kutch. But then the information unravels as a probate notice for a Peera Dhunji late of Bagamoyo is placed in the *Zanzibar Gazette*[1] for December 4, 1894. Quite how this character connects with Peera Dewjee is a mystery – unless of course Dhunji and Dewjee Parpia were brothers or cousins who both settled in East Africa. So far no recorded mention of a Dewjee Parpia has ever come to light.

Historically, Indian merchants had always kept agents in Muscat and Aden, key ports in the Indian Ocean trading circle. Their relationship with Oman was particularly close as the Sultan employed Indian merchants to run his finances. Gujarati ledger keepers were renowned for their exact calculations and neat rows of figures and the *banyans*, as the Hindu merchants were called, had brought the art of doing business to a pinnacle of refinement. The Omani Arabs, who in general had little interest in business affairs, were happy to rely on Indian expertise and they profited from this arrangement.

From the 1830s trade between India and East Africa grew significantly. In 1832 the Sultan of Muscat and Oman, Seyyid Said, established the capital of his African empire in Zanzibar and then brought his East African possessions, consisting of the coastal towns between Mogadishu and Mozambique, more securely under his control. Seyyid Said was a shrewd and enlightened ruler and during his rule of more than twenty years, Zanzibar's fortunes increased dramatically. It was his deliberate policy to invite Indian traders over to stimulate commerce and he encouraged them to settle as he regarded them as wealth creators and positive assets for his kingdom.

The story of Tharia Topan, one of the earliest Khojas from Kutch to settle in Zanzibar, is typical of many. He was born in 1823 in Lakhpat, not far from Mandvi, the son of a poor vegetable seller. At the age of 12 in 1835 he came to Zanzibar as a stowaway. The story went that, accused of theft, he ran down to the harbour to escape the hue and cry and hid on a dhow amongst the cargo. Safe in his hiding place, the terrified boy fell asleep and when he awoke the vessel was already under way. Fortunately the captain was sympathetic and did not throw him overboard, but agreed to take him to Zanzibar. Once there he introduced himself to a relative, who was working in the Customs House, who got him a job as a garden boy to the Customs Master, Ladha Damji, the richest and most important person on the island – barring the Sultan. Tharia had fallen on his feet and showing himself both intelligent and willing to work hard, he made his fortune. Though illiterate when he arrived, he quickly learnt the art of the ledger and how to add up and calculate values of items rapidly in several currencies in his head. He was employed by the Hindu firm of Jairam Sewji, which farmed the customs from the Sultan.

The administration of Zanzibar under Seyyid Said was very simple. There was no paperwork or bureaucracy; it was all done by word of mouth and the customs master acted as his minister of finance. Profits from trade made up the main part of his income and, as the Sultan famously said, 'I am nothing but a merchant.' The Bombay-based firm of Jairam Sewji paid the Sultan an agreed fee, which gave them a monopoly on all import and export duties collected on behalf of the Sultan and thus effective control of the port and finances of Zanzibar. The customs system was arcane and arbitrary and different amounts were charged not only on different items but also depending on separate treaties and agreements, or how the customs master felt that day – or probably how much he was bribed. Western visitors were impressed by the volume of trade passing through Zanzibar, but they also complained about the unequal tariffs, noticing, for instance, how the duty on slaves bought by Europeans was more than double that charged to Arabs and Indians. The post of customs master in the early years was extremely lucrative and anyone working for the Customs of Zanzibar had ample opportunity to become rich.

For his first solo venture in business Tharia imported a donkey cart and drove it out to the villages and purchased cloves and coconuts and brought them into the city for sale. Transporting his goods by cart, he carried larger quantities more swiftly than the local sellers, who travelled on foot and carried the produce in traditional baskets. He made a profit, and from that small start he moved on, gradually building up a trading business while still working at his day job in the Customs. By 1845 he was rich enough to return to India and find himself a wife. Sadly she died within two years and in 1848 he returned to India to find a second wife. On his trips back to India, he painted a rosy picture of the opportunities in Zanzibar and encouraged many of his fellow Ismailis to come out and join him. He offered to pay their voyage costs, assist with loans and even employ them. It is probable that Peera's father was one of many who came out as a result. In 1840 there were only 165 Ismailis resident in Zanzibar, including 26 married women, but by 1866 there were over 2,000.[5]

Dhows set sail from the coastal ports of western India as soon as the 'Star of Agastya' (Canopus) had been sighted and the northwest monsoon winds began to blow steadily. Agastya was the saint of the pioneer sea pilgrims and travellers to East Africa, and they knew the time had come for them to leave India and make for Zanzibar when they saw his star appear in the sky in the month of December. Though the northwest monsoon begins in November, which was when Arabian dhows set sail for East African ports, the winds did not reach India and blow in a more southerly direction until slightly later. This was when the wealthy merchants loaded up their goods in *baghalahs,* large dhows decorated with carved sterns and high curved wooden sides, copied from the western designs of East Indiamen. The capacity of their deep bottoms was convenient for carrying heavy jars of cooking oil, rice and wheat and quantities of merchandise, but made them uncomfortable and slow to travel in as they rolled and wallowed in the high seas. Nicknamed the sea mule, the *baghalah* was the main Indian Ocean trading vessel until the arrival of steamships. By contrast, the traditional Kutchi dhows, *ghanjahs* and *batelas,* the transport of choice for the lowly piece good trader, with their raked prows and sterns, travelled low and fast in the water.

When the time for leave-taking came, the whole village assembled at the shore the night before. Some of the passengers as young as 10 or 11 years old were leaving home for the first time. The seamen performed their *puja*, or prayers in the case of Muslims. The voyagers with their families bowed to their gods bringing offerings of coconut and sweet rice. The Hindu women placed a *tilak* or red dot on the forehead of a travelling husband or son for luck, while the Muslim women gave their men a *taweez* (an amulet bearing a verse from the Koran) to wear either tied on an arm or around the neck. Both groups gave their menfolk presents of sweetmeats to bring them safely home, pledging to fast and perform prayers on the second day of each new moon.

Passengers slept on deck grouped by religious communities. Each man sorted out his belongings, chose his spot to roll out his sleeping mat and arranged special places for cooking according to his caste.

The ship's master, *malam,*[6] steered the ship by the sun during the day and by the stars at night. He carried enough food and water for the journey. The passengers came on board with their bundles containing trade goods to exchange for African products on arrival. As they approached the Equator, the wind became stronger and whipped up high waves. When the boat began to toss, the passengers stood up and joined hands in a circle and sang verses from the holy books. This helped calm them and they forgot differences in religion and caste. The dhows took about 26 days to reach Zanzibar.

The dhows returned to India at the start of the southeast monsoon, which blew from April to September. All those who wished to remit money or send letters home packed them in sealed addressed bags and handed them over to the firm of Jairam Sewji. No commission was charged and the *malam* handled these packages with great care. The return journey took from two to eight weeks depending on the winds.

The newly arrived traders joined established relatives or contacts in Zanzibar and did the most menial jobs working dawn to dusk. The majority started out with little or no capital. They took a 90-day loan on which they paid no interest and then concentrated on maximising profits, so as to repay their debt as soon as possible. They ploughed all profits back into the business after meeting the cost of living. They lived a spartan lifestyle to begin with and not all were as successful as Tharia Topan.[7]

Richard Burton wrote a good eyewitness account of Zanzibar in 1857 and the sights he described would have been familiar to the young Peera Dewjee. Burton arrived just after the death of Seyyid Said in December 1856. He and his companion John Hanning Speke had come to Zanzibar to procure a travel permit from the Sultan and find porters and buy equipment for their famous expedition to find the source of the Nile.

In volume one of his *Zanzibar: City, Island and Coast*, Burton wrote in detail about his arrival and described the town and people of Zanzibar city.

All travellers were struck by the extraordinary beauty of the approach to Zanzibar, and after a long hazardous sea journey, they welcomed the lush green of the vegetation and the shimmering white of the buildings seen from afar. Burton had the same reaction. The sight of Zanzibar captivated him and he wrote: 'Truly prepossessing was our first view of the...island of Zanzibar set off by the dome of distant hills...The sea of purest sapphire lay basking...under a blaze of sunshine which touched every object with a dull burnish of gold.'

As Burton drew nearer he smelt the heavy spicy perfume of cloves from the plantations and saw the puritanical plainness of the buildings and the square-curtained fort dominating the front, with the palaces and various consulates on either side. Coming closer he saw the Sultan's flagship, a 50-gun Bombay built frigate, modestly named *Shah Allum* or King of the World. Strangely, it showed no colours nor did it acknowledge, as was customary, the approaching British warship.

Burton was a passenger on the *Elphinstone,* an East India Company sloop-of-war, and in accordance with diplomatic protocol she ran up the blood red ensign (the flag of Oman) at the mainmast and the Union Jack at the fore and delivered a 21-gun salute to announce her arrival. Thereupon, as Burton recounted, a gay bunting flew up and the brass carronades of the *Victoria* (another ship in the Sultan's fleet, named in honour of the British Queen) at last roared the prescribed greeting of 22 guns. They had arrived on the fortieth or last day of mourning for Seyyid Said, the reason for the unusual silence.

Trading dhows did not follow such an elaborate ritual when entering Zanzibar waters. They signalled their arrival in the traditional way by blowing on a large conch shell. The sights and sounds of ships coming and going were music to the ears of a Zanzibari. His eyes were forever trained towards the sea, searching the horizon for a vessel bearing the next cargo, and his whole life revolved about the activities on the waterfront.

Burton found the waterfront thick with various trading craft, but on closer inspection he noticed how the Sultan's navy looked dilapidated and ill-kept at its moorings. The new Sultan, Majid, apparently showed no interest in maintaining his father's fleet of ships.

The Arab stone town of Zanzibar was built on a sandy triangular point, called Ras Shangani. Behind the main harbour, which faced directly onto the sea, there was a second harbour in Darajani Creek for unloading cargoes. Beyond that was the area called Ngambo, the African town, a maze of *makuti* roofed huts.[8] There was no breakwater to protect the town in Burton's day, so during the rainy season the lower part was often flooded.

Once on dry land, Burton's initial favourable impression was soon dispelled and he did not mince his words. The main shore of the city, he said, was a cesspit. Cows wandered around, corpses floated at times upon the water and offal and worse strew the beach. A continuous stench arose from the piles of cowries drying and stewing in the sun,

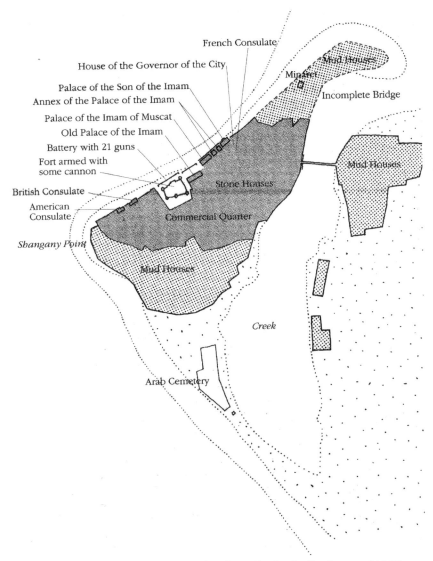

French Consulate

House of the Governor of the City

Palace of the Son of the Imam

Annex of the Palace of the Imam

Palace of the Imam of Muscat

Old Palace of the Imam

Battery with 21 guns

Fort armed with some cannon

British Consulate

American Consulate

Shangany Point

Minaret

Incomplete Bridge

Mud Houses

Mud Houses

Stone Houses

Commercial Quarter

Mud Houses

Creek

Arab Cemetery

A sketch plan of Zanzibar Town taken from Charles Guillain's map of 1846

41

waiting for the mollusks inside to decay away, and from the washing and scraping of ivory ready for shipment. Copal, the outer husk of the coconut used in the production of varnish, had to be washed in a solution of soda, which produced an unpleasant smell. Copra – the white coconut meat – split to dry in the sun, produced a nausea-inducing odour. Zanzibar had no sewage or drainage system and people simply left refuse to pile up in the streets or to wash away naturally when it rained. At night the waterfront often flared as if on fire from lime burning on the shore in small round built up heaps. They used lime for whitewashing the houses and there was a great deal of building going on.

The west end of town was the most salubrious area with pavements of tamped lime. Burton described the houses built of coral ragstone, with the wood and ironwork imported from India. There was nothing straight or level in the buildings and on top of some of the flat roofs he spotted thatched penthouses to catch the breezes. He noticed the carved wooden doorframes inscribed with sentences from the Koran to protect the house from witchcraft, or decorated with a yard of ship's cable to drive away thieves. He thought the houses looked like jails with bars in the small windows instead of glass. Inside, the rooms were long, high and narrow – 40 feet by 15 feet by 20 feet being the usual proportion. Dr Christie, who lived in just such a house, felt it was like living in a narrow hallway and it took him some time to get used to it. There was no furniture inside except a few hard wooden chairs, but ornaments of porcelain and glass filled the lines of niches set in the walls. Burton knew the women's quarters, upstairs, were more elaborate but he was not admitted so didn't see them.

Burton then described the shops – mere holes in the wall raised a foot above the street – where the owner sat or squatted, writing upon his knee with a reed pen in his ledger, doing his accounts.

Walking further he came to the area called Forodhani (meaning Customs in Swahili) and saw the Customs House where the customs collector sat within a simple open structure under a matting roof, even though huge sums of money and many valuable goods continuously passed through his hands. They intended to build a proper building, and a start had been made, but the *Bhattia*⁹ customs officer from the firm of Jairam Sewji preferred his old style of office due to superstition – anything too fine or modern might be a temptation to fate and bring him bad luck.

At the market place just past the Customs House, the town became congested. 'Motley is the name of the crowd,' wrote the sarcastic, cynical Burton. He saw one officer in the service of His Highness stalk down the market carrying a long whip trailing behind him ('followed by a Hieland tail,' as Burton puts it), proudly as if he were Lord of the three Arabias (not just a small island in the Indian Ocean!). African slaves who disliked the whip cleared out like frightened pigeons. He was a yellow man with short thin beard and high, meagre and impassive features, well dressed and gorgeously armed, wearing a knee length loose tunic under a knee length coat and thonged sandals on his feet, which gave him his distinctive gait.

Right meek by the side of the Arab's fierceness appeared the Banyans (Bhattias from Kutch), unarmed burghers with placid satisfied countenances. They wore long moustaches, no beard and a Chinese pigtail springing from the top of a carefully shaven head. The pigtail was folded back, when the owner was formally dressed, under a high turban of spotted purple or crimson stuff edged with gold. These turbans were bound round in transverse plaits – not twisted like the Arabs – and peaked in the centre, hornlike, above the forehead. Their snowy cotton shirts fitted close to the neck and were short-waisted, the full sleeves tight at the wrist, while the immaculate loin cloth displayed the lower part of the thigh leaving the leg bare. Slippers of red leather, sharp toed with points turning up, completed the outfit.

Another conspicuous type noticed by Burton was the Baluchi mercenary, distinguished from the Arab by the silkiness and length of his flowing beard. He carried an old matchlock inlaid with gold and silver decoration and pouches of gunpowder in his belt and provided an armed guard for the Sultans. A force of Baluchi mercenaries were permanently stationed in the Fort, next to the Customs. Burton then mentioned the Gulf Arabs with their unkempt locks falling over saffron stained shirts armed with straight sword and daggers. They were much feared in Zanzibar as pirates and were unwelcome seasonal visitors. Next under the spotlight came muscular Hadramaut porters (from the Yemen),[10] carrying huge bales of goods and packs of hides suspended from poles – ever chanting the same monotonous grunt-song and kicking out of the way the humped cows munching fruit and vegetables under the shadow of their worshippers, the Banyans.

'Add half a dozen pale-skinned "Khojahs," tricky-faced men with evil eyes, treacherous smiles, fit for the descendants of the "Assassins," [with] straight, silky beards, forked after the fashion of ancient Rustam, and armed with Chinese umbrellas.' And complete the throng by throwing in a European. How ghastly he appeared, with his blanched face and how frightful his tight garb, as he walked down the street in the worst of tempers and used his stick upon the mangy pariah dogs and the naked shoulders of the Africans that obstructed him.

At times the Arabs, when someone trampled on their toes or heels, turned fiercely and fingered their daggers but no more, as they knew if they were to kill a man or slave they would get no help from the sultan but be at the mercy of the man's family or master.

'Far more novel to us is the slave population, male and female,' says Burton, who is not usually an admirer of the African race or indeed of any of the human kind. This is what he had really come to see, he tells us – not the others! However, unlike later writers who went into grisly detail about the horror and cruelty of the slave market, knowing that was what readers back home wanted to hear, he gazed with detachment at the 'lines of Negroes stood like beasts.' Instead Burton described the domestic slaves of Zanzibar going about their daily business in town. He was an old fashioned 'Orientalist,' who accepted slavery as part of Islamic traditional society, much in the same way that serfs were part of Russian life of the same era. He respected Arabic and Indian culture and was fascinated by the different customs and peoples he saw on his travels, but he did not seek to change their way of life, only to describe it. Though Britain had banned the owning of slaves amongst its own people, at the time of Burton's visit they had not yet started to actively interfere in the practice by other nations – that was yet to come.

What struck Burton most about the African domestic slaves he saw, was the scrupulous politeness and ceremonious earnestness of greetings between friends. He gave an example of the elaborate greeting ritual in Swahili, with all its repetitions and longueurs. In fact, he said, the slaves went about saluting their friends in order to waste time, running unnecessarily from house to house. He noticed how even freemen in Zanzibar usually began their morning thus and idled through working hours. The men dressed very simply, with a yard of cotton tied round the waist and allowed to fall to the knees. Bead necklaces completed the costume. Burton noticed the wide variety of tribal marks tattooed into the skin, signifying the different areas of Africa from where the slaves had originated. Female slaves wore a single loose piece of chequered cotton, with their hair twisted into pigtails and if well off or married they had earrings run through the shell of the ear, thumb rings and massive bangles of white metal on wrists and ankles, and sometimes a stud in the nose.

Later on Burton gave his forthright opinion of Khojas:[11]

> Zanzibar contains about 100 Khojahs, who are held to be a 'generation of vipers, even of Satan's own brood.' Here, as in Bombay, they are called Ismailiyyahs. They practise the usual profound Takiyyah (concealment of tenets)…The Imam to whom they now pay annual tribute is one Aga Khan Mahallati, a Persian rebel, formerly Governor of Kirmán [now living in Bombay].

He described how Khojas were the principal shopkeepers in Zanzibar and were by no means deficient in intelligence (high praise from Burton).

> They are popularly accused of using false weights and measures; they opposed the introduction of a metallic currency…Many have applied themselves to slave dealing, and lately one was deported for selling poison to negroes; they are receivers of stolen goods, and by the readiness with

which they buy whatever is brought for sale, they encourage the pilfering propensities of the slaves.

Despite determined attempts at denigration, Burton could not avoid some praise of the Khojas. He described how they travelled far and wide and how several had reached the Lake regions deep in the interior of Africa well before the Europeans had even thought of going there. Burton met Musa Mzuri, handsome Moses, and his brother Sayyan in the interior in 1857 and they told him how they had started travelling in central Africa almost thirty years previously (that is in the late 1820s). As a fellow traveller and explorer, Burton could not fail to admire the adventurous spirit and successful journeys of the two brothers.

Burton finished his description of the Khojas with these words, 'At Zanzibar all not in trade are rude artisans, who can patch a lantern and tin a pot; one of them, who had learned to mend a watch, repaired the broken wheel of my pocket pedometer.' Of

The very intelligent oriental

all the people he met in Zanzibar, the Khojas impressed him most favourably. Burton probably knew the Aga Khan, as Burton, too, had served under General Napier during the wars in Sindh. He had a greater understanding and sympathy for Muslims than any of the other early European explorers in Africa. He had gone under cover and in disguise amongst them on a number of occasions, most famously when he visited Mecca.

Burton's description of Zanzibar is a valuable first hand depiction of the early period before western influences made too many inroads. Despite his various inconsistencies and jaundiced views, his account is a fascinating read. Burton soaked up information and gossip like a sponge and wrote it all down in a white heat of enthusiasm without much editing or chronology. Most was written in 1857 when he stayed in Zanzibar for six months trying to arrange his expedition to find the source of the Nile. Delay followed delay and, frustrated by his enforced wait, he occupied himself by taking copious notes about Zanzibar and finding out all he could about the island and surrounding coast. He wrote most of the two volumes, totalling 1,000 pages, while staying at the British Consulate. When Burton finally started for the interior of Africa, he left his manuscript in the care of Atkins Hamerton, the British consul, with instructions to send it on to the Royal Geographical Society for publication. Hamerton died before he could send it and his successor, Rigby, did not approve of Burton and sent it instead to Bombay where it was lost and languished until 1871, when it finally turned up again and was sent back to Burton. Burton brushed it up with a few topical additions and published it in 1872 – just when there was renewed interest in Zanzibar and the slave trade. At the back of the book there is an appendix explaining and defending his dealings with his former expedition partner, the unfortunate John Hanning Speke, whose argument with Burton over the source of the Nile and subsequent accidental death had been a *cause célèbre*. Many had taken Speke's side and thought him badly used by the elder man. Colonel Rigby, the Zanzibar consul, was one who was pro-Speke and had no hesitation in calling Burton 'a cur and a liar.' Rigby and Burton had been rivals at language school in India and held opposing views. They heartily disliked each other.

1 Richard Burton, *Zanzibar: City, Island and Coast*, 2 vols, London: Tinsley Bros, 1872

2 James Christie, *Cholera Epidemics in East Africa*, London: Macmillan & Co, 1876, p 337-340

3 Later in the century this term also came to be used for a trade operating in the opposite direction and was applied to cotton lengths produced in the mill towns of England and exported to Africa.

4 Officially *The Gazette for Zanzibar and East Africa*, the paper's title was usually shortened.

5 Kassamali R Paroo, 'Pioneering Ismaili Settlement in East Africa,' 1990, p1 http://ismailimail.files.wordpress.com/2013/12/untitled-attachment-00031.pdf, accessed 3 December 2104

6 *Malam* is the Indian word, the Swahili equivalent is *mwalim*.

7 Much of the information for the description of the dhow voyage has been taken from Blanche Rocha D'Souza *Harnessing the Trade Winds*, Nairobi: Zand Graphics, 2008.

8 *Makuti* – thatch made of dried coconut palm leaves.

9 Bhattias are a Hindu trading caste, originating mainly from Kutch region.

10 Later in the century Zanzibari stevedores tended to be African slaves, employed by the previous Yemeni porters, who in turn had become rich and slave owners.

11 Burton, *Zanzibar*, Vol 1, p 336-339

Chapter Three

The Early Years

The writings of Dr James Christie[1] give us a more detailed picture of how Peera Dewjee would have lived during his early years in Zanzibar. Dr Christie arrived in Zanzibar in 1865 as a doctor attached to UMCA, The Universities Mission for Central Africa, but he also worked at the Sultan's sugar plantation at Mkokotoni and had his own private practice in town. He lived in Zanzibar for almost ten years and in 1870 was appointed personal physician to Sultan Barghash. His descriptions of life in Zanzibar are particularly interesting because as a doctor he went inside the houses and saw the intimate lifestyle of the various communities. He was not part of the British diplomatic or military service so had no political axe to grind nor was he a missionary with a religious message to impart. Instead he was a scientist, with a trained eye for detail and sympathy for the human condition.

He visited many Khoja houses and knew the community well as he devoted several pages of his book *Cholera Epidemics in East Africa* to describing them in detail. He used them as a case study for his investigation of the causes for the spread of cholera, which he correctly identified as a waterborne infection, and in so doing, left a unique vision of how the Khoja community lived and worked in Zanzibar during the 1860s. It is more than likely he met and knew Peera Dewjee and his family, but unfortunately he makes no mention of him in his writings or letters.

Here is a summary of what Christie had to say about the Khojas of Zanzibar. By the mid 1860s they were the most numerous and influential of the Indians permanently resident in the town.

They are natives of Cutch…They are rigid Mohammedans, and, although they disregard the pilgrimage to Mecca, large numbers annually make the pilgrimage to Meshed 'Aly and Meshed Hussein,[2] a religious duty incumbent on all Shia'ahs…A journey of this kind…frequently occupies two years.

The Khojahs of Zanzibar are exclusively engaged in business, wholesale and retail, being the principal merchants and shop-keepers of the place. They have thus extensive business connections with all the ports on the mainland, both in the sale of European goods and in the purchase of native produce; and thus they are brought into intimate connection with the European and American merchants as middle-men, and also with the natives in the city and on the main-land, as retailers.[3]

The Khojas, said Christie, were essentially a business caste; their entire time from their earliest years was devoted to mercantile transactions, leaving little or no time for other pursuits. They opened their business early in the morning and did not shut until late in the evening or until there were no more customers. The outside business was conducted by the husband who was in the shop only when not otherwise engaged and the retail or shop keeping part of the business was carried out by the wife or a junior member of the family. Not only was the wife the domestic partner in life, she was also the indispensible business partner. As every Khoja youth was expected to engage in business, so he needed a wife to help him. Since the wife devoted her time to the business, she ignored household duties and the comforts of domesticity were quite unknown.

One or two wealthy wholesale Khoja merchants lived apart in more luxurious settings, but the majority lived together in one area of town in houses arranged in narrow streets converging towards the market place and customs house. Their houses were built adjoining one another (as in a terrace) and were usually two storeys high. Along each side of the street and in front of the shops ran a high broad bench of masonry used as a step and as a place to display goods for sale. A narrow *makuti* roof shaded the bench from sun and rain. The frontage of the shop was seldom more than 12-14 feet wide and was left open during the daytime. The goods were exposed for sale on the floor and on some narrow shelving surrounding it. The wife sat within on a low stool with rolls of copper money beside her.

The purchaser stood outside in the street so his movements could be observed.

In John Hanning Speke's *Journal of the Discovery of the Source of the Nile* published in 1863 there is an illustration entitled Banyan contemplating his Account-book. This shows an Indian wearing reading glasses, sitting cross legged on the floor of his small shop. On his lap are his written accounts. It must be after dark as there is a lit candlestick by his side. Though this depicts a Hindu, dressed only in his loin cloth and with his distinctive headgear, a Khoja shop keeper would have sat and waited for custom in similar fashion.

Behind the shop there was a general storeroom and a narrow passage, which led to an open courtyard behind. If the business was small, the family used the storeroom as the sleeping apartment and the open courtyard became the kitchen. In many houses the second floor was merely a room over the shop accessed by a small hole in the floor and an almost perpendicular ladder. In larger houses the second story extended further back over the storeroom below. The entrance was again a steep ladder into a combination of kitchen/bathroom and closet with a door leading to the bedroom at the front.

A stout rope fastened to a beam in the roof passed through the hole of the entrance by the side of the stair to be grasped by anyone going up or down. Christie commented that fractured skulls were a

Banyan contemplating his account book

common form of accident amongst Ismaili children. The bedroom only held essential furniture – a bedstead, a few stools, a swinging cradle, a rickety chair or two and a chest. Christie found it difficult to understand where all the members of the household were stowed away at night, for the family was often large and often included a grandmother or grandfather.

Their cooking apparatus consisted of earthenware jars, tinned copper cooking pots, coconut-shell ladles and some tinned platters or trays for the rice and curry. There were no forks or knives. There were always two water jars, one for drinking and one for use in the bathroom or closet. Christie noted the sanitary arrangements were particularly bad as the latrine was only separated from the main living room by a low wall, worse than the poorest slave huts, which at least had no latrines within them.

Generally there were two female domestics who did the cooking – Christie said they were often called *Marashi* or rosewater, but the odours around them were anything but sweet. The sight of a *Marashi* cleansing her cooking dishes or carrying on her culinary operations or ladling out the drinking water seriously upset the good doctor, who found it a sickening sight and vowed never to eat in a Khoja house and never to accept a drink unless it be the water of a coconut.

Though living conditions were not hygienic, the Ismailis were most particular regarding personal cleanliness and clothing. An Ismaili man considered it shameful to appear in anything except a snow-white garment. In daytime they usually wore a calf length white tunic with wide cotton trousers beneath. On special occasions they wore a long sleeved overrobe, often red or black in colour, with embroidered lapels. The richer the individual, the more elaborate and extensive the decoration. They wore turbans (called *pagadi*) and Ismaili officials wore gold turbans. Ismaili women dressed very plainly, except at weddings and on festive occasions when 'there [was] a great display of wealth… silks and satins of decided hues and patterns, massive gold bracelets, anklets and necklaces being worn.' Christie thought the community suffered more than others from fever, dysentery, hypertrophy of the liver or spleen, hydrocele and various skin diseases. The children were sickly and delicate and the mortality rate amongst their children was high.

Christie concluded the condition in which they lived was not the result of poverty. In fact, many would have liked to see a better state of affairs. But invariably the answer came: 'It's our custom.' As Christie reasonably pointed out, 'limited as these people are to certain streets, occupied solely by themselves, it would not be unreasonable to compel them to do, as a body, what would be invaluable to them, namely, to put their locality in a sanitary condition compatible with ordinary health.' This was done a few years later and living arrangements were improved, though elements of similar houses can still be seen in the stone town area of today.

Christie went on to describe the social organisation of the Khoja community in Zanzibar. He said they had many public gatherings and festivities and on Fridays they met in a public building set apart for the purpose, where after prayers, they all ate together. The place where Ismailis meet for worship is not called a mosque. They gather in a Jamatkhana, a building which usually houses a large prayer hall, another hall for social gatherings, plus a large kitchen. The congregation is known as a Jamat. The Ismaili community in Zanzibar was first established in 1838 and, according to Burton, to begin with the faithful met in a disused Sunni Mosque, before building their own customised Jamatkhana. The present Ismaili Jamatkhana in Zanzibar was opened in 1905 and replaced an earlier building.

Christie was impressed with the way the Ismailis ran their affairs. Although, as he pointed out, the community spent much of its wealth in communal feastings and celebrations, the system was not without special and important advantages. At the Jamatkhana everyone met on common ground and they encouraged kind feelings between individual members. They took care of their own poor, exercised supervision over conduct and looked after the interests of all. Members in disgrace or bankrupt were generally sent back to India. But the downside was that the communal living made them more careless about the comfort of their own homes. According to Christie, 'a more cheerless, uninviting abode, is not to be seen than a Khojah dwelling-house.'

Christie was not the only one to be interested in the structure and organisation of the Khoja Ismaili community in Zanzibar. Sir John Kirk, the British consul, also recorded information, which can be seen in his papers now housed in Edinburgh at the National Library of Scotland. He noted the names of the officials, how much money they sent back to the Aga Khan and to the Rao in Kutch and gave numbers for the Khoja population of Zanzibar.

Kirk said a committee of five men or headmen called *Amuldani* ran the Jamat in Zanzibar and they rotated the main posts amongst themselves on an annual basis. The *Mukhi* kept the register and authorised public feasts in the Jamat, while the *Kamaria* kept the accounts. No deed of the Khoja Jamat, said Kirk, was valid unless sanctioned by all five of the *Amuldans*. When Kirk wrote in 1870, these five headmen were: Randulla Hamad of Nuggah, Tarya Topan of Kutch, Lalji Mukhi of Kutch, Alibhai Sunji of Nuggah and Gulam Hussein Tidepa of Kutch. In addition there should have been a *Vari,* the chairman or leader of them all, but he had died and Randulla Hamad, his son, was signing in his father's name.

In 1870 the Khojas sent 60,000 rupees to the Aga Khan, an increase on the previous year when they had sent 45,000 rupees. They also remitted a small annual tax, from ivory and copal traded, to the Maharao of Kutch.

In February 1870 Tharia Topan gave Kirk, in response to his inquiries, an estimate of the Khoja population of Zanzibar. He reported there were 425 families from Kutch, 100 families from Jamnuggah, seven or eight from Banuggah and five from Bombay making up a total of 537 families – approximately 1,500-2,000 adults. He said thirty years earlier there had only been 160 households and only 20 married Khoja women, but now the number of married Khoja women had risen to 700. By far the greatest number of Khojas originated from Kutch. This was due, according to Kirk, to the destruction of the old cloth trade and the ruin of many families.[4]

Being a doctor, Christie noted the specific customs of the Khojas for caring for the sick. Visitation, he said, during illness was incumbent upon all relatives, male and female, and the care and treatment of a sick person devolved more upon the congregated relatives than on the individual household. He commented on the great kindness and affection they displayed towards each other, when ill. This was in contrast to other communities who did not show such compassion. Though the 1858-9 cholera epidemic had not affected the Ismaili population so greatly, the epidemic of 1869-70 hit them with extreme severity. Many businesses were suspended and shops closed.

When young Peera Dewjee first arrived, he would have lived in one of the simple shop houses described by Christie and helped his mother in the business. As the family expanded and the business grew, perhaps the house grew as well with added rooms upstairs. All indications are, however, that Peera's father was not successful. Possibly he died early, succumbing to one of the many diseases to which (according to Christie) Ismailis were prone, leaving Peera as the main breadwinner for the family. Peera's personality in later years showed all the traits of a self-made man, who as a youngster had to struggle hard to earn a living and had used his wits to survive and prosper.

Some idea of how a Khoja shopkeeper conducted his business transactions and made a profit can be gathered from this colourful description of a Khoja buying copra in Pemba. It comes from Henry Stanley Newman's book *Banani* and, though set much later in the century, the haggling process is a timeless one and Peera Dewjee would have known it well.

> He waylaid the country folks as they came into town laden with sacks of copra. Tired with their load they were glad to rest. Then came the long haggling about the price, the Khoja beating them down to a pice and wasting more words on a pice than Englishmen would spend on a sovereign. Many an outburst of laughter would arise from the onlookers as one joke after another passed, the Khoja never yielding but making up for it by abundant chatter. At last the price is fixed, and the load laid upon the weighing machine. Vain are the protests that come from the countryman that the weight is incorrect. Thump go the weights upon the scales. The

money jingles merrily in the Khoja's bag of coins. It is irresistible. The transaction is complete. The ready money changes hands and another customer appears as a stalwart black servant…carries to the rear of the shop the copra purchased, to make room for the next parcel.[5]

When Peera Dewjee first came to Zanzibar in the 1850s there was no set coinage or fixed weights and measures. Everything purchased involved a long bargaining process and money was calculated by weight and sometimes manufactured or cut up to suit. It was not until the mid-1860s that the Indian Rupee became the main currency of choice, and they introduced a fixed exchange rate of 128 pice to the silver Maria Theresa dollar. The Maria Theresa dollar, a large silver coin bearing the head of the Austrian empress, had formerly been the most widely accepted currency, functioning like the American dollar of today. It was also used as a measure of weight. Burton explains how the *Wakkiyat* or ounce, the unit most commonly used, was equivalent to the weight of a Maria Theresa dollar. Ivory was weighed in *farsalah (frasila)*, grain was measured in *Kibabah*, small scoops, while distance was usually reckoned in marches by the day.

Burton tells us with disapproval that the Indian trade is carried out by dhows and batelas of which there are neither registers nor returns. Khojas and Banyans insured vessels and often acted as underwriters making a fortune as they avoided paying out unless the vessel was completely lost. But as the century progressed shipping movement became more closely regulated and monitored and by 1870 all dhows were required to register with the port authority in Zanzibar and fly a flag of nationality. One of the British consul's duties was to keep a list of British-registered ships entering Zanzibar. This consisted mainly of Indian dhows, which was a source of grievance to the traders, as British shipping paid higher port dues than other countries – notably France. The Indian shippers tried to avoid the charges by registering their dhows under flags of convenience such as Mozambique or Madagascar, which were either exempted or paid considerably less, but the British consul was having none of it and in the end a set tariff was introduced which applied to everyone.

The seemingly haphazard and arbitrary method of doing business frustrated Burton and other European observers, who could not understand how it operated and worked so well. There appeared to be no reliance on precise computation and written contracts, and the lordly approach of the Arabs and their dislike of exact facts and figures bemused the Western traders. They thought they were being deliberately misled and disadvantaged and as trade with the West increased the European merchants became more determined to put their own systems in place and exercise control. They saw how the export of slaves and ivory in exchange for Indian piece goods and Western guns and luxury items was increasing yearly and they cast envious eyes on the profits to be made from the expanding trading opportunities. Though French and American traders were the first to enjoy the benefits of a close trading partnership with Zanzibar, it was ultimately the British who triumphed and gained overall control of Zanzibar and its trade. One of the ways they achieved this was through manipulation of the Indian merchants, many of whom were British protected persons due to British colonial control of India. The 1860s heralded a sea change for Zanzibar and East Africa, with increasing Western intervention and settlement from India.

---

1 A collection of Christie's Zanzibar letters can be found in Cambridge University Library, GB 12MS, Add 8163. Much of the information for this chapter comes from these, and from his book, *Cholera Epidemics in East Africa*, London: Macmillan & Co, 1876.
2 The main Shia holy sites: the mausoleums of Ali at Najaf and Hussein at Karbala, now in Iraq.
3 Christie, *Cholera Epidemics*, p 336-7
4 Information from Kirk's papers, Acc 9942/35
5 Henry S Newman, *Banani: The Transition from Slavery to Freedom in Zanzibar and Pemba*, London: Headley Bros, 1898, p 72-3

Chapter Four

Peera Joins the Service of Barghash

From an early age Peera Dewjee worked for Barghash, the fifth surviving son of Seyyid Said, Sultan of Zanzibar. Peera's obituary states: 'Peera Dewjee at an early age joined the service of HH Seyid Burgash bin Said by whom he was thoroughly trusted for his great zeal and honesty.'[1] Barghash was still a minor when he accompanied the Sultan on his last visit to Oman (1854-6). When the Sultan died unexpectedly at sea on 19 October 1856, Barghash, the senior son travelling with his father, went against Arabic custom and had the body embalmed and brought back for burial in Zanzibar. Barghash did not set up his own independent household until after his father's death when he received his inheritance. This occurred at some point in 1857, when Peera would have been about sixteen years of age and Barghash nineteen or twenty. Barghash was born circa 1837.

The royal household in Zanzibar was extensive. When Sultan Seyyid Said died at the age of 63, he left 100 wives, 36 living children, out of an original 57, countless horses and more than 5,000 slaves who worked on his 45 plantations. He also owned a number of palaces in Zanzibar town. On his death, in accordance with Islamic law, his concubines were freed and his property was divided between his children. Each of them inherited a plantation with a residence, and in addition each son received 57,917 Maria Theresa dollars, a handsome fortune in those days, and each daughter received half that amount. It took several months to sort out the late sultan's affairs to make sure all the family members received what was due. A decision was reached to divide the kingdom. The eldest son, Thuweini, became Sultan in Muscat, another Turki became governor of Dohar, while Majid became Sultan in Zanzibar. Thuweini felt he had been short-changed as the African kingdom was so much wealthier than his desert lands.

He threatened an invasion, but the British intervened and brokered an agreement whereby Majid paid his brother a certain amount each year in compensation.

With so many demands on his purse, Majid ended up heavily in debt. He was a sickly, gentle prince, who suffered from epilepsy and had a taste for opium. He found his role as Sultan onerous and he spent much of his reign trying to avoid family arguments and making unpleasant decisions. He left the management of affairs of state to an unpopular individual called Suleiman Ali.

Barghash thought he was better suited to be Sultan of Zanzibar, but his hopes were dashed by the British consul Atkins Hamerton, who supported the older Majid. Majid had been acting as regent in Zanzibar since the death of another more senior brother, Khalid, while Seyyid Said was in Oman. The British thought the easy-going Majid a safer prospect than the fiery unpredictable Barghash and they threw their weight behind his claim as did most of the Arab population. Barghash had been out of the country for almost three years and was an unknown quantity. He didn't yet have a power base of his own. Nevertheless, Barghash persisted. He tried shooting his brother as he passed by in front of his house, but missed, and was given a severe reprimand. Forced to accept the inevitable for the time being, Barghash's resentment rankled and he plotted and planned, waiting for another opportunity to usurp the throne.

Information about this period comes from a lively account written by one of Sultan Said's youngest daughters called Salme. She eloped and married a German national and in her old age wrote about her early life in Zanzibar when she had been an Arabian princess.[2] She left a glowing account of her idyllic early childhood at Beit el Mtoni, the old Sultan's favourite residence, and then in town when she moved at the age of seven to live with her brother, Majid. She was 11 when he became Sultan of Zanzibar and she received her inheritance. He, like her, had a Circassian mother and was light skinned, almost European in appearance, unlike several of the other royal children who had African or Abyssinian mothers. Barghash's mother was an Abyssinian.

With so many royal children there were bound to be factions and Said's offspring were exceptionally quarrelsome. They divided into groups depending on the origins and allegiances of their mothers and favourite sisters.

The princes and princesses lived in a group of palaces built along the waterfront in Zanzibar and clustered around the Sultan's main town residence – Beit el Sahel. The buildings stood so close together family members could hold conversations from the open windows and some buildings were connected by passages built over the street below. There were so many in the royal family that brothers and sisters had to share the available living quarters and they lived in separate apartments within the houses, which often consisted of no more than a single room. They reserved the upper floors for the women, while the men had rooms on the ground floor. At the front of the house there was always a *baraza* or meeting room, where the menfolk could drop in for coffee and to talk business and politics. The open central courtyard was the main hub of the house. The courtyard led to other rooms and stairs went to the upper floors. Cooking was done in the courtyard and there was always a crush of servants and slaves and tradesmen and a great deal of noise. Salme most likely first saw Peera Dewjee in one of these town palaces. Many years later, when Peera Dewjee had become one of the most powerful men in the kingdom, Salme recalled him as a clever, but low born, former lamp cleaner and court barber.

While a lamp cleaner conjures up images of the boy Aladdin polishing his magic lamp and summoning up the genie who gives him his wishes, in Zanzibar, in the nineteenth century, before the age of electricity, the job of a lamp cleaner was a menial, but essential occupation. Keeping the lamps burning bright in the Sultan's palaces was a responsible duty, perhaps comparable to that of an in-house electrician for a hospital or big office block of today. Light came not from a flick of a switch, but from innumerable candles and oil lamps, all of which needed daily attention. Lamps played an important part in the Islamic religious and daily routine, from the traditional lighting of the first small oil lamp at break of dawn when morning prayers were said, to the elaborate candelabra illuminating the mosques and palace audience chambers.

Salme tells us oil lamps were kept burning in all the rooms and corridors of the palaces throughout the night. Outside lanterns served as street lights. After sunset in the cool evening, the princesses went out visiting their friends. Fully veiled and protected by an entourage of armed guards and slaves, they ventured out into the dark streets. Salme left a wonderful description of the decorative lanterns they carried on long poles to light their way, imported from China and designed like Russian churches with brightly coloured domes and apses. The main festivals, Eid-ul-Fitr, Eid-ul-Adha, and *Nairuz* or *Siku Ya Mwaka*, the Swahili New Year, all involved special lighting displays and fireworks. In the early part of the century they used coconut oil in the lamps, but later they imported kerosene (paraffin). Wicks had to be trimmed and adjusted, candles lit and lanterns repaired – it was a full-time job for several lamp cleaners to service all the lights in the royal palaces.

They used the soot, the by-product of lamp cleaning, to make *kohl*, the black eye mascara worn by all Arabs and thought to have medicinal and cosmetic properties. Soot was also the main ingredient in making lampblack, a popular ointment used to blacken gentlemen's moustaches and beards. They also used soot in manufacturing shoe polish and ink.

It is probable the Dewjee family business was originally built on soot and that Peera's mother and younger siblings made ointments and ink from the soot collected from the Sultan's palace by Peera, and then sold these products in their shop. If Dewjee senior had died or failed to succeed as a general trader, then capturing this niche market made sense. Much later on a member of the Dewjee family owned a famous perfume shop selling the latest scents imported from Paris as well as created from his own closely guarded recipes – perhaps this was how it started.

The intelligent and industrious Peera caught the notice of Barghash who promoted him to be his personal barber and valet.

Peera's knowledge of ointments and cosmetics and shoe polish, no doubt helped in this job. His close proximity to the royal prince was an enviable position. In medieval Europe the office of gentleman of the bedchamber was always a coveted post as it gave access to the ear of the sovereign, an opportunity to ask for favours and to influence political outcome. In Europe the office declined with the introduction of a constitutional monarchy, when important decisions were no longer made by the ruler, but in Zanzibar policy making and the process of government still depended on the Sultan and the advice he received. The role of barber and valet carried with it exceptional opportunities.

In addition to his official duties, Peera Dewjee was a messenger and spy for Barghash. As a lamp cleaner he would have had access to all areas, including the women's quarters, which were usually off limits for most men. Few people could read or write, so verbal messages were continuously sent from house to house, usually by slaves. Salme tells us special runners were employed to take messages and messengers were well rewarded as a misreported message could lead to all kinds of misunderstandings and it was important to keep them on your side! Nevertheless, mishaps did occur and the conspiratorial goings on within the Sultan's court sometimes degenerated into a bad case of Chinese whispers. Peera with his superior intelligence and linguistic abilities was well-placed as the perfect courier on occasions when important matters needed to be transmitted quickly and accurately. As an Indian he had more social mobility than an Arab and more status than an African slave and could move between the spheres of the Arab, African and European, without attracting undue attention. He could speak Swahili, various Indian languages, English and quite possibly some French as well.[3] Peera was perfect spy material.

No written evidence has ever come forward, but it is likely Peera was involved in Barghash's unsuccessful plot of 1859, when he would have been working as a lamp cleaner in Barghash's household. Salme gives us most insight into the conspiracy. She was one of the main players. It had important repercussions for her later life, and she covers it, in detail, in her memoirs.

Salme's mother died of cholera early in 1859. The orphaned Salme, aged just 15, came under the influence of an elder sister called Chole. Chole had been the favourite daughter of the old Sultan, who had given her special privileges and left her in charge of the household during his absence in Oman. His death had hit her hard and her nose was seriously put out of joint as her brother Majid, the new Sultan, favoured another sister, who now had the more honoured position at court. She quarrelled with Majid and turned to Barghash and urged him on in his conspiracy to oust his brother. She seems to have been an energetic and headstrong woman, the spoilt darling of an indulgent father, who enjoyed the excitement of intrigue, heedless of the consequences of her actions. The young motherless Salme fell completely under Chole's captivating spell and she was drawn into the small group of conspirators who surrounded Barghash. These were two nieces, Shembua and Farshu, who were daughters of the dead Khalid, and Abdul Aziz a younger brother of Barghash, aged just twelve. The two nieces were very wealthy and had inherited a splendid plantation with a fine house, which their father, an admirer of all things French, had called Marseilles. Marseilles served as the headquarters of the planned revolution. The French consul's wife Madame Cochet was also involved in the plot. Presumably the French hoped to benefit from a change of Sultan as Majid favoured the British.

The six main conspirators lived in three adjoining houses. Chole and Salme lived in Beit al-Tani the former residence of a glamorous Persian princess called Sherazade, who had been married to Seyyid Said for a short time, before divorcing him and returning to Persia. It was connected to Beit al-Sahel, the Sultan's town palace, by a bridge over a bathhouse built between the two houses. Sherazade had brought with her a large entourage of Persian cavaliers, who had lived down below and in a separate house opposite. Barghash had recently moved into this house. Shembua and Farshu, the two nieces, lived next to Barghash's house across a narrow lane.

The disaffected Barghash began to hold secret meetings to win over the tribal chiefs to his side. His supporters mainly came from the al-Harthi tribes and once a large enough group of malcontents had gathered around him he started to plan an uprising to overthrow Majid. Barghash could not keep his plotting secret or conceal his jealousy and he stopped attending Sultan Majid's official audiences, a sure sign of his discontent and making him liable for punishment. As Salme explained, Barghash as a young man was too excitable and quick-tempered and a stronger more ruthless Sultan than Majid would have arrested and imprisoned him at this stage and nipped the conspiracy in the bud. But Majid hoped his brother would be won over with forbearance and kindness. For a long time he ignored the plotting and turned a blind eye, although he was well aware of what was going on.

The British consul and great friend of the old Sultan, Atkins Hamerton, had died in 1857, but his replacement Colonel Christopher P Rigby, Arab scholar and military man, did not arrive in Zanzibar until 1859. The delay was due to a serious accident Rigby had in Bombay just before his scheduled departure, when his coach overturned. He suffered severe injuries which took months to heal, leaving him with a permanent limp and he had to use a stick to walk. In his absence the French consul Ladislas Cochet, the next most influential foreign representative, had taken the lead amongst the Europeans. France's interest in Zanzibar lay in trade, not in political domination, and they wanted the slave trade to continue undisturbed as they needed labour for their sugar plantations in Mauritius and the Comoro Islands. They were content to maintain a status quo. Majid's position was weak, but Barghash was not popular. Watchful inaction seemed the best policy. The brothers and sisters meanwhile squabbled amongst themselves and indulged in petty rivalries and intrigue, spending their inheritances on jewellery and informants.

The four princesses worked themselves up to a fever pitch, arranging for supplies to be sent and stored at Marseilles and preparing for a rebellion. Salme, the only one who could write, did all the correspondence with the various chiefs and ordered the ammunition and guns. Their excitement only grew when, as she tells us, 'Our spies informed us that the Government had at last decided to put an end to our doings.' They redoubled their efforts for the success of the enterprise.

Rigby, the new British consul, finally arrived and decided to take a hold of the situation in Zanzibar and stiffen the resolve of the Sultan. Unlike his predecessor, who had largely ignored the slaving activities of the Muslims as long as the Christians complied, Rigby enforced with extreme vigour the anti-slaving treaties Britain had made with Zanzibar. He made the Indians register at the Consulate as British protected persons and free their slaves. It is quite possible Rigby's arrival gave extra impetus to Barghash and his plotters, as members of the Indian community and the Arab merchants disliked the new determined stand against the slave trade. They were alarmed by Majid's compliance with British policies and his dependence on Rigby's advice.

The plotters fixed a day for the coup and then suddenly several hundred soldiers surrounded Barghash's house. Majid had finally reacted, and he shut up Barghash in his house along with some of the Arab chiefs who supported him. Chole spoke to Barghash through the open windows wondering what to do next, but Barghash refused to submit or ask his brother's forgiveness. He had plenty of food, but was short of water. The princesses solved the problem by devising an ingenious canvas hosepipe to channel water from their houses to his.

With Barghash a prisoner in his house, Chole and her female conspirators took charge and put together a daring plan to free Barghash, so he could escape to Marseilles, the rebel headquarters, and lead the rebellion from there. They decided to disguise Barghash in women's clothes and sneak him out. One dark evening the princesses went together with a retinue of slaves to plead for permission to see their brother and his sister Meje, who was living with him in the house. The soldiers did not know how to refuse the royal ladies and reluctantly allowed them to go in. Once inside, Barghash, despite protests, was wrapped up in a *buibui* (the black outer dress of Arab women) which left only his eyes free and they clothed little Abdul Aziz in a similar fashion, with their weapons concealed beneath their robes. They put the tallest women of the retinue beside Barghash to make his height less conspicuous and walked out together. They carried on walking further and further into the narrow dark streets, beyond the guards, to the outskirts of the town. No one stopped them; it seemed the plan had worked. Barghash threw off his women's clothes and hurried to Marseilles to join his armed supporters, who had gathered there. The princesses ran back exhausted to their houses, worn out by the unaccustomed exercise and excitement.

But the Baluchi guard had recognised Barghash despite his disguise and had reported it to Majid. The situation forced Majid into action. He sent his soldiers to Marseilles to fight the rebels, but the battle was inconclusive and he could not dislodge them. He turned to the British for help to save him and keep the peace. Six ships of war happened to be in port, four British and two French, the *Assaye, Clive, Lyra, Isis, Cordeliere* and *Estafette*. A detachment of marines from the British ships was sent to capture the plantation. They bombarded the house at Marseilles and reduced it to ruins. Several hundred of Barghash's supporters were killed and they admitted defeat. Barghash escaped and returned a fugitive to his house. But, proud and stubborn to the last, he refused to submit to his brother and barricaded himself within his house. He spurned the emissary sent by Majid and his offer of generous terms and remained obdurate. Lacking the will or means to force his brother into submission, Majid again turned to Rigby and the British for help. The British gunboats used to police the slave trade had a shallow enough draft to get close to Barghash's seafront property. They anchored one opposite Barghash's house and the marines began firing bullets through the windows. One bullet narrowly missed Barghash, but he still refused to give himself up, instead retreating to the back of the house.

Chole, now in a terrible state, cried and cursed the British, afraid they would all be killed. Finally, she persuaded the obstinate Barghash to give in and tender his submission. Salme wrote that Chole ran at once to the British Consulate to announce this and demand a cessation of hostilities, but the Consul was not at home. Fortunately, the marines stopped firing when the people from Barghash's house called out, 'Peace, Peace.' But still Barghash's pride prevented him from submitting to his brother in person. He would only do it through the mediation of a foreign power. Consul Rigby went up to his front door and banged on it with his walking stick. Shamefaced, Barghash came out and he was put on the British gunboat *Assaye*. They took him to Bombay the next day. These events took place in October 1859, when Peera was eighteen.

What part Peera played in all this drama will never be known, but judging by his subsequent career, he was probably in the thick of it, carrying messages and receiving payments as an informant. With his love of dressing up, he may even have had a hand in Barghash's disguise. Bearing in mind his later position of trust with Barghash and how he rose in his service, it would not be unreasonable to suppose that it was this episode, which first opened the Sultan's eyes to the talents and abilities of his lamp cleaner, Peera.

Barghash was not gentle or forgiving and when his little sister Salme, who had risked so much to help him, made peace with Majid, he never forgave her and cut off all contact with her. He was ruthless and could be cruel – imprisoning his brother for a minor offence and whipping one of his wives within an inch of her life because she dared to wave to a French gentleman in the street. He was fiercely proud, stubborn, sincerely religious and intelligent. He was a man's man, who prized honour and kept his word and wanted to rule. Somehow Peera, the young ambitious Khoja, and the turbulent Arab prince hit it off and found a common understanding and friendship, which lasted thirty years.

Norman Bennett, in his *History of the Arab State of Zanzibar*, suggests Majid was not the feeble, lacklustre Sultan often portrayed, but wily and manipulative, who successfully used the British to secure his position in Zanzibar and outmanoeuvre his brother. However, it is more probable the British took advantage of the Sultan's weakness and used the opportunity of the dynastic quarrel to tighten its grip on Zanzibar. Zanzibar, like a princely state in India, had to dance to a British tune to keep up an appearance of independence. There was a heavy price to pay for British help. Consul Rigby now required the Sultan to enforce the slave-trading treaties in the fullness of their terms, which had not been done previously. Rigby insisted that British naval ships had the right to seize, search and destroy any suspected Arab slaver operating in Zanzibar waters. The embattled Sultan Majid was in no position to refuse his protector, despite the protests of his subjects and the financial losses suffered.

The Indian community of Zanzibar also felt the heavy hand of Consul Rigby. By the time Rigby left, he had freed over 8,000 Indian-owned slaves,[4] and had acted to prevent Indians under British protection from either possessing slaves or from dealing directly in their sale or transfer. When at first the Indians protested, saying they were now citizens of Zanzibar answerable only to its Sultan and didn't want British protection, Rigby refused to listen. He announced that all their slaves had to be emancipated immediately and then registered at the British Consulate. Many Indians reluctantly complied as they could not afford to lose their commercial ties with British India.

Rigby on his return to England was praised by his superiors for 'meritorious labours characterised by great judgement and resolution.'[5] Sultan Majid heaved a huge sigh of relief when Rigby left in September 1861 due to ill health and the Indians of Zanzibar regarded Rigby's departure as equal to the termination of a great catastrophe.

------

1 *Zanzibar Gazette*, August 31, 1904
2 *Memoirs of an Arabian Princess* by Emily Said-Ruete, was originally written in German and published in 1886, but since then there have been several translations into English all of which differ slightly and have alternative editor's introductions and notes. The most comprehensive version is *An Arabian Princess Between Two Worlds: Memoirs, Letters Home, Sequels to the Memoirs, Syrian Customs and Usages*, edited with an introduction by E van Donzel, Leiden: E J Brill, 1993.
3 Evidence that he could speak French comes from a report on the

arrival of Bishop Courmont in Zanzibar in 1884, when he was welcomed by 'the Indian Pira, one of our former students and the representative of the Sultan.'

(*Annales de la propagation de la foi*, Vol 58, 1886, p 197) Fr Armand Fava had been sent to Zanzibar to establish a French mission as early as 1858, though it was not formally opened until 1860. Amongst other functions it ran French language courses.

4 Mrs Charles E B Russell, *General Rigby, Zanzibar and the Slave Trade*, London: Allen & Unwin, 1935, p 95

5 Norman R Bennett, *A History of the Arab State of Zanzibar*, London: Methuen, 1978, p 69

Chapter Five

The Waiting Years

Barghash's banishment was short lived. In October 1861, after spending two years in Bombay, he returned to Zanzibar in the company of Major Lewis Pelly of the East India Company, who had just been appointed British consul. Majid had agreed to his brother's return, but under strict conditions, as he now regarded his younger brother with great suspicion. Barghash was required to attend the Sultan's formal public audiences – *baraza* – no doubt so an eye could be kept upon him, but otherwise none of his former Arab friends were allowed to visit or speak with him. The American Consul, William C Webb, noted that 'his reception was very cool and his situation here is very unpleasant.' [1]

Barghash spent much of his time at one of his country properties, as he was not welcome in town. This gave him ample opportunity to reflect on the error of his ways and he appears to have learnt his lesson. The generally accepted conclusion is that he had enjoyed himself in Bombay and the exile had done him a lot of good. The British had treated him well, giving him accommodation, a carriage and a generous living allowance during his enforced stay. The experience had opened his eyes to the power of the British Raj and had given him a reality check. He had seen the wonders of India at close quarters and realised how backward and parochial Oman and Zanzibar were by comparison. A chastened and reformed character, he now hunkered down and waited for his sickly brother Majid to die. Barghash knew, if he could just keep out of trouble and be patient, the sultanate would soon be his. He blamed his sisters for the failure of his rebellion and would never again accept the advice of women. He turned against female influence and kept his own wives in strict seclusion under virtual lock and key.

Barghash devoted himself to country pastimes, hunting and generally keeping a low profile. He received no allowance from his brother, so he did not have the funds to indulge in costly luxuries or high living. His main hobby was cookery. He was always fond of his food and apparently liked to do the cooking himself. Cold-shouldered by his former friends, and kept away from public attention by order of Majid, his main companions became his servants and slaves. Peera Dewjee, his barber and valet, was one of those who kept him company during the lonely years of waiting.

British consuls came and went. Lewis Pelly, the next consul, realising how unpopular Rigby's anti-slaving policies had been, quietly allowed them to lapse. He introduced a system whereby dhows captured by the British Navy on suspicion of slavery were to be brought into Zanzibar for investigation to determine if they were actually slavers or not. They were no longer to be destroyed on the spot as sanctioned by Rigby. On the practice of Indian slave holding, he showed sympathy to those who complained that Rigby's emancipation measures had caused their landed property to fall sharply in value. He did nothing to prevent them from reverting to their old ways.

By 1862 nearly all that Rigby had achieved had been reversed. This 'softly-softly' policy was continued by Pelly's successor, Robert Lambert Playfair (1863-5), who excused his stand on slavery by saying Sultan Majid lacked the authority to compel his subjects into obedience. There had always been a divergence of policies and rivalry between the India Office and the Foreign Office as each tried to promote its own views and personnel. Zanzibar affairs came under the direction of the India Office, but the Foreign Office controlled British diplomacy overseas and became increasingly interested in the region as the century progressed. Pelly and Playfair represented the last gasp of the old guard of the India office – the old fashioned Orientalists, and pragmatists who thought Rigby's emancipation policies had been overly enthusiastic and ill-judged, likely to precipitate unrest. They preferred a more conciliatory approach.

The political life of Zanzibar was enlivened in 1865 by Abdul

Aziz quarrelling with Majid and then in 1866 by Salme's elopement with a German trader. Abdul Aziz argued with Majid, accusing him of withholding his share of the inheritance of a brother who had recently died. Majid grew so annoyed that he slapped his brother in public. Angered by this insult, the hot-tempered Abdul Aziz plotted to have his followers ravage Majid's clove plantations until he relinquished the legacy. But before he could carry out his intentions, he was arrested and thrown into prison. Barghash came under suspicion, because Abdul Aziz had been his fellow accomplice in the 1859 plot. Barghash was also arrested and brought in for questioning but protested his innocence vigorously. He was believed, because he was ill and suffering from an immense scrotal swelling at the time.

Barghash had the medical condition known as elephantiasis, which is caused by an infection with *Wuchereria Bancrofti*, a filarial worm which is common in the tropics, and is transmitted by the bite of a mosquito. An infected mosquito will inject larval worms, which travel in the lymphatic channels to the lymph nodes and develop into mature worms two or three inches long. In men, the lower limbs and the groin nodes are usually affected. Initially the disease is symptom free, but with repeated infections the body reacts with fever and transient infection of the lymphatic tracts. Over many years of infection, some sufferers will develop elephantiasis.

As the lymphatic drainage is obstructed, fluid accumulates in the tissues under the skin of the lower legs making it thick and fissured like the skin of an elephant. In men, this can also cause hydrocele, a large fluid collection in the scrotum. This was the case with the unfortunate Barghash. Another disturbing symptom is chyluria, when lymph gets into the bladder and the urine turns milky. Elephantiasis is a slow insidious disease, which usually starts in childhood and takes several years to manifest itself.

Nowadays treatment with anti-helminthic drugs can kill the worms, but once elephantiasis has developed it cannot be reversed. In the nineteenth century all that could be done was to alleviate the symptoms by massage, careful hygiene and drainage of the excess fluid. Barghash suffered a great deal from this embarrassing condition and he tried to hide his swollen misshapen lower limbs under flowing robes. As he aged and the disease worsened, attacks of acute sepsis became more frequent, leaving him in agony for days. (Burton noted that elephantiasis was common amongst Arabs in Zanzibar and he attributed it to poor hygiene and climatic conditions – though this was not strictly true, as it was caused by mosquitoes).[2]

It is tempting to speculate that his trusted barber and valet, Peera Dewjee, helped with the treatment of this unpleasant condition – perhaps he performed the surgical incisions necessary to drain off the accumulations of fluid, when the swellings became severe and painful. The role of barber and surgeon has always had a close affinity and dexterity with the razor was no doubt a prerequisite of Peera's job. Though Barghash always wore a beard and moustache, his head under his turban was kept close shaven. His turban, which was twisted around his head in Omani fashion and tied in a knot with the end hanging loose, required daily re-tying, unlike the folded turbans of the Hindus and Ismailis, which could be simply lifted off and worn again like a hat.

Family life amongst Arabs is kept strictly private. Barghash kept his domestic arrangements well away from prying European eyes and his attendants were loyal. Dr Christie, who acted as doctor to the Sultan's household from 1865 and was later employed as Barghash's personal physician, never described his patient's illnesses in his letters home, nor how he treated them. He did complain, however, that Arabs were bad patients, who expected to be cured as if by magic. He disliked their habit of paying him in kind rather than money, as he had no use for embroidered scarves and shawls. His favourite patients were the Hindus, who paid him in cash promptly and followed his instructions exactly.[3]

Barghash on this occasion asked the Sultan for permission to go to Bombay to consult a doctor. Barghash said that if Majid released Abdul Aziz, he would personally accompany Abdul Aziz to Bombay on the understanding that the rash young prince was never again to return to East Africa. Consul Playfair supported Barghash's request and persuaded Majid to agree. Moreover, he arranged for the Indian Government to give Barghash specialist medical attention in Bombay and be treated like a sick friend.

Abdul Aziz, who Salme described as one of her more energetic and vigorous brothers, went on to have an adventurous life, living in Oman and Baluchistan. He never returned to Zanzibar.

During September-October 1865, on the recommendation of the British Consul, Majid also visited India. It was hoped an Indian visit would have a good effect on him too, help his epilepsy and rouse him from the fatal apathy that afflicted him (opium addiction). He returned with many purchases, including furniture, two carriages, for which Zanzibar had no roads, and a band of musicians, which became a permanent feature of the Arab sultanate. There is a photograph of Majid seated in an elaborate Indian-style carved chair beside a side table (a novelty item for an Arab household) with a vase of flowers (also unheard of in Arab households of the time). The India visit unfortunately did not cure him of his 'apathy.'

After the failure of the 1859 palace coup, Salme and the other royal women involved were in deep disgrace. Even the Indian shopkeepers feared dealing with them and only did so after dark. Salme retired to her plantation at Kisimbani, where she lived quietly for a while. Then Majid visited her and offered forgiveness. She admitted her fault and came back to live in town. But Salme was not content.

Majid made no effort to find her a suitable husband, and her former friends no longer trusted her. Her involvement in the plot had tarnished her. She amused herself with the visits of European ladies, who were fascinated by her and came to see her often. In one of Elizabeth Jacob's letters, dated February 1865, there is a good description of an audience with Sultan Majid and a visit to two of his sisters.[4] Henry Jacob with his wife had come to Zanzibar to work for Captain Fraser on the sugar plantation at Mkokotoni. Their stay in Zanzibar was short, but the letters Elizabeth wrote home provide a fascinating glimpse of Zanzibar life. She described how the day after

A reception at the Sultan's Palace

her husband had been with the British Consul Playfair and the other English residents to pay respects to the Sultan, she went with Mrs Playfair to pay her respects to the Sultan and his ladies.

'He received us in a long plain marble paved room which had two crimson chairs at one end on which we were seated. He sat on one side and his four brothers at the other, his women folk being banished to a distance of about fifty feet so that we could not possibly speak to them.' The English women spoke in Hindustani, and the Sultan replied in Arabic and an interpreter translated, which did not make much conversation possible. The usual ceremony of sweet drinks, coffee and attar of roses poured on handkerchiefs followed and then they set off to see his other sisters who had houses of their own.

Their first visit was to Asche, the elder sister of Chole, who according to Elizabeth Jacob 'lived in the dirtiest house you ever saw. First a dirty courtyard with ducks gobbling in pools of dirty water and dirty slaves cooking omelettes etc. for the royal table, then a staircase so narrow and dark and dirty' that Elizabeth's best clothes were covered with black dust. Asche was a disappointment. She sat squatting on a mat chewing betel nut and spitting out of the window and didn't say a word. The guests were plied with the usual refreshments – sweetmeats, sherbet, coffee and attar of roses.

The next visit to Salme was far more entertaining. She came clattering down the stairs to meet them and greeted them in English and laughed with glee at their surprise. Elizabeth Jacob described her as most picturesque, 'and must be very pretty indeed if one could see her face without her mask which hides all but her eyes, mouth and chin.' She was dressed in a silk crimson and silver striped tunic with trousers underneath, but the dress was hardly visible for all the gold and jewels. Her nose, ears, arms, hands, legs, neck and head were literally laden with heavy gold jewellery set with innumerable precious stones. In each ear she had six earrings all about a foot long. She told the ladies that though they were uncomfortable, she never took them out, and slept fully clothed in all her jewels. She served them coffee with milk and sugar in European cups and spoke a little Hindustani as well as a few words of English. Elizabeth Jacob was impressed with the Eastern luxury and fine furnishings of her room, which she said 'was the only place in any of these royal residences that looked fresh and clean even!'[5]

Salme enjoyed the attention of these Europeans and their chatter about life in Europe seduced her. She must have thought a new life in Europe would solve all her problems. Majid and her family seemed to have no interest in her future – she was yet another supernumerary princess destined for spinsterhood and nonentity. Salme wanted more out of life. It was shortly after this in 1866 that she began her affair with Heinrich Ruete, a young German trader who lived in an adjoining house. It caused an excited flutter amongst the gossips of Zanzibar. Flouting conventions, she took her chance and charmed the young German. They fell in love. When the evidence of her pregnancy could be concealed no longer, terrified for his safety, Heinrich Ruete fled Zanzibar and Salme attempted to stow away on one of her lover's company ships, but she was spotted and brought back to Zanzibar.

Informed by the British Vice Consul, Dr John Kirk, that her

behaviour would inevitably lead to the death penalty for her and the child, Captain Pasley, a senior officer in the Royal Navy's East African Anti-Slave Trade Squadron, took pity on her. With the help of Mrs Seward, wife of the surgeon attached to the British Agency, he organised a daring rescue. A trusted servant of Mrs Seward's took the secret message to Salme, telling her to come to the beach on 26 August, the date of Swahili New Year, when as part of traditional ritual all citizens of Zanzibar went down to the sea to wash themselves and their belongings. A ship's cutter was despatched to a prearranged spot with orders to embark the princess and her servants. The princess was waiting ready on the beach, with her boxes of Maria Theresa Dollars and jewellery, and sprang willingly into the boat, but her two servants were terrified and screamed loudly as they knew nothing about the rescue plan. One was bundled into the boat but the other ran away.[6]

Captain Pasley and the crew of the frigate HMS *Highflyer* carried the princess and her servant to the safety of the coaling station in Aden, where there was a small British settlement. Here she gave birth to a son and received Christian instruction. She was baptised and given the Christian name of Emily. Her little boy was named Henry after the father. Heinrich Ruete and Salme were eventually married at Aden on 30 May 1867. Sadly little Henry died between Lyons and Paris on the way to Hamburg, but Salme later had three further children, a son, Rudolph, and two daughters.

Suspicion fell on the British Agency and in particular Vice Consul, Dr Kirk, though he denied all knowledge of the rescue operation. Captain Pasley's chivalrous intervention, though humane and admirable, could have backfired badly and indeed the British community in Zanzibar lived in fear of reprisals for some time afterwards. A British warship had to be stationed offshore as a precaution. However, Salme's removal from Zanzibar was probably a relief to Majid and he made no effort to punish his sister or those who had helped her. Her impulsive actions later had political ramifications and caused problems, but they did not impact upon Majid, who took the credit for his clemency and forbearance. As for Salme, her husband died in an accident in Germany just three years after the marriage. On her own, she became disillusioned with Europe and spent the rest of her life trying to get back to Zanzibar.

With the arrival of Henry Adrian Churchill (1865-70), an official appointed by the Foreign office and not the Indian government, the awkward question of Indian slave holding reasserted itself. Churchill resurrected Rigby's policies and began issuing regulations prohibiting Indians from slave trading activities and requiring the registration of slaves. But the Indians from Kutch protested strongly and insisted the British had no hold over them. The precise legalities were investigated and the answer came back from Bombay that Britain did not have the right to interfere in Kutchi slave holding without the express authority of Kutch's ruler the Rao. Reluctantly Consul Churchill backed down. He did, however, secure a promise from Sultan Majid that he would punish Indians engaging in the slave trade and recognise that all future Indian arrivals in Zanzibar would be subject to British authority. He also managed to persuade the Sultan in 1868 to allow the Royal Navy to step up their surveillance of slave ships.

Churchill put more pressure on the Indian community and increased the anti-slaving patrols, but he did not manage to make significant changes. He was frequently ill and on sick leave and his deputy Dr John Kirk had to stand in for him.

Under the sultanate of Majid slave trading continued as a profit making and legal activity and the economy of Zanzibar grew at a healthy rate. But astute observers were becoming nervous of British intentions towards Zanzibar. They feared the prosperous slave trading days were coming to an end.

Majid was never reconciled to his brother Barghash, although as he had only one daughter and no male issue, he realised Barghash would succeed him after his death. As Sultan Majid's hold on life slowly ebbed away, Barghash's contact with powerful sectors of Zanzibar's community increased. He married the daughter of one of the wealthiest Arab chiefs in Zanzibar, thus ensuring his support. He spoke with Acting British Consul Kirk on a number of occasions and surrounded himself with a pious grouping of Ibadhi imams or *Muttawa,* who gave religious legitimacy to his claim. This time there was to be no mistake. He would be Sultan.

What was Peera Dewjee doing during these years? The normal growing up process for a young Khoja Ismaili in Zanzibar at this period was to start his own business and once it was established, to find himself a wife to help him run it. This usually occurred around the age of twenty but Peera Dewjee does not appear to have married until much later, when he was over thirty years of age. His eldest son was not born until about 1878. Was this because he was so busy in the service of Barghash he had no time to attend to his own business activities or marry? Did an earlier wife and family all die of cholera? Or was there another reason?

It is hard to imagine Peera did not start a trading business of some kind. Like most of his generation he was a businessman to his fingertips. It was what he had been trained to do from childhood. In the foreground of Johnson's photograph of Khojas, depicting Nansi Parpia and his family, a younger man elegantly dressed, also seated in a chair, stares confidently out of the picture. The occupant of the chair (a sign of status), explains Johnson, is an example of the new generation of Khojas, who had recently started trading with London.[7] There is something about the direct gaze of the young man, (despite the glasses), and the dark eyebrows that meet over the nose, which seems similar to the only known photographs of Peera Dewjee taken over thirty years later. If this is Peera, he would be in his early twenties, exactly the right age when, as Burton explains, the young Indian merchant, having established himself in business, returns to India to find himself a wife.

But 1863 was a dangerous time for businessmen in Bombay. Cotton exports from Bombay boomed when the American trade failed due to their Civil War. Everyone bought into cotton furiously, prices went sky high, the market overheated and then crashed. The Bank of Bombay failed. Many who had bought cotton stocks lost everything, while others, who had borrowed money on easy terms, had their loans and mortgages withdrawn and were ruined. Was this the fate of Peera

Dewjee? There is a tantalising entry for 2 September 1864 in the *London Gazette* under notices from Bombay which mentions a Peera Dewa, Khoja, currently in the Bombay gaol requesting insolvency relief. If this is our Peera, then he would have had to start all over again, defer all thought of marriage and continue with his day job until his debts were paid. It would explain why Peera remained in the service of Barghash as his barber and valet, a position not usually taken by Ismailis who preferred to run their own shops and businesses.

More circumstantial evidence for this scenario comes from General Rigby's biography written by his daughter Mrs Charles E B Russell in 1935, which was based on his journals and writings. Under notes on trade dating from 1862, Rigby complained how British trade in Zanzibar lagged behind that of France and America due to a lack of organisation on the ground.[8] He cited as an example, which he said happened more than once, how a businessman in Bombay would charter a ship to load cargo for London, but when the ship arrived the agent had no cargo ready, because no communication had been received and the letter of instruction from Bombay arrived after the ship. The ship waited in vain for cargo and then left in ballast entailing a heavy loss for the charterers in Bombay. It is possible that Peera Dewjee, who later ran a shipping line for the Sultan and worked as a shipping agent, suffered a similar misadventure, compounded by the crash in Bombay, leaving him bankrupt and heavily in debt.

1 Norman R Bennett, *A History of the Arab State of Zanzibar*, London: Methuen, 1978, p 70
2 With thanks to my sister Dr S A Hull for the medical information.
3 Letters of Dr Christie, Cambridge University Library MS, Add 8163
4 Yvonne Bird, ed, *A Quaker Family in India and Zanzibar, 1863-1865: Letters from Elizabeth and Henry Jacob*, York: William Session, 2000
5 *Ibid*, p 163-4
6 Tim Jeal, *Explorers of the Nile*, 2011, p 360-1. Tim Jeal is a descendant of Captain Pasley. I thank him for giving me additional insights into the rescue operation.

7 William Johnson, *The Oriental Races and Tribes, Residents and Visitors of Bombay*, Vol I, London: 1863, plate 24

8 Mrs Charles E B Russell ed, *General Rigby, Zanzibar and the Slave Trade*, London: G Allen & Unwin, 1935, p 103

Chapter Six

A Few Words about Slavery

Although this book is not about slavery, it is impossible to write about nineteenth century Zanzibar without some mention of the infamous trade. The trade in slaves was the most profitable business in Zanzibar until the closure of the slave markets. Zanzibar became rich because the main market for slaves was situated on the island and the Sultans drew their chief source of income from duties from slaves.

The first slave treaty of consequence made between Britain and Oman was the Moresby Treaty of 1822, forbidding the sale of slaves to Christians anywhere in the dominions of Seyyid Said. The Hamerton Treaty of 1845 followed, prohibiting the export of slaves from his African dominions. It gave British naval vessels the right to seize and confiscate any vessels, which were the property of His Highness or of his subjects carrying on the slave trade. The only exception was for boats transporting slaves between ports within the Sultan's own dominions in Africa, primarily the port of Lamu in the north and the port of Kilwa in the south.

The important let-out clause was this exemption for slaves being transported between Lamu and Kilwa. This allowed slavers to take their human cargo to these far-flung ports of the Sultan's African territories under pretext of legal transportation and later smuggle the slaves out from there. As British ships could not legally board ships of other nations, those flying the French or Portuguese or American flags of convenience avoided search.

The Sultan groaned in mock despair. Lord Palmerston said grand words about putting an end to the African Slave Trade, but with cynicism, as he knew the treaties were mere face-saving measures to satisfy the lobbyists in Britain who were baying for action. It would take more than a few nicely worded legal phrases to stop an age-old trade, which was deeply entrenched in the region and in the 1840s the political will was not yet there. The British valued their friendship with Oman and did not wish to alienate an important ally. Maintaining peace in the Middle East was the overriding factor for the time being.

The loopholes meant that the 1845 treaty was honoured more in its breach than in its compliance. Trading vessels came and went as before and instead of legal cargo, the Arab merchants smuggled the slaves destined for Oman, Egypt and Persia, while the French and Portuguese traders carried on buying slaves in ever greater numbers for their plantations on the Comoro Islands, Madagascar, Mauritius and Mozambique.

The Royal Navy had permission to harry slave ships in Zanzibar waters, board suspected slavers and capture any slaves they found. This made slave trading a more risky business, but the rewards were correspondingly higher and the conditions of transported slaves were made worse as a result of the efforts to avoid capture. The patrols by the Royal Navy were not very successful. The fast sailing dhows could out-manoeuvre the more cumbersome naval gunboats, and if challenged they had plenty of tricks up their sleeves. Some claimed the slaves were sailors. Others landed their cargo in secret when a naval ship appeared on the horizon. When the British searched they found no slaves and the slavers simply reloaded the slaves again when the danger was over. This caused maximum discomfort for the live cargo, hidden in damp caves and in the undergrowth of sandy coves. The slaving dhows flew a number of flags of convenience and thumbed their noses at the British as they sailed by, running up an American or French flag as they went. The British expended a great deal of public money and manpower for very little result. According to Tim Jeal, 17,000 members of the Royal Navy died as a result of their service with the West and East African anti-Slave Trade Squadrons.[1] No figures are given for the numbers of the slaves they freed, but they were few by comparison. The romance of *Dhow Chasing in Zanzibar Waters*, (the title of the famous book by Captain G J Sulivan, RN published in 1873) was anything but, in reality. However it was good propaganda. The British back at home believed Britain was taking the lead in the fight against slavery and its iniquitous trade, and that was what mattered. But in Zanzibar, the first round had gone to the Arabs. The slave trade had always existed in the Indian Ocean and it always would. Nothing could stop it, – or so they thought.

The Indians of Zanzibar owned many slaves. They owned plantations and had slaves to work the land; they had transportation companies providing porters, who were slaves, and some directly traded in slaves and ivory. In addition, almost every family in Zanzibar owned domestic slaves.

One testimony by a former domestic slave, in the collection written down by A C Madan, is that of a young man of the Yao tribe, who was owned by an Indian ivory dealer based in Saadani. He seems to have been treated well by his owner who would leave him in charge of his house and property during his visits to Zanzibar. Once, when the Indian went to Zanzibar, ten dollars were stolen.

> When he came back I told him that ten dollars had been stolen but he only said 'Never mind.' After this we went to live at Uvinje...In this town the Banyan built a hut of cocoa-nut leaves, but did not get as far as plastering it, when he left this house to me and wages for labourers, charging me to collect earth and direct the work. He went to Zanzibar to buy doors, lime and other things. When he came back he found large heaps of earth ready and was much pleased...
> Then came the time when all slaves were registered. The consul came to the district of Saadani and other districts on the mainland. On the arrival of the consul he registered all slaves belonging to Hindis as free. [2]

Richard Burton mentions meeting Indian slave traders in the interior of Africa, most famously of all the Khoja Ismaili, Musa Mzuri. He and Speke were given a letter of introduction to Musa, who was the leading ivory trader in the region of the great lakes and lived at Tabora in splendour surrounded by his wives and 300 slaves. They finally caught up with Musa in Tabora (then known as Kazeh) in 1857, and Burton had a long conversation with him and gleaned valuable information about the geography of the area. Musa offered to take the two explorers to Uganda, where he was heading for his next trading trip, but Burton was too ill to travel, much to Speke's disappointment. Three years later, in 1860, Speke, on his second expedition to find the source of the Nile, met up with Musa again in Tabora. He helped the two explorers, Speke and Grant, and supplied them with porters, as theirs had all deserted, but then unfortunately died, before he could go with them to Uganda. Speke described how Musa looked horribly ill despite dosing himself with what he described as his pills – small dried poppy heads taken with alternate bits of sugar candy. Musa had been an opium addict for more than forty years, but finally repeated attacks of malaria combined with the opium caused his death. The opium addiction had not affected his business acumen, as Speke complained that he charged 400 per cent more for trade goods and porters than was charged at the Coast.[3]

In 1860, Consul Rigby deported a British Indian called Kanoo Manjee, who owned 69 slaves working for him on his plantation. He had been asked to register them, but he refused. Rigby fined him ten Maria Theresa dollars a slave and sent him on the first dhow back to India.[4] The Indian merchant Rush Ramji, the Chief of Customs' clerk, rented nine slaves to Burton for his expedition. Their only object according to Burton was to capture further slaves.[5] Even the saintly Livingstone as late as 1871 referred to his 'banian slaves,' porters sent to him by Dr Kirk, the British Consul. These were ten slaves owned by an Indian trader, who rented them to Kirk. They proved to be a troublesome and mutinous lot, who joined the Arab slaving raids and helped murder fellow Africans, much to Livingstone's distress.[6]

Slavery in Zanzibar was endemic and permeated every sector of society. Every Arab and Muslim of standing owned slaves, and wealth and respect was counted in slaves. As there was very little 'free' labour to be had on the island, Christians and Europeans often had no other option but to employ slaves rented from their owners.

There is the interesting case of Captain H A Fraser, who in 1864 at the request of Sultan Majid set up a sugar plantation at Mkokotoni. As a British subject, he was not allowed to own slaves or employ them – slave trading by British subjects had been outlawed in 1807 and slaveholding by British subjects had been forbidden under the Emancipation Act of 1833. To get round this Fraser employed other people's slaves, slaves owned by the Sultan and others. He engaged them on contract, paid them a set wage and trained them for the work. To begin with all went well and no objection was raised by British Consul Playfair. However, in 1867 he was accused of underpaying his labour and profiting by slavery. Sultan Majid tried to save the situation by buying up the whole workforce and freeing them, so Fraser could employ them legally on proper wages. But the freed slaves were confused by their new status and many refused to work. Fraser ended up bankrupt and the sugar cane factory project failed.

Captain Fraser was a rude and overbearing man with a bad temper, who made more enemies than friends. Dr Kirk, the deputy British Consul, did not approve of him. He shopped him to his brother-in-law, the Reverend Horace Waller, a missionary and slavery abolitionist. Waller brought Fraser's misdeeds to the notice of the general British public, who were horrified to hear one of their own had been involved with slave labour in Zanzibar.

Fraser's defence, which was eventually brought before the British parliament in 1872, reads as if he was a philanthropist rather than a businessman. (The pamphlet produced with the help of Dr Christie is entitled 'A letter to the Honourable Members of the Select committee of the House of Commons appointed to inquire into the Question of the Slave trade on the East Coast of Africa in reply to allegations by Horace Waller stated in evidence to your Committee on 24th July 1871.') In it he explained how he provided a doctor (Dr Christie) and housing on the plantation so his staff would work to the best of their ability. He said when his staff first arrived many suffered from horrible diseases, but after he had looked after them and fed them for a few months their health improved. He explained how he rarely lost staff as they appreciated the working conditions and he only dismissed those who were incorrigibly work shy. He explained how he had no other option but to employ slaves as they were the only labour to be had in Zanzibar. He described the large amount of money he had put into the operations, building a factory and putting in machinery, employing British engineers and overseers and was most aggrieved by the way the missionary Waller had made an example of him, especially as he claimed he had cleared his position with the British consul before going ahead with the project. He was disappointed that this same ex-consul had then changed his mind and now disowned him.

It seems Fraser had a point and the British Anti-slavery League was being somewhat disingenuous. If there was no other labour to be had, what was he supposed to do? No doubt Fraser had an unfortunate manner, but others in a similar situation found they had no option but to employ slave labour, not directly, but indirectly. Ropes, the American merchant, in 1883, described his band of women garbling cloves and bashing coir fibre from coconuts on the roof of his office and singing and dancing while they did the work.[7] Though he did not specifically mention it, they too would have been slaves, employed at a daily rate from their owners, who kept a proportion of the pay. (Slavery in the US had been abolished in 1865.)

There were precise laws governing slave ownership in Zanzibar – the amount they could keep from the money paid to their master for work done, and two days off each week when they could work for themselves and keep all they earned. Some Zanzibari slaves did quite well out of the system and even owned slaves themselves. There are descriptions of feast days, when slaves dressed up in rich clothes, ate, drank and made merry. Salme described how at the feast of Eid ul-Fitr, the most important holiday in the Muslim calendar, bands of slaves went round the households demanding presents and would not leave unless coins were pressed into their hands. The terrible picture of slaves in chains, cruelly treated and starving, was not always accurate, and the anti-slavery acts forced on the Sultans paradoxically sometimes made conditions worse rather than better.

The demand for slaves and ivory from East Africa increased after 1840. Prior to this, the trade had been largely in African hands. Slaves captured from rival tribes and as a result of tribal conflict were brought down from the interior as part of large trading caravans and sold to overseas buyers, mostly from Arabia and other Muslim areas. Abyssinian slaves were particularly prized. But after 1840 foreigners, mostly Arabs and Swahili, began to travel into the interior actively seeking ivory and slaves to meet the increased demand. As the supply dried up, the traders went further and further inland and used more and more force to gain what they wanted. There was an insatiable demand for ivory in the West and the plantations in Zanzibar and the French colonies, producing cloves and sugar, depended on a large workforce, which needed continual replenishment.

Even Dr Livingstone, the most influential voice in the campaign against slavery in East Africa, conceded that traditional Arab treatment of their domestic slaves was relatively mild. He said it was the process by which Africans were torn from their homes, which was unspeakably brutal. The terrible land and sea journey they suffered to get to Zanzibar and the Gulf were the cruellest features of the trade. On arrival they were often treated better by their Arab masters than workers in British factories by their employers and Livingstone could vouch for this as he had been a mill worker as a boy.

Livingstone's explanation for this conundrum was the corrupting evil of the profit margin. Once profit entered into the equation, then the lot of the slave became much harder, as in the case of plantation workers in the American Deep South. Livingstone thought that as society became more sophisticated and wants multiplied, the distance between master and the common man widened and the treatment of slaves grew correspondingly harsher. He understood that the responsibility for the cruelties of the slave trade did not lie solely with the Arabs and Swahili.

It is ironic that the slave traders eventually engineered their own downfall. Many of the famous European explorers travelled with Arab slave traders and relied heavily on their help. They could not have reached the Great Lakes or found the source of the Nile without their assistance. It was the descriptions sent home by such men as Livingstone, Speke and Stanley, who saw first hand the atrocities perpetrated by the slave traders, which finally persuaded the British Government to act with greater firmness.

Consul Rigby (1860-2) was the first to confront the problem head on in Zanzibar. Up until this point the India Office had turned a blind eye, but now India, directly under the rule of the British government since 1858, felt powerful enough to uphold its principles, particularly in the case of its own subjects. British subjects and British protected persons were not allowed to own slaves. This had been clearly stated in the treaty of 1833 and in the more extensive one of 1845, which also restricted the export of slaves from Zanzibar. But in Zanzibar the law was being flouted. Indian merchants from Bombay and Kutch openly owned slaves. They had slaves working on their *shambas* (plantations), manning the dhows, and working in their offices and homes. The blunt speaking Rigby said this could not continue: all British protected persons were required to release their slaves forthwith on pain of prosecution.

Rigby's initial efforts failed, as many Indians refused to accept British status. Instead they declared themselves citizens of Zanzibar under the protection of the Sultan. They challenged the legality of the British consul's interference and initially their point of view was upheld. Indians from Kutch were declared answerable to the Rao, not to the British Government. But the British were determined to bring the recalcitrant Indians in line, as they saw it, as an essential first step in a solution to the wider problem of slavery in Zanzibar. A new dispatch of 1866 ordered that they be treated as British subjects.

Slaveholding in British India and in Kutch had been outlawed as early as 1836, but this ruling did not apply to those Kutchis living overseas. In 1867 Sultan Majid tried to protect his Indian friends from British interference by claiming that Kutchis who had entered his services had automatically acquired rights to possess slaves in his dominions. He asked what was the status of those Kutchi children born in Zanzibar? Surely they were Zanzibari and his subjects, not British ones.

In 1869 there was a high profile quarrel over an Indian arrested by British Consul Churchill for selling a slave in the market in Zanzibar.

Sultan Majid said the British consul had no right to arrest one of his subjects. He sent two envoys, Hamid bin Suleiman and Sheikh Mahommed bin Abdalla, to India to see the British Governor General in Simla to clarify the position. Their mission was unsuccessful. The Governor General upheld the Consul's action and said that since 1866 all British subjects had been required to enrol on the Consular register in Zanzibar. Furthermore, the Indian in question was a British protected person because he originated from Kutch, and was therefore answerable to British law.

In the same year the Rao of Kutch, under pressure from his political agent Major Shortt (no doubt prompted from Zanzibar), was persuaded to issue a more comprehensive proclamation saying that any Kutchi found to have engaged in the slave trade would be deemed a criminal and punished accordingly. This new proclamation was extended to all his Kutchi subjects, wherever they lived. Kazi Shahbuden, the Rao of Kutch's chief advisor, told Major Shortt that to the best of his knowledge by 1869 Kutchi traders were not known to be openly engaged in the slave trade, although he admitted that most of them owned slaves at least outside of Zanzibar town.

This finally clarified the position of Kutchi Indians living in Zanzibar, who were now deemed to be answerable to British law and would have to comply with the British veto on slave dealing and slaveholding. Sultan Majid had failed to withstand British interference within his realm and a significant number of the population of Zanzibar had been removed from his jurisdiction. This humiliated him. It signified a further loss of independence for the state of Zanzibar, and a further increase in British influence.

Amongst the Indian population more slaves were confiscated from Indian owners and sent to a freed slave settlement outside Bombay called Nasik. But many Indian owners simply denied they had slaves and continued to hold them illegally or by proxy. Slave owning by the Indian population went underground. This unofficial status provided fewer channels of recourse, and the slaves suffered.

In 1868 the British Government sanctioned the building of their own gaol in Zanzibar and paid 10,000 rupees towards construction costs. There had been a British consular court in Zanzibar since 1861, but now they expected a surge in legal actions and convictions. The gaol was designed with two storeys, the upper floors for European offenders – mainly drunk and disorderly British sailors – and the lower floor for 'natives,' presumably British Indians who had failed to declare and emancipate their slaves.

Did Peera Dewjee own slaves? Almost certainly, yes, if he could have afforded them! Working in the service of Barghash, the Sultan's brother, he would have claimed exemption from compulsory registration at the British consulate and been part of the Kutchi lobby, who protested against their enforced status of British protection. After 1870, Indians in Zanzibar gradually distanced themselves from overt slave trading and slave ownership.

1 Tim Jeal, *Explorers of the Nile: The Triumph and Tragedy of a Great Victorian Adventure*, London: Faber and Faber, 2011, p 362
2 A C Madan, ed, *Kiungani; or, Story and History from Central Africa; Written by Boys in the Schools of the Universities' Mission to Central Africa*, London: George Bell & Sons, 1887, p 54-9
3 John H Speke, *Journal of the Discovery of the Source of the Nile*, Edinburgh: William Blackwood and Sons, 1863, p 99-100
4 IOR/L/PS/6/560 note on slaveholding by Kutchis
5 Jeal, *Explorers of the Nile*, p 71
6 *Ibid*, p 27
7 Norman R Bennett, ed, *the Zanzibar letter of Edward D Ropes, Jr 1882-1892*, African Studies Center, Boston University, 1973, p 10

Chapter Seven

A Poisoned Chalice: Barghash the Unlucky

Sultan Barghash

Sultan Majid died in 1870 aged 36. His epilepsy had worsened and the fits came more and more frequently. In the morning of 7 October he was found lying on the floor, barely conscious, but dressed in his robes and wearing his sword. Family members and courtiers rushed to the palace at the news and clustered round him waiting to hear his final instructions and choice of successor. But he was too weak to speak. His hand feebly moved until it rested on his sword hilt and then he died. When Barghash leant over to check whether Majid was still breathing, his dagger fell from its sheath to the ground and Khalifa, a younger brother standing close by, picked it up and returned it to him. This friendly gesture surprised the Arabs in attendance as a more ruthless man in a previous age would have seized the chance and with one thrust taken the sultanate for himself. The auspices were not good and the superstitious Arabs muttered in their beards.[1]

Nonetheless the handover went smoothly and Barghash was proclaimed sultan. He prided himself on being more like his father, in contrast to his feeble and soft living brother, Majid, who had neglected his duties as a Muslim ruler. Barghash wanted to turn the clock back and return to the old ways of his father, who had made the Islamic religion central to his government and sought the counsel of his Arab clerics.

Barghash followed the Ibadhi faith, which still is the traditional religion of Oman. It is a breakaway branch of Islam, founded circa 700 AD by Abdullah bin Ibadh, a Kharejite migrant from Persia, who had refused to recognise the authority of the Caliph in Damascus. Ibadhis differ from both Sunni and Shia Muslims in that they recognise only the first two successors of the Prophet Mohammed – Abubaker and Omar. (Sunnis acknowledge the first four – Abubaker, Omar, Othman and Ali, while traditional Shias recognise the first three.) Ibadhi mosques are simple and unadorned without minarets and the teachings eschew outward show and luxurious living, emphasising the spiritual over the material world. Not only is alcohol banned but tobacco as well. The puritanical and egalitarian nature of Ibadhi teachings was unusual within Islam. The Ibadhi Imam or head priest was elected by a council of chiefs, who also had the power to depose him if they wished. Originally the position of Imam represented temporal as well as spiritual power. As the centuries passed, the office of Imam became less democratic and in the nineteenth century had fallen into the hands of one ruling family in Oman, the al-Busaidy, whose sons were given the honorific religious title Seyyid, as descendants of the Imam. The full title of the first Sultan of Zanzibar was: Seyyid Said bin Sultan, Imam of Muscat and Sultan of Muscat and Zanzibar. Barghash inherited the religious role of Seyyid and when he became sultan of Zanzibar he was expected to oversee the religious conduct of his people as well as looking after their temporal needs. To a devout Muslim religion was all encompassing and there was no separation between the aspirations of mosque and state.

At first glance the world of the Omani Ibadhi Sultan Barghash and the Khoja Ismaili Peera Dewjee had little in common, but yet they worked together well. Both religions had their roots in Persia and were considered unorthodox by most Muslims and had a history of persecution – and perhaps because of this sense of being outsiders, were more tolerant of other religions and beliefs. Like the Khoja Ismailis, Ibadhis have the doctrine of pious concealment, which allowed them to misrepresent the true facts under duress or if the ends justified the means. The organisation of the Ismaili jamat, with its governing body of officials, had similarities to the Ibadhi council of elders, who controlled the community and reported to the Imam – however with the important difference that the office of the Aga Khan was hereditary, not elective. Khoja merchants had been established in Oman since the early eighteenth century and had been given the freedom to worship and live as they wished according to their customs, within their own settlements. There was a long history of friendship and co-existence and certainly Peera Dewjee and Sultan Barghash did not find their religious differences an obstacle to developing a close working relationship.

In John Martineau's biography of Sir Bartle Frere, there is an interesting description of a visit to the Khoja quarter or moholla in Muscat. Called Matrah, this settlement was in effect a fortified walled town, situated just outside the Arab city. Here according to Frere 'they all live and allow no-one else to live.' He noted an inscription over the main gate dating to 1733 and inside saw a thriving community with many healthy-looking women and children and numerous shops and businesses. They flew their own flag which was dark blue with a star and scimitar in white, in contrast to the red flag of Oman, and by the time of Frere's visit in 1873 had cast off the supremacy of the Aga Khan, but remained British subjects.[2]

According to traditional Ibadhi custom, Barghash's position as sultan in Zanzibar depended on the approval and agreement of his fellow chiefs and holy leaders. He ruled by means of *baraza* or open court, where citizens could come with their grievances and be heard whatever their station in life and receive justice according to *sharia* law.

The *baraza* or public audience was an extremely important function of the Sultan's government in Zanzibar, and there were many complaints whenever it failed to meet.

Barghash's first inner circle of councillors was a group of six pious reformist Ibadhi clerics known as *Muttawas*. Kirk, who referred to them as fanatics, lists them as follows:

Hamood bin Seif,
Alibhai Amin (Kathi,)
Mbarak bin Khalfan (Khadi),
Mohammed bin Suleiman, Mundevi,
Salim bin Khalfan,
Hamud bin Ahmed bin Seif.[3]

This council of six were all stern Ibadhi Muslims, who wanted to banish the Europeans and all European habits from the island and return to strict principles of Koranic law. Three days after he had succeeded to the Sultanate, on 10 October 1870, Barghash publicly repudiated the promise he had previously given to the British Consul Churchill to support the suppression of the slave trade in return for the British backing his candidature for Sultan. Urged on by his Arab council, he felt secure enough to adopt a hostile attitude towards the British and their anti-slavery policies.

Following the example of his father, Barghash devised a daily schedule devoted to prayer and duties of state and ran to a strict programme. He ruled in person and this ordered routine provided a framework and system for his government. Majid had allowed favouritism and corruption to take over at the palace, and although his reign had seen the prosperity of the island increase, it had not been due to any active participation on his part. Barghash thought he could do better and prove himself a worthy successor to his father by taking a more hands-on approach.

Every morning he arose at 4 am and entered the throne room carrying a lamp and the Koran from which, seated on the throne, he read certain passages aloud. At 4.30 his pious Arabs joined him taking it in turns to read from the Holy Book. They then prostrated themselves for the morning prayer and further readings took place until the sun rose. Now they broke their fast; tea, milk and cakes were brought to them. After this Barghash's confidential agents came to him, giving him news of events which had occurred during the night; they were succeeded by the Treasurer and the Customs officer, who each gave their reports. These interviews continued until 8 am, when the Sultan left the throne room to eat his first full meal of the day. In his private dining room Barghash sat alone at a large table covered with food. All around the room stood his slaves with their arms crossed on their breasts awaiting orders to carry morsels of food to the favourite ladies of the moment. Returning to the throne-room, the Sultan remained there from 9-11 am patiently and courteously listening to swarms of officials, merchants, travellers, plaintiffs, beggars and slaves who brought him greetings, requests and complaints.

After midday prayers, he retired for a two-hour siesta in the harem palace. He then had a short period when his friends came to talk to him and to eat sweets and fruits. Once afternoon prayers were over by 4.30 pm Barghash again retired to his own apartments for the second meal of the day. Then it was time to examine the work of the judges called *khadi* who dispensed justice in the Palace Square.

> At 6 pm there took place the beautiful and picturesque ceremony of the Closing of the Day. While the sun sank into the ocean, turning sea and sky to gold, the Seyyid, and his nobles, stood watching from a verandah. When the last red rim had disappeared, he raised his arm; guns fired a salute, the band played the anthem, and the crimson flag of Islam came fluttering down the staff.
>
> Now came the moment for evening prayers, after which visitors were received, and sometimes the Royal Party were entertained by a professional reciter of poems, who declaimed of war and courage. At last it was time for the night-prayers [at 8.30 pm], and then the weary Sultan could retire to sleep.
>
> This exhausting programme was strictly adhered to, but every month Barghash took at least a week off and rested at one or another of his country palaces.[4]

Zanzibar under the Sultans had a different time system from that used in the West. It ran from sunrise to sunset, therefore the first hour or *saa moja* was one hour after sunrise, the equivalent to the European time of 7 am and so on. The six hour difference caused much confusion to Europeans and appointments were often missed due to misunderstandings over time. The traditional rhythm of Islamic daily life, with the call to prayer five times a day, was completely alien to most Europeans living in Zanzibar, while the Arabs found the Christians equally puzzling with their entirely different customs and way of life.

It is not certain when Peera Dewjee graduated from court barber to Chief Steward, but certainly from the moment Barghash became Sultan, his duties became more onerous and responsible. It is not unreasonable to suppose Peera Dewjee helped orchestrate this elaborate daily programme, made sure the schedule ran to time, that meals arrived punctually and that all ran smoothly. Later he became Barghash's chief confidential agent, who kept him informed of events and crucially had a half hour conversation with Barghash before the start of each day.

According to Kirk, during the first month of his reign Barghash was busy with the sale and distribution of Majid's goods, most of which he seized for himself.

As the British Consul Churchill was on sick leave at the time of Majid's death, Dr Kirk, the deputy consul, found himself in charge at a critical moment. He reminded Barghash of his promise to stop the slave trade in return for British support, but Barghash brushed him aside. Back in England, Consul Churchill recommended to the home government that Barghash be replaced as Sultan by his brother Turki. When Barghash heard this he was furious. He called the German Consul to a secret parley and asked the German Government to ally with him against the British, but the Germans refused as they were loath to be drawn into a quarrel over Zanzibar.

Kirk was left in the hot seat to solve this bitter dispute, but heal it, he did. A man of calm and patient temperament, he set himself to win over the Sultan by degrees, continuously making himself useful by giving Barghash information and friendly advice, seemingly without ulterior motive or strings attached. The situation in Oman turned to his advantage. A civil war had broken out and Barghash received letters from both sides asking for his assistance. Turki, one of his elder brothers, had seized the Sultanate of Oman, but was facing opposition from religious reformists linked to Barghash's Muttawa advisory group, who claimed the Imamship and wanted to separate the religious office from that of the sultanate. In 1866 Sultan Thuweini of Oman had been murdered by his son, Salim, who took power, but was so unpopular that Turki had taken the opportunity to invade and claim the Sultanate instead. To add to the complexity of the situation, there was also the perennial worry that Zanzibar might be re-integrated with Oman and Barghash would then be deposed or left as a junior ruler paying tribute to his brother. Suddenly he needed to re-establish friendly relations with the British Consul as he required the reassurance of British support.

It was probably Peera Dewjee, his most trusted personal attendant, who took the secret messages Barghash did not want his Arab councillors to know about and evidence for this comes from Kirk himself who writes in one of the Consular reports:

> His Highness being desirous that…these letters should reach me unknown to his matawa advisers sent them by the hand of a confidential messenger and so also were they returned with my acknowledgement and remarks thereon.[5]

These were letters from his two brothers Turki and Abdul Aziz asking for help against the Muttawas and a letter from the religious fundamentalists asking for assistance against his brothers. Barghash was in a quandary and did not know how to answer. He needed a knowledgeable outsider to give impartial advice. Kirk did so discreetly, but to the point. He warned Barghash that the Imam's claim to be master of Zanzibar would not go away and he should be careful before committing himself to any demands. He signed himself off with the words: 'Should it ever be in my power to counsel you further on this or any other matter of State, I shall always deem it a privilege to hold myself at Your Highness's orders.'[6]

In this instance Barghash took Kirk's advice and refrained from hasty action. His brothers gained control of Oman without his help. The wily British Consul had succeeded in re-establishing an amicable relationship with the Sultan and Barghash began to seek his counsel with increasing frequency with Peera Dewjee as the go-between.

Beside political worries, Barghash had severe money problems. Majid had left many debts and owed an enormous sum of money to the Bombay firm of Jairam Sewji, which farmed the customs. Barghash refused to honour his brother's debt. Ladha Damji, the head of customs in Zanzibar, pressed for payment in full and a bad tempered argument ensued. Eventually when Barghash offered the post to another Indian company, Wat Bhima, Ladha Damji backed down and they reached an agreement. Ladha Damji continued in the post and Barghash handed over one of his father's ships in lieu of payment. Mohammed Bakashmar, who had been treasurer for Majid, was involved in these negotiations, and Barghash was pleased with the outcome. Bakashmar became one of Barghash's most trusted palace officials, second only to Peera Dewjee.

The 1870s saw the formerly obscure island of Zanzibar enter upon the world stage. A sleepy backwater no more, the island of Zanzibar became increasingly significant both commercially and politically as the century progressed. But with this new importance came the harsh spotlight of international scrutiny and increasing western influence and interference. The opening of the Suez Canal in 1869 halved the travelling distance from Europe to East Africa and India. The communication revolution had started and there was a surge of interest in East Africa and an increasing number of European visitors to Zanzibar. Ships from Europe to India no longer needed to go round South Africa, but could come via Egypt and Aden, and Zanzibar. Letters, which in previous years had simply got lost or taken months to come, now arrived in a matter of weeks. In December 1872, the

British India Steamship Company started a regular service to run mail between Aden and Zanzibar, once a month. This service, though it sounds unremarkable to us today, was for the citizens of Zanzibar a life changing moment. It helped stimulate the business life of Zanzibar. For the first time there was a reliable and regular means of contact with Europe and India. The Sultan complained he would have preferred a liner service between Zanzibar and Bombay, rather than Aden, but he was being picky and in no position to be choosy.

One famous visitor to Zanzibar, whose mission was to have momentous consequences for Barghash and Zanzibar, was Henry Morton Stanley, who arrived on January 7, 1871 aboard the American whaling ship, the *Falcon*. He had come to look for Dr Livingstone, who had headed deep in the interior in 1865 on his quest to determine the source of the Nile and to report on the slave trade. No one had heard from Livingstone for over a year. His many admirers and fellow abolitionists had become increasingly anxious about their favourite missionary and explorer.

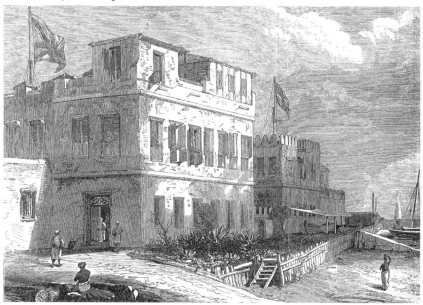

The British Consulate in 1872, with the American Consulate next door

Stanley, the brash Welsh-born opportunist, now an American citizen, was a very different man from the cynical Burton, but he too felt the need to write down his impressions of Zanzibar. It was, he said,

> the Bagdad, Ispahan, the Stamboul, if you like, of East Africa... Bagdad had great silk bazaars, Zanzibar has her ivory bazaars; Bagdad once traded in jewels, Zanzibar trades in gum copal; Stamboul imported Circassian and Georgian slaves; Zanzibar imports black beauties from Uhiyow, Ugindo, Ugogo, Unyamwezi and Galla.

He was particularly impressed by the Wangwana (the free African inhabitants of Zanzibar) whom he hired as captains, guides and *askaris* for his expedition. They were according to him 'an exceedingly fine-looking body of men, far more intelligent in appearance than I could ever have believed African barbarians could be.'[7] Unlike Burton, Stanley admired the people of Africa. It was his fellow Europeans whom he was to find most disappointing and difficult to deal with.

Stanley called on Francis Webb the American consul. By this time American influence was waning and Britain had become the pre-eminent foreign power in Zanzibar. Dr Kirk despised Webb because he was in trade and dried the animal skins he exported on the flat roof of his residence. 'American stinking hides' was Kirk's disparaging comment. Stanley had arrived with only 80 dollars in his pocket but Webb without hesitation pledged his own word to the local merchants that his countryman's credit was good. Due to Webb's help, Stanley ran up expenditures amounting to many thousands of rupees. He purchased six tons of supplies which the kindly Webb and his wife stored in their courtyard until Stanley was ready to sail for the mainland.

Stanley took advice about what he would need for his expedition from a retired Arab slave trader, Sheikh Rashid, who told him he would need ten *dhoti* or forty yards of cloth a day to buy food for 100 men. He learned how different tribes preferred different types of beads, copper wire and cloth as trade goods. The most popular cloth was, white *Merikani* from the US, blue *Kaniki* from India or coloured *Barsati*, also from India.

Stanley was secretive about his real mission, only telling Webb. He had an audience with Barghash and was a given a *firman* (a travel permit and letter of introduction to show to the Arab traders he might encounter). Barghash received him graciously and presented Stanley with a horse from his own stables. He was always mystified by the European passion for exploration and travel in the wilds of the African interior but, as he knew it was good for business in Zanzibar, he happily sanctioned the expeditions and helped the explorers on their way – mentally rubbing his hands as he thought of all the porters employed and trade goods purchased.

Stanley waited for a further two months at Bagamoyo as there were delays in mustering the 140 porters or *pagazi* he had ordered from Sewa Haji Paroo, an Ismaili Khoja from Kutch, who had the main transportation business on the mainland. Sewa Haji gave him valuable advice on how to organise his caravan, recommending that he split his men into five smaller parties so they did not all travel together.

In Bagamoyo Stanley managed to anger the increasingly influential Dr Kirk. Stanley accused Kirk at a public dinner of not expediting the porters and stores he should have sent to Livingstone, three months previously. Stanley had been shocked to find these stores still waiting in Bagamoyo. When he caught up with the Livingstone caravan at Tabora, Stanley had more harsh words to say about its tardy dispatch in letters he sent home. Kirk was an old Africa hand, who had travelled with Livingstone on the Zambezi expedition of 1858-62, while Stanley, the former workhouse boy, had no experience of African travel at all. Kirk was extremely annoyed, but concealed his displeasure, merely pointing out that delays were inevitable in Africa and Stanley would soon learn. The caravan trade was booming and reliable porters were in short supply. Kirk, with his non-confrontational style, appeared to brush off Stanley's accusation, but he did not forgive or forget and when the opportunity came, he punished the upstart American with great vindictiveness.

Sewa Haji's caravan business was a remarkable success story and his family became one of the most famous East African Ismaili dynasties.

One of four brothers, Sewa Haji was born in 1851. His father Haji Paroo Pradhan had migrated from Bhuj, Kutch to Zanzibar with his brother Jaffer and established a small general store in Zanzibar in 1852. Haji then crossed over to the mainland, where he opened a branch in Bagamoyo in 1860. Bagamoyo, situated on the mainland directly opposite Zanzibar Town, was the favoured starting point for caravans to the hinterland and Haji's new shop proved to be a successful venture. In the next few years the family business expanded enormously. They supplied porters and general trade items to Arab traders going to the interior and the business grew as the number of trading caravans to the interior increased and their services were needed more and more. They acquired the reputation of being efficient and honest and were popular with European travellers. In 1869 tragedy struck. Two of Sewa's brothers (Sajan and Kasam) died during the cholera epidemic and, short staffed, a cousin Allidina Jaffer Paroo was called over from India to help manage the business. Despite his youth Sewa Haji took over the reins of the family business in Bagamoyo and showed himself to be an astute operator. Money flowed into the merchant's pockets as he progressed to greater things and went into partnership with another successful Ismaili trading family. The business consortium of Haji, Kanji & Bros became famous as dealers in arms and ivory and financiers for trading caravans.

Later Sewa Haji worked closely with the German Colonial Government. He was deeply religious and charitable with his money, and in his last years helped build a leper hospital in Bagamoyo and finance a general hospital in Dar es Salaam. In 1896 Sultan Hamoud appointed him his chief financial agent, but sadly he did not enjoy this lucrative contract for long as he died the following year in February 1897, of carbuncle[8] aged only 46. His obituary from the *Zanzibar Gazette* described him as 'one of the keenest of businessmen in the modern sense of the word...and a prominent figure from Zanzibar mercantile life.'[9] As he had no children, it was the talented young relative and assistant Allidina Visram who then carried on his business empire, moving it to Mombasa and Uganda.

It is likely that members of Peera Dewjee's extended family were also involved in the Bagamoyo caravan business. Dhunji Parpia traded in partnership with Manek Haji, who was probably related to Sewa Haji. When his presumed son Peera Dhunji died in Bagamoyo in 1894, Alidina Kanji, the business partner of Sewa Haji Paroo, acted as trustee for probate.[10] Later the grandchildren of Peera Dewjee and the Paroos intermarried and there seems to have been a long standing history of friendship between the two families. They both originated from the same region of Kutch and had arrived in Zanzibar at the same time. The story of Sewa Haji Paroo demonstrates how East African Asian settlers at this time still maintained close family connections with India and often called out young relatives from India to help in their African businesses, whenever a need arose. The tradition of the close-knit family business network continued to operate in Africa and contributed much to the Khoja merchants' success. Trained from early childhood in business, they often took on responsibilities at a young age. Sewa Haji Paroo was barely out of his teens when he headed his own company and supplied the porters for the famous expeditions of Livingstone and Stanley, ensuring his name would go down in history.

The success of Stanley's expedition and his meeting with Livingstone in Ujiji is well known. Stanley brought back Livingstone's papers and letters. These contained first-hand descriptions of the brutal way in which the slave traders were now attacking African villages in order to capture slaves and provided the evidence, which finally galvanised the British Government into action. It was clear the treaties and naval patrols were not working. The East African slave trade was actually increasing and the methods used to obtain slaves becoming ever more cruel. The truth could no longer be avoided. Already in 1870 a committee had been set up in England to investigate the East African Slave Trade. This was followed by a select parliamentary committee, which met the following year to report back to Parliament. Finally in the summer of 1872 the Anti-Slavery Society convened a public meeting at Mansion House in London. Feelings ran so high that in response to the public outcry Parliament prorogued a special meeting to decide what action to take to finish the hateful trade once and for all.

'Barghash the Unlucky' was the name given to him by local historians, and certainly things were not going well for the new Sultan. His brother Majid had all the luck. He had inherited vast riches but had squandered his inheritance, leaving the affairs of government in the hands of others. Yet Zanzibar had grown richer under his watch and he was loved and respected, while Barghash, energetic and full of good intentions, was thwarted at every turn. He did not have the charm and lovable nature of his brother and his subjects feared rather than respected him. The coffers of the kingdom were empty, political troubles beset him and now a fresh catastrophe struck.

In December 1871 Barghash went on pilgrimage to Mecca in his steamship *Sea King*, taking his younger brothers with him. During his absence he left two of his relatives, Seyyid Suliman bin Hamed and Hamad bin Hamed to deputise for him. He was away for 60 days and returned on 29 March 1872. Barely three weeks later on 15 April 1872, a cyclone swept through Zanzibar directly over the town and island. This terrible storm raged for a whole day causing immense destruction. All the ships in the harbour sank except for one. The Sultan lost his entire fleet. The narrow streets of the town became impassable torrents, houses were blown down and the clove and coconut plantations were levelled to the ground. It was a scene of total devastation. Dr Christie described how the leaves on the few remaining trees were left brown, and withered, as if scorched by fire.[11] A foot of water flooded the British consulate and Dr Kirk wrote how at the height of the storm howling wind burst his office open and a solid teak chest, in which he stored documents, as well as the bureau where he held his correspondence were ripped open and gutted of their contents.[12] Livelihoods were ruined and the death toll rose as disease and despondency spread. The Island of Pemba escaped relatively unscathed but clove production on Zanzibar Island was wiped out and the plantations took several years to recover. As if this disaster was not enough, disturbing rumours came to the ears of the Sultan; the

British were putting together a plan to close the slave markets and ban the slave trade – his last remaining dependable source of income.

Scene of the hurricane of 1872

1 Genesta Hamilton, *Princes of Zinj: The Rulers of Zanzibar*, London: Hutchinson, 1957, p 133-4
2 John Martineau, *The Life and Correspondence of Sir Bartle Frere*, Vol 2, London: John Murray, 1895, p 105
3 See the letters of Sir John Kirk, National Library of Scotland, Acc 9942/25
4 Genesta Hamilton, *Princes of Zinj*, p 158-9
5 FO 84.1344 – see Alastair Hazell, *The Last Slave Market: Dr John Kirk and the Struggle to End the East African Slave Trade*, London: Constable & Robinson, 2011, p 197
6 Hazell, *Last Slave Market*, p 198
7 John Bierman, *Dark Safari: The Life Behind the Legend of Henry Morton Stanley*, London: Hodder & Stoughton, 1991, p 81-2
8 An infection of boils

9 *Zanzibar Gazette*, February 10, 1897
10 Zanzibar Archives, HC 1/319
11 James Christie, *Cholera Epidemics in East Africa*, London: Macmillan & Co, 1876, p 24
12 Hazell, *Last Slave Market*, p 232

Chapter Eight

Bartle Frere and the Closure of the Slave Markets

On 27 September 1872, Lord Granville, the Foreign Secretary, wrote to Sir Bartle Frere asking him to undertake a temporary mission to Zanzibar to negotiate a treaty with the Sultan. The three main provisions were to be:

1. All transport of slaves by sea should cease absolutely.
2. The public slave markets should be closed.
3. The subsidy due to Muscat which was in arrears should be paid immediately.

The last clause was a sweetener: Frere was given the option of offering to pay a part of the subsidy, providing the first two articles of the treaty were agreed.

Sir Bartle Frere, member of the Council for India and a former Governor of Bombay, seemed the ideal man to head the mission. He had long been an admirer of Livingstone, whom he had hosted in Bombay on a number of occasions. He was an expert on the subject of the East Coast slave trade and had been a prominent member of the committee which had successfully lobbied the British government for action against the slave trade. Now he was to be given the opportunity to put into practice the recommendations he had pressed for.

Frere laid his plans with great care. He was determined the project would be a diplomatic tour-de-force, a display of British power and righteousness in action, with himself at the helm. His governorship of Bombay had ended in disappointment as an economic collapse had happened on his watch and he had left India under a cloud in 1866. The Zanzibar Mission was a chance to retrieve his reputation, but he needed a free rein to be sure of success.

He asked and obtained from the Foreign Secretary a promise of wide ranging powers and support from all relevant ministries. He personally selected the members of his delegation and left England on 21 November, taking with him Clement Hill of the Foreign Office, Charles Grey of the India office, Captain Fairfax RN, Major Euan-Smith as his Private Secretary, Dr Badger, Arabic scholar, as interpreter, and his son Bartle junior, who had just left Eton.

He travelled via France, Rome and Naples paying courtesy calls on the heads of State, including an audience with the Pope, to seek backing and approval for the aims of the British mission. He also paid visits to institutions which provided shelter and refuge for freed slaves. He knew the slaves would need follow-up care after being set free. One of his cherished aims was to provide training and teaching facilities for ex-slaves. Frere had been an enthusiastic promoter of the freed slave settlement at Nasik near Bombay and when a similar settlement was later opened near Mombasa it would be named Freretown in his honour. On reaching Brindisi he boarded the Admiralty yacht, *Enchantress*, a paddle steamer of 800 tons, and proceeded onwards to Egypt.

In Cairo he held talks with the Khedive, who assured him he was not a semi-barbarian like the Sultan of Zanzibar, but a thoroughly civilised ruler who understood the benefits to be accrued from the principles of free labour. However, the Khedive explained, although he was enlightened, not all his subjects were, and he could not stamp out the slave trade and tradition of slavery in the country with a *coup de sabre*, despite his earnest desire, as slaves had existed in Egypt since before Mohammed. The way forward in his opinion was to extinguish slavery gradually, as people became more enlightened and a class of free labourers to do the work grew up. He told Frere the slave trade in Egypt was diminishing and if the British Government was serious in stopping the trade it should exert more pressure. Egypt at this point was governed under a dual French and British mandate propping up the puppet ruler, the Khedive, an appointee of the Ottoman Empire. It was also a major importer of slaves and the Khedive's information about the declining trade was misleading![1]

Frere re-joined the *Enchantress* at Suez and then steamed on to

Aden. At Aden he picked up Colonel Pelly, an old friend and protégé, now British Representative in the Persian Gulf, who was waiting for him on board the BISN Co mail steamer, the *Punjaub*, which was about to depart on its second voyage to Zanzibar. Passengers included Mr Muthoridass, a Hindu merchant of Bombay formerly resident in Zanzibar and Kazi Shahbudin the ex-Diwan or prime minister of Kutch, who were part of the official Zanzibar delegation. They had been asked to explain the terms of the treaty to the British Indians in Zanzibar. Frere left no stone unturned to ensure the mission was all-inclusive and successful.

After eight days sailing, the two ships arrived off Zanzibar on 12 January 1873 and anchored opposite the British Consulate. Vice Consul Kirk first, then Nassir bin Said, representative of the Sultan, came on board and they arranged a formal visit to the Sultan for the next day, when the royal letters would be presented. In the harbour also were three British men-of-war, HMS *Glasgow, Briton* and *Daphne* and an American warship the *Yantic*.

Despite Frere's careful preparations, none of the other foreign consuls showed support and the French acting consul, M Bertrand, and the American consul were particularly non-cooperative. Only the American naval captain agreed to join the palace visit and show solidarity with the British mission. M Bertrand was the leading French merchant in Zanzibar and according to Frere was a young Levantine more Syrian than French.[2]

The next day Bartle Frere at the head of an impressive retinue of 48 British officials and naval personnel walked the short distance from the consulate to the Palace. Never before had Zanzibar been visited by such a grand assembly of high officials. In honour of the occasion the Sultan met them 30 yards from his door. He usually stayed inside his palace when visitors came, so this was exceptional. Customary greetings were exchanged and he shook hands most cordially with Frere, whom he had met in Bombay. The Sultan's guns fired a salute, answered by those of HMS *Glasgow*. With perfect politeness, the party walked up to the Reception Room, with Bartle Frere given precedence over the Sultan. The Sultan seated himself at one end of the audience room, with his brothers and two of his ministers, Suleiman bin Hamed and Nassir bin Said. Also present was Ali bin Sud a relative. When the royal letters were presented, the Sultan stood up and raised them to his forehead as a mark of respect.

The ensuing conversation touched on the Sultan's ship, *Sea King*, which had been lost at sea on its way to Bombay for repairs. They did not discuss the matter in hand. It is quite possible Barghash was uncertain of the precise reason for the visit. With great courtesy Barghash accompanied his important visitors back into the street and Nassir bin Said came with them as far as the consulate. Barghash was invited to pay a return visit to Frere the next day. The Royal Navy sent a steam tender, which towed the royal barge to the *Enchantress*. The second meeting was again a model of politeness and diplomatic protocol. Barghash offered to put Frere up in one of his palaces, but he refused the offer, though it was later taken up by Dr Badger. Barghash then voiced his concern about Egyptian designs upon his northern territories. Frere reassured him and spoke instead about the new British India Steam Navigation Company steamers, subsidised by the British Government, which he hoped would provide a most useful service to Zanzibar. Barghash was in excellent spirits and Dr Badger, who knew Barghash, translated.

The Reverend Dr George Percy Badger (1815-1888) was an Anglican priest and Arabic scholar. The son of an army sergeant, he had grown up in Malta in poverty with little formal education, but he had a natural aptitude for languages. As a young man he studied in Beirut and acquired a mastery of colloquial Arabic that few of his contemporaries could match. Ordained in 1842, he then served as a military chaplain and Arabic interpreter in Bombay and Aden. In 1862 he retired to England and devoted the rest of his life to his studies and writing. Considered an outsider by the establishment, with a reputation for being short tempered and difficult, his expertise in the Arabic language proved useful to the British government on a number of occasions. He got on particularly well with Barghash who liked and trusted him. Badger was nearly 60 when Frere brought him to Zanzibar as the official interpreter.

All doubts as to the intentions of the visit were removed during the next few days, when Barghash fully digested the content of the letters and negotiations began. As Frere explained in his written reports, Barghash's information was imperfect. 'He has newspapers, especially Indian ones, of which the substance is translated for him by an old Arab ship captain, [who was excluded from the British Consulate for his intemperate ways and] who was for some time in England and understands nautical English' but not much else.[3] With Badger on hand Barghash no longer had any excuse for misunderstanding.

Meanwhile there was a meeting of the Indian residents with an address by the two representatives brought over from India, who explained the contents of the treaties and put pressure on their fellow countrymen to cease all involvement with the slave trade. Kazi Shahbudin warned that any Kutchi found owning a slave or trading in slaves would in future have his property in India confiscated according to the law.

For a whole month during which Frere, Kirk and Badger had long and repeated interviews with Barghash, the Sultan hesitated and deferred his answer. Barghash was most perplexed and worried and wished to help his friends the British, but he was concerned about the ruined state of the island due to the hurricane. He had to listen to the wishes of his Arab subjects and he definitely could not afford to pay the arrears of the Muscat subsidy. At one point he pleaded with Badger as an old friend to help him find a middle way. He broke down in tears before Frere, so agonising was his situation, which he said was as if 'a spear is held at each of my eyes, with which shall I choose to be pierced? Either way it is fatal to me.'[4] Frere thought that left to himself, Barghash would have agreed the treaty, but his Arab council threatened to depose him and French support stiffened his resolve. The French faction in Zanzibar had no wish to see the end of the slave trade as it would affect their plantations. They came up with a compromise, a 50 per cent reduction in the amount of slaves sold in a year. It was estimated Zanzibar and its subsidiary slave markets exported about 20,000 slaves a year. Frere refused to alter the terms of the treaty.

Finally on 13 February 1873, after four weeks of prevarication, the Sultan gave a point blank refusal to sign, saying he wanted to keep the 1845 treaty and didn't need another one. Four days earlier the French consul M de Vienne had returned to Zanzibar and Kirk attributed the timing of the rejection to his return. The French had been spreading malicious rumours for some time that British missionaries were political merchants who used tracts and Bibles as a cover for smuggled Manchester goods, which they used as bait to tempt Africans who they then captured and took away as slaves. The British and French were traditional enemies and rivals in the region and always adopted a deliberately hostile attitude towards each other. In 1862, as a sign of temporary rapprochement, both sides had signed an agreement to guarantee the independent sovereignty of Zanzibar. France now hinted that Britain would be infringing this agreement if they resorted to force, and warned that any move to annex the island would be met by strong objections from France. Barghash and his advisors did not realise France was no longer the superpower she once had been and this political posturing was bluster. Germany was the new emergent superpower and her consul, Herr Schultz, supported the British initiative against the slave trade. Herr Schultz initially had not been in favour of the new treaty, but after receiving a directive from Berlin, he changed his tune.[5] However, the French intervention was not making negotiations any easier.

On 25 January Badger had received a message from the Sultan attached to a cutting from a Bombay newspaper. It was an article in which a correspondent had suggested the mission to Zanzibar would never be successful unless Britain took over the island by force. Was this Britain's real intention, asked the Sultan? Badger sent back a scribbled message denying it. He described the writer as a 'babbler' and told the Sultan to pay no attention to his folly.[6] This use of a newspaper cutting may indicate the hand of Peera Dewjee, as a few years later he regularly scoured the newspapers for relevant articles and marked them for the Sultan's attention. Badger was surprised how much Barghash had improved since he had first met him twelve years ago, during his exile in India. Then he had been a sullen and ignorant youth, but now he had a library of Arabic books printed in Cairo and showed himself to be educated and well-informed with a particular interest in Egypt.

On 15 February Bartle Frere sailed away south with HMS *Briton* as an escort. The two Indian representatives returned to India and Dr Badger went home due to ill health. The effort of translating complex messages from Frere so the Sultan could understand the underlying meaning and then relaying back the evasive replies from Barghash had severely tested his temper and nerves and the stress had inflamed his gout. Frere announced he would be back in a month, giving Barghash ample time to dwell on the error of his ways and come round to a proper decision. Barghash appears not to have recognised the danger signs and thought he had been let off the hook and that the British would not compel him to sign the treaty.

Frere spent a pleasant and productive month inspecting the chief slaving ports along the East African Coast. He visited Mozambique, Madagascar and the Comoro Islands. The only place he met with marked hostility was at Kilwa. As Frere sailed down the coast he recorded his impressions and thoughts in a voluminous set of letters and reports, sitting at a small table in his cabin, holding on with one leg as the small steam yacht tossed about in the ocean. He was particularly struck by the enormous increase of Indian commercial interest and saw how Africans, Arabs and Europeans all used an Indian agent to manage the details of buying and selling. Without the Indian middleman little business could be done. He saw how Indian merchants occupied every place there was any trade and were in charge of the Customs Houses along nearly 1,000 miles of the coast. He was intrigued by the 'silent occupation' of the coast from Socotra to Cape Colony by Indian merchants and commented that 'it was a most curious phenomena.'[7]

He saw that though German, American and French trade was larger by far than that with England, all these foreign nations conducted their trade through Indians with Indian capital and Indian firms, and much of their African profits ultimately ended up in India. Frere realised England through India had an immense practical hold on East Africa and pondered on how this could be used to abolish the slave trade, especially as the Sultan and his Arabs were in thrall to Indian money lenders.

He was also surprised by the superficial character of the Sultan's hold on the East African Coast, seeing how his authority was confined to a few garrisoned seaports and did not extend inland. The so-called African empire of the Sultan was unlike any empire Frere had known.

One of Frere's recommendations to the home Government was for a new survey of the East African Coast to be done as a matter of urgency. He had seen with his own eyes how cut off the East African Coast was. Many of the places he visited had been without news from Europe for as long as seven months. He attached great importance to the new British India steamship line and wanted a regular service to be extended to all the principal ports down to the Cape. He felt better connections with Britain and the West would be the key to facilitating legitimate trade and discouraging the trade in slaves. He, like Livingstone, believed that the three Cs – Christianity, commerce and civilisation – were the answer for Africa.

On his return to Zanzibar, Frere found everything in a state of suspense. Trade was at a standstill and the Sultan affected an air of indifference. He still refused to sign the treaty. Frere's patience was at an end. He wrote that Barghash's refusal to sign the treaty was 'a studied policy of disregard for the wishes of England,'[8] and decided to take off the velvet glove and bring out the iron fist.

After a last letter of warning to Barghash, Frere left Zanzibar on 14 March to proceed to Muscat and on 28 March sent a series of despatches from Mombasa. These consisted of letters of instruction to Dr Kirk and Captain Malcolm, the senior British naval officer in Zanzibar, and an ultimatum for the Sultan. Frere wrote that no transport of slaves by sea would be permitted any longer. Henceforth from 1 May, the existing system of Customs House passes would be stopped and every slave was to be examined by the British Consul. Furthermore, the prohibition on conveyance of slaves by sea was to be enforced by the British Navy. Polite negotiations were at an end, now came the threats. Zanzibar with its harbour facing the town was vulnerable to a naval blockade and Barghash, who had lost all his ships in the hurricane, was completely defenceless. Frere sent copies of these letters to the British Government for their approval, and added further that if the Sultan still refused to sign, he recommended taking charge of the Sultan's Customs Houses and employing the officials, who were almost all British Indians, to intercept the slaves, collect the customs and account to the British Government who would only then account to the Sultan.[9] This was annexation in essence!

When the letters reached England, they fell like a bombshell on the British Cabinet, who were horrified at the content. They had expected willing compliance from the Sultan, without resort to such blatant bullying tactics. But they had no option but to give their reluctant approval as the orders had already been given. They had to trust their envoy knew what he was doing and hope the threat of force would get the desired result. The Home Government had not contemplated such determined resistance from the Sultan and the ministers were alarmed that matters had been allowed to escalate and might escalate even further.

It was Dr Kirk, now promoted by Frere to British Consul, who was left behind with three British men-of-war as enforcement agents, to coerce and cajole the unfortunate Barghash into signing the treaty. Frere steamed off for some more sight-seeing and fact-finding towards Muscat. Consul Kirk rose to the occasion. This was Kirk's finest hour and he saved the situation for both Frere and the British Government. His input proved crucial for the success of the Zanzibar Mission. His good relationship with the Sultan and intimate knowledge of how Zanzibar society worked helped him find the best approach.

He understood it was the Arab councillors who were the chief stumbling block, not the Sultan, and it was those men he must convince. He had several meetings with the Sultan in full council and explained to the councillors clearly and simply why it was in their best interests to sign the treaty. Was it not better to have some trade rather than none at all? Could they not see how the months of indecision and suspense had already proved disastrous for business? Kirk's eloquence was reinforced by the naval blockade. The ships on the station were so cleverly disposed that hardly any slavers succeeded in getting past them, and the number of slaves and trade goods passing through the Customs House had already been much reduced. Commerce was the lifeblood of Zanzibar and eventually the Arab councillors gave ground and withdrew their objections thanks to the persuasive Dr Kirk. The French were exposed as mere mischief-makers and their bluff was called. No French ships appeared to the rescue, as they did not have the will or the might to protect the Sultan. On 5 June 1873 with the approval of his councillors, Sultan Barghash signed the treaty and the main slave market in Zanzibar was closed three days later on 8 June. The treaty negotiations had taken almost six months.

The closure of the slave markets in the Sultan's dominions was a significant milestone for the abolitionists and their fight against slavery, but it was by no means the end of the battle. The East Coast slave trade continued, but clandestinely, as it became more and more difficult both to transport and dispose of slaves without getting caught. Arabs in Zanzibar were allowed to keep their domestic slaves for the time being, while the formation of a paid labour force gathered momentum. Fortunately for the cash-strapped Sultan, the booming ivory trade made up for his lost revenue from slaves.

On his return to England Frere took full credit for the success of the Zanzibar Mission and he was made a privy councillor in recognition of his services. In 1875 he was chosen to accompany the Prince of Wales on a tour of India and in 1877 was appointed Governor of Cape Colony, South Africa. Sir Bartle Frere was undoubtedly a clever man, with sincere intentions for good, but his character contained flaws, which became more serious as he grew older. As his biographer said, he was reported 'to promise more than he performed.'[10] He had a desire to make all things smooth and shied away from arguments and confrontation. His biographer described how when he had to refuse a request, 'he instinctively threw into the manner of his refusal an ever larger measure of courtesy than usual, so that…the petitioner… sometimes went away from the interview with a sense of being consoled rather than rebuffed.'[11] His lack of plain-speaking and arm's length method of dealing with Barghash, leaving most of the negotiations to minions and go-betweens, served only to confuse and make the Sultan more obdurate and obstinate.

After his Zanzibar Mission Frere was criticised for this lack of frankness and of being an advocate of 'equivocal and entangling engagements' but he defended himself by saying that 'the semi-civilised chief rarely understands our power; my doctrine would be to teach it to him by friendly communication before the necessity of unfriendly remonstrance arises.'[12] Frere's career eventually ended in failure and in retrospect harsh words have been said about his arrogance and high-handed methods, but it is hard to see how a better result could have been achieved. Military action was avoided and the closure of the slave markets was a notable success. As Frere pointed out, the long and difficult route gave more effect and strength to the treaty, which a quicker and easier result may not have done.

Tharia Topan worked closely with Kirk and according to an Ismaili source, it was 'by Tharia Topan's efforts that Sultan Bargash was able to ink an accord in 1873 for the suppression of the slave trade with Sir John Kirk…His inestimable services in connection with the abolition of the slave trade were highly recognized by the Queen of England.'[13] Topan was the leading businessman in Zanzibar and his opinion carried credence on the island, not only amongst his fellow Indian merchants but also with all others involved in commerce, whatever their creed or colour. He was so powerful in Zanzibar that it was noticed that his fellow countrymen trembled in his presence as he had the means to make or break them.[14] The support he gave to Dr Kirk swung the argument in favour of the British position and as a mark of appreciation he was given a knighthood, an exceptional honour for an Indian at this period. This recognition is evidence as to how important his input was for the successful signing of the treaty. But despite the voluminous amount of correspondence and reporting on the Zanzibar Mission, little light is shed upon this aspect of the negotiations. Tharia Topan became one of Barghash's inner circle of councillors and was made chief collector of customs, as the Sultan realised the value of his influence and wealth.[15]

Kirk wrote to Frere in a letter dated June 7, 1873,

> Well, we have got the treaty, thanks to the orders you gave at Mombasa, and that I carried out with rather an iron hand…From the beginning I dealt with the Sultan in Council, never meeting him in any other capacity, and forced the Arabs to give an opinion on which he might act. This succeeded admirably, but it was hard work.

Barghash, as his previous form demonstrated, did not respond to friendly suggestions, which he interpreted as weakness. He and his Arabs were obstinate and difficult men to deal with, who needed firm handling. The elderly Arab chieftains and religious leaders were largely ignorant of the Western world and the terms of the treaty seemed to them totally unreasonable. Barghash summed it up, during one of his exchanges with Frere: 'It is quite in your power to destroy us, but you ask us to destroy ourselves, and that we cannot do.'[16] The threat of military action was the kind of negotiating tool they understood, but even this failed to elicit an immediate climb down. In the end, as Frere had predicted, it was the British Indian factor which forced the issue as negotiations dragged on into the second phase and there was a protracted stand-off. When trade ground to a standstill and businesses suffered, the Indian merchants withdrew their credit and remonstrated with the Sultan and his councillors to give way and sign. It was the economic squeeze which carried the day.

This episode shows that Barghash at this period was still under the thumb of his Arab councillors and still retained his old tendency of turning to France for protection when relations with Britain soured.

Whether or not Peera Dewjee helped the Sultan in his conversations with the French is unknown, but it is highly likely he acted as a messenger and go-between. As an Ismaili, he would have had divided loyalties. The Aga Khan supported British policies and Tharia Topan, the chief Ismaili merchant in Zanzibar, backed Kirk. Support for the Arab slaving faction drained away as the months of indecision dragged on and business interests suffered and the serious intent of the British became apparent. Notice was taken of those like Tharia Topan, who was optimistic that commercial life in Zanzibar could flourish without the slave trade and refused to lend money to slave traders. He was the richest and most astute financial operator in town and where he led others followed.

The 1873 treaty marked a turning point in the history of Zanzibar. The Arab state had been in decline for some years but this was the moment of realisation, when the Arab chiefs felt the pinch of their diminished power and the extent of their dependence on Britain and the financial influence of the British Indian merchants. The negotiations over the slave trade represented a final phase of the power struggle between the old Muslim ways of the East and the new ideas based on Christianity coming from the West. After 1873 Barghash no longer relied on his Arab councillors but turned increasingly to British advice and protection. The Indian money-lenders switched their funds to financing the ivory trade, and prospered further, while Sir John Kirk became known as the uncrowned king of Zanzibar.

---

1 Martineau, *Life and Correspondence of Sir Bartle Frere*, Vol 2, London: John Murray, 1895, p 76
2 *Ibid*, p 85
3 *Ibid*, p 86
4 Hazell, *Last Slave Market*, p 247
5 Martineau, *Life and Correspondence of Sir Bartle Frere*, Vol 2, p 84
6 Hazell, *Last Slave Market*, p 246
7 Martineau, *Life and Correspondence of Sir Bartle Frere*, Vol 2, p 97
8 Zanzibar Archives, AA1/10

9 Martineau, *Life and Correspondence of Sir Bartle Frere*, Vol 2, p 101

10 *Ibid*, Vol 2, p 28

11 *Ibid*, Vol 2, p 28

12 *Ibid*, Vol 2, p 117

13 Mumtaz Ali Tajddin Sadik Ali, *101 Ismaili Heroes*, Karachi: Islamic Book Publisher, 2003, p 416

14 Norman R Bennett, ed, *The Zanzibar letters of Edward D Ropes, Jr, 1882-1892*, Boston: African Studies Center, Boston University, 1973, p 27. 'The power TT has here is more than you can possibly imagine. Why I have seen insolent big headed fellows like Praggia Dossa actually tremble in TT's presence simply because they know that he could reduce them to paupers in a few months.'

15 Topan received his knighthood in India in 1890 and was the first Indian to be knighted for services in Africa.

16 Hazell, *Last Slave Market*, p 249

Chapter Nine

The Sultan of Zanzibar's European Tour

One of the rewards offered to Barghash for signing the treaty and enforcing the anti-slavery regulations was an invitation to visit England and meet the Queen. Barghash, true to his word, had closed his slave markets and was doing his best to uphold the provisions of the treaty he had signed, so he was disappointed when no royal letter came during the course of 1873, nor in the following year. In the end Dr Badger intervened, writing to the Foreign Office to say how pained the Sultan was by the delay in the promised invitation, which reminded the British government of their promise. Badger pointed out that the Sultan's visit could do the work of a gunboat as a means of fostering good will and compliance. A visit was at last arranged for June/July 1875. It was to be a private visit, not an official one, as the British government feared setting a precedent. Barghash would be entertained as a guest of the nation, but he was expected to pay for his own transport from Zanzibar. The British Government, having got the result they wanted, seemed reluctant to honour their side of the bargain or behave with undue generosity. Nevertheless the Sultan's European Tour would be a personal triumph and a key event of Barghash's reign.

British Consul Dr Kirk returned to Zanzibar in April 1875, after a year of sick-leave, bearing the long awaited invitation and presented it to the Sultan, who was most pleased to receive it. This excerpt from a letter to W H Wylde of the Foreign Office, dated 24 February 1875 and written on board ship while Kirk was travelling back to Zanzibar, gives an insight into the pre-planning involved in such a visit and the cautious Scot's diplomatic style:

It is to be hoped Dawes has called in or written to say by this time. I knew he telegraphed to Mackinnon[1] on getting my letter and on landing at Aden possibly I may have a message.

By this time also I suppose you have been in communication with Dr Badger as you proposed. You were very right in thinking he can be of use to us, or just the opposite, as we happen to take him, there is no one to fill his place as interpreter and probably no one the Sultan will trust.

I shall do my best to keep down the number of the Sultan's attendants and let you know as soon as possible how many they are to be, that the arrangements may be made at the Hotel where he is to be lodged – It will also be for someone at home to get an order to pass his luggage at the customs when we know where he is to land – but on all this I shall write again.

I had a note from Lord Stanley of Alderley asking me to inform him as soon as possible of the Sultan's plans as he wishes to entertain him at Crewe – this will relieve us a little and be a good way of getting him to see the works at Manchester, although Lord Stanley is personally very much disliked by the people of that place.

I think Mackinnon too will help us if H. H. goes to Glasgow.

In looking over the letters I am very pleased to see his reception is to be strictly private. I hope it will be kept so throughout – he will see so much more in this way. [2]

First and foremost the Sultan needed a ship. He had none suitable, as his fleet had been destroyed in the hurricane. Edward Dawes on behalf of Mackinnon arranged the charter of the SS *Canara* for the Sultan's use. Built in Glasgow in 1874, it was one of the largest and newest of Mackinnon's mail ships.

The Sultan left Zanzibar on 9 May 1875. He was accompanied by Dr Kirk, his chief minister Nassir bin Said bin Abdullah (signer of treaties), and four of his Arab chiefs: Hamed bin Suleiman, Hamud bin Mohammed, Mohammed bin Hamed, Mohammed bin Suleiman and Tharia Topan, the Khoja merchant. Other members of the party included the unreliable nautical interpreter Mohammed bin Khamis, a scribe Zahir bin Said, a cashier (probably Bakashmar), a priest, a couple of barbers, a butcher and four cooks as well as a number of unspecified personnel and servants. Ali bin Sud acted as regent during the Sultan's absence and Major Euan-Smith was called over from India to deputise for Kirk. This is the first time there is documentary evidence for Peera Dewjee's movements. It is recorded in his obituary that he went with the Sultan to England, though it does not say in what capacity, but probably as his valet and barber.

They sailed through the Suez Canal, into the Mediterranean and round by Gibraltar to Portugal, their first port of call, arriving there on the morning of 4 June. Admiral Seymour, with the Channel Squadron, which had been ordered to Lisbon to escort the Sultan to England, had already arrived. The sight of the warships anchored off Lisbon provided the Sultan with an impressive reminder of Britain's naval might.

The Sultan's time in Portugal was not without incident. Oman and Portugal were old enemies, and there were still unresolved boundary issues involving Mozambique. But the city of Lisbon, Barghash's first sight of Europe, gave him a tremendous welcome with full military honours. Cheering crowds filled the streets. They waved flags and threw flowers. The colourful scene astonished the Zanzibari Arabs, but as befitted their dignity they kept up an impassive demeanour showing nothing but polite pleasure.[3]

The Sultan was invited to an audience with the King and Queen of Portugal in their palace. Seeing the splendour of Lisbon, Barghash became concerned that his retinue was not large enough to impress the Portuguese monarch, and he devised a cunning plan to swell the numbers, dressing up his servants as Arabs and including them in his entourage. The story goes that Dr Kirk, who had arrived beforehand, was surprised to see such a large crowd accompanying the Sultan. He realised what he was up to and prevented the entry of the 'kitchen contingent' into the Royal presence, managing to steer the impostors into an adjoining room.[4] It is highly likely Peera Dewjee the Sultan's valet and barber had a hand in this ingenious subterfuge.

At the royal audience, conducted in French, the remainder of the Sultan's suite also caused some embarrassment. The Portuguese Queen seated herself and the King invited Barghash to a seat, but the rest of the courtiers were expected to remain standing. This was unheard of in polite Arab society – a woman seated whilst men stood – so they decided to all sit down – on the floor. Nothing was said and this breach of etiquette was politely ignored but both parties inwardly deplored the other's barbaric manners.

More awkwardness followed, but this time of a political nature, when it became clear the Portuguese wished to use the visit as an excuse to settle the boundary dispute. Barghash's reply that 'these things are drawn with the sword not with the pen' alarmed Kirk and he felt it prudent to set sail at once for England. They left the next day on 5 June.[5]

HH Seyyid Barghash and his entourage reached England on the morning of 9 June and landed at Gravesend in the pouring rain, where Dr Badger waited for them. From there they were transported up the Thames in boats belonging to the Thames Steamboats Company and disembarked at Westminster Palace Steps that afternoon. Here they were met by an official greeting party and an enthusiastic crowd of Londoners eager to catch a glimpse of the exotic visitors. There was a guard of honour and a band which played 'God Save the Queen.' Sir Bartle Frere was the first to come forward to welcome the Sultan, followed by Mr Bourke, Under Secretary of State for Foreign affairs. Mr Wylde, Head of the Consular Department of the Foreign Office, and Clement Hill, also of the Foreign Office, were amongst the officials who formally greeted the Sultan.

There is a good description of the Sultan's arrival in the *Standard* newspaper for 10 June 1875. This mentions how the African servants (slaves) unloading the luggage from the boats were heckled by the onlookers and how they nodded and smiled, enjoying the attention. The Sultan was described as being of rather robust constitution and not above middle height with a winning smile, who acknowledged the greetings of the crowd by frequently raising a finger. This was in contrast to his Arab councillors who pretended not to notice their surroundings and kept their heads down and preserved their grave expressions. 'Among the suite were several aged men with grey beards and stooping forms; one of them wore sandals and one was perceptibly lame.' They wore turbans and were dressed in long flowing dark robes beautifully embroidered and a cummerbund carrying sword and dagger. 'Amid the excitement of the landing, so self-possessed was a member of the retinue that he immediately recognised and spoke to Dr Christie, an English physician, who for some time past has been a resident in Zanzibar.' Quite possibly this was Peera Dewjee.

The Sultan's party was then directed to several open carriages waiting for them in the Palace yard. The Sultan, Kirk and Badger got into the first one while the rest of the party, their luggage and the Foreign Office officials filled the others. Thousands of curious spectators lined the streets as the Sultan of Zanzibar and his retinue drove slowly through central London to the Alexandra Hotel in Hyde Park Corner, where they stayed.

This hotel no longer exists, but in its time it was a spacious and fashionable hotel with all modern conveniences and a grand entrance portico with banded columns. It also boasted a lift and the *Illustrated London News* ran a picture of the Sultan in a lift. He was apparently fascinated by it and thought it a magical contraption.[6]

There were apartments on the ground floor and the upper floors were divided into bedrooms with en suite dressing rooms. A newspaper report in the Melbourne newspaper the *Argus* says the hotel provided the Sultan with his own slaughter-house and a place for his own cooks to prepare his meals with due regard to his religious scruples. 'The religion of our guest, it must be said, makes a heavy demand upon the working day. Long before London is stirring the Seyyid, with his nobles and priests…has been up and praying for an hour and a half.' The article goes on to explain how the customary five prayers a day were reduced during travel, when only obligatory prayers were recited. During his stay in England the Sultan cut down his religious observances to three times a day; once at sunrise, once between noon and sunset and a final evening prayer within two hours after sunset.[7] The long daylight hours of the English summer must have made it unusually exhausting for the pious Ibadhi Muslims. Peera Dewjee as an Ismaili had more flexible religious requirements and it is likely he spent much of his time on errands for the Sultan and out shopping.

THE SULTAN IN THE LIFT

The Sultan's visit was to be a notable success, but it got off to a sticky start and was nearly derailed altogether by the intrigues of his wayward sister Salme, who had inconveniently re-surfaced. After the death of her husband in 1870, she had been living in Germany in somewhat straitened circumstances. She now wanted to return to Zanzibar and claim the inheritance she said was owing to her and complained bitterly that her cruel brother the Sultan refused to reply to her letters or recognise her. Her unusual case and romantic background attracted attention and she had acquired powerful friends at the court of the German Emperor in Berlin, who sympathised with her plight. Amongst her sympathisers was Queen Victoria's daughter Vicky, the wife of the crown prince of Germany and another daughter, Princess Alice, married to the Grand Duke of Hesse, who took up Princess (as she now styled herself) Salme's cause.

When Salme heard her brother the Sultan was coming to England she decided to confront him. How could he ignore her appeal, if they met in London? She booked into a London Hotel and made herself known to the German Consul and others who might assist her to arrange a meeting with the Sultan. Dr Playfair MP, a brother of the erstwhile Zanzibar Consul Playfair, concerned for her reputation and perhaps the political implications, hurried to take her under his wing and she stayed with the Playfairs, under their watchful care, for the rest of her trip.

Kirk was asked to tell the Sultan his sister had come to England to see him. Kirk with Badger's help reluctantly brought the subject up, but the Sultan became angry and said he did not wish to hear her name mentioned in his presence. She had dishonoured the family and her apostasy under Muslim law had annulled her inheritance and that was the end of the subject. However the British Royal family, who had heard of her story through their German relations, pitied Salme and thought Barghash was wrong not to forgive his sister and heal the rift. Queen Victoria was so upset by his lack of forgiveness that she refused to invite the Sultan into the Royal Enclosure at Ascot when he went to the races the next day. Barghash was further insulted when two military gentlemen accosted Kirk in the Sultan's presence at Ascot and began 'dilating on the disgraceful way in which the Sultan was treating his sister.' Kirk told them to mind their own business before being informed by a detective that they were the Duke of Cambridge and Count Gleichen, two members of the British royal family. The Sultan, when he learnt of this snub, wanted to leave England immediately. Kirk and Badger had trouble persuading him to remain.[8]

Meanwhile Salme had an important and unexpected visitor – Sir Bartle Frere. He was concerned the Salme effect might spoil the visit and sour British relations with Zanzibar and he wanted Salme out of the way. After some small talk he came to the point and asked her to choose between her own ambitions and those of her children. If she agreed to avoid Barghash during her time in England, then he would ensure that her children's inheritance rights were restored. Salme, as a devoted mother, chose to accept this offer for her children and true to the agreement she remained discreetly out of sight during the rest of her stay. She was to be bitterly disappointed when Frere did not keep this promise. The excuse was that her children were German citizens and did not qualify for British help, so nothing could be done.

Dr Kirk achieved further damage limitation when he explained to the Prince of Wales the Sultan's reasons for his lack of sympathy with his sister's plight. Once he had heard Barghash's side of the story, the Prince said he understood the Sultan's position and the Sultan's subsequent invitation to meet the Prince and Princess of Wales at home with the royal children broke the ice.

There may have been an added edge to these intrigues. Chole, the arch conspirator, and Salme had recently started to correspond again and Chole offered to look after Salme's fatherless children and bring them up in Zanzibar. But in 1875 Chole died in suspicious circumstances – of suspected poisoning – and so the children remained in Europe. The ambitious Salme wanted to get back her influence and place her son as a possible heir to the Sultanate, especially as there was a shortage of direct male heirs. This was not acceptable either to the Zanzibari hierarchy or to the British diplomats, neither of whom relished the thought of a half German Sultan in Zanzibar.

There was a report of the visit to Ascot in the *Illustrated London News*:

> ...at ten o'clock, the Sultan went to Ascot, to witness the racing for the Gold Cup. Two open landaus, each drawn by four horses, ridden by postillions, conveyed the Sultan and his party. In the first carriage were, besides the Sultan, Dr. Kirk and Mr. Clement Hill; the second contained the Sultan's Prime Minister and councillors...Just as the leading carriage was passing Tattersalls' one of the traces snapped. A delay of nearly a quarter of an hour ensued to get this replaced. His Highness arrived at Ascot rather later than the English Royal Princes and Princesses. His carriage was stationed opposite the Royal Stand, and he had a good view of the race. He got back to London at eight o'clock in the evening.[9]

This was the official version of events, which leaves out any hint of the undercurrents previously described. The drawing accompanying the article, which appeared on the front page of the periodical, showed the Sultan watching the races through a pair of opera glasses, standing in a carriage. This became one of his favourite images and a copy of it later appeared in an illustrated book written in Arabic for the Sultan commemorating his visit to England, which he liked to show to foreign visitors.[10] What his true feelings were about that day can only be imagined.

The Sultan's tour continued as follows:

Friday 11 June: In the morning he received visits from Lord Salisbury and Mr Ward Hunt, Lord Hertford and Lord Stanley of Alderley. Lord Stanley, who had converted to Islam in 1862, was the first Muslim member of the House of Lords. In the afternoon the Sultan visited Lord Derby, the Foreign Secretary at the Foreign Office. This was to draft an alteration to the restrictions placed upon the slave trade, to save embarrassing the Sultan, who had brought several domestic slaves with him. An additional clause was inserted to allow household slaves to accompany their master at sea without the ship being confiscated, but if they were carried against their will, then they were to be set free. From the point of view of the English this extra clause was not a success as it provided another loophole for the slavers; hundreds of personal servants were soon to be found making the Mecca pilgrimage, whence only a few returned, the rest having been profitably disposed of.[11]

On his way back to the hotel Barghash drove through Hyde Park, where he was much astonished at the display of carriages, flowers and ladies walking about in revealing dresses. 'Verily,' he remarked to Dr Badger who accompanied him, 'the present world is undoubtedly yours; whether the next will be yours also is, to say the least, uncertain.'[12] He stayed quietly in the hotel that evening.

Saturday 12 June: The Lord Mayor paid him a brief private visit and then the Prime Minister, Benjamin Disraeli, came for half an hour in the evening.

In a letter to Lady Chesterfield, dated 13 June 1875, Disraeli described how earlier in the day he had given his cabinet ministers a good telling off for the inauspicious start of the Sultan's visit to England. The letter continued:

THE ILLUSTRATED LONDON NEWS

REGISTERED AT THE GENERAL POST-OFFICE FOR TRANSMISSION ABROAD.

No. 1871.—VOL. LXVI.   SATURDAY, JUNE 19, 1875.   WITH EXTRA SUPPLEMENT   SIXPENCE. By Post, 6½d.

About four o'clock, by appointment, I paid my visit to the Sultan myself. He received me at the door, or rather in the hall, of his hotel with all his chiefs. They were not good-looking, but he, himself, is an Arab with a well-favoured mien, good manners and pleasing countenance and the peculiar repose of an Oriental gentleman. Being used, from my travels, to these interviews and gentry, I addressed him directly, looking in his face as I spoke and never turning to the Interpreter. This greatly pleases them, but is very difficult to do. The audience was successful.

It seems that Disraeli's personal meeting with the Sultan helped make amends.[13]

Sunday 13 June: Day of rest.

Monday 14 June: The Sultan visited the Prince and Princess of Wales at Marlborough House and met the royal children. Barghash appreciated the intimate domestic occasion, when he was welcomed like one of the family. He was surprised to see the two little princes dressed in sailor suits, copying the dress worn by working men on board Royal Naval ships. The choice of costume remained a source of puzzlement to him and in later years he often commented on it. The jovial pleasure-loving Prince of Wales knew how to put people at their ease. It was not the first time his diplomatic skills proved his worth, despite the opinion of his disapproving mother.

Also that morning the Sultan had his photograph taken by Maull & Co of Piccadilly for a *carte de visite*. Pestered by rival photographers who wanted to take his photograph, the Sultan exclaimed to Badger his interpreter – 'For the sake of Allah do conduct me somewhere to have my face taken, in order that I may be able to show a copy of it to the numerous face-takers who apply to me for it.'[14] Visiting cards with photographs were the fashion and everyone of consequence had one and the Sultan had his own made and then handed them out to the officials he met, in the same way that business cards are used today. Traditional Islam, however, frowned on portrayal of the human form and the photographs and pictures of the Sultan which appeared in the newspapers, some alongside European women, shocked the stricter Muslims in Zanzibar, who felt his behaviour unbefitting.[15]

Cartoon, 'More Slaveries Than One'

Tuesday 15 June: The Sultan received a visit from the Archbishop of Canterbury, and then went to the British Museum. The enormous circular reading room greatly astonished him. 'It is a city of books…I must come again soon,' he said in translation by Badger.[16] In the evening he went to the Princess's Theatre and saw *Around the World in 80 Days*.

Wednesday 16 June: He visited the Botanical Gardens in Regent's Park, then went by train to Brighton, where he visited the Aquarium, enjoyed the beach, attended a soirée at the Brighton Museum and stayed the night at the Grand Hotel.

Thursday 17 June: Back in London again, the Sultan received a visit from the Central African Mission committee and the Bishop of

London. In the afternoon he went to the Alexandra Park Horse Show before attending Lady Derby's party in the evening. At the Horse Show it was noticed that he walked about among the people without any ceremony and even rescued a little girl from the crush of the crowd by handing her over to an attendant, 'which called forth an admiring cheer.'[17]

Friday 18 June: In the morning he visited the Regent's Park Zoo. In the afternoon he drove through a tremendous rainstorm to visit the General Post Office where he was shown the telegraphic machine room. When attempts were made to explain the working of the apparatus he simply shook his head in amazement. What most impressed him was the speed with which a reply was received to a message he sent to his agent in Aden, the telegraphic station closest to Zanzibar.[18] In the evening the Sultan attended a reception given by the Royal Colonial Institute in South Kensington.

Saturday 19 June: Sultan Barghash spent the afternoon at Lady Frere's Garden Party in Wimbledon and in the evening dined at the Crystal Palace and saw a fireworks display put on by Messrs Brock. One of the set pieces included his monogram in Arabic letters.[19]

Sunday 20 June: Day of rest.

Monday 21 June: The Sultan with his full entourage went by train to Windsor Castle to meet the Queen, who received him 'with gracious and dignified kindness' according to the *Illustrated London News* report on 26 June 1875. A more lively report from the Melbourne *Argus*,[20] wrote that the Sultan had described the royal presence as magnetic, and compared her to the mountain of lodestone in the Arabian Nights which drew the nails out of the sides of the ships which passed that way. In the evening he attended the opera at Drury Lane – *Lohengrin* by Wagner.

Tuesday 22 June: The Sultan went to the Globe Theatre for a production of *Bluebeard*.

Wednesday 23 June: He visited St Thomas' Hospital and the Houses of Parliament with Dr Kirk, Dr Badger and Mr Hill, and three of his entourage. At the hospital he met the Treasurer Sir Francis

The Sultan of Zanzibar at Lady Frere's garden party.

Hicks, the chief surgeon, Mr Simon, and a large group of medical students. He saw the Nightingale Home for training of nurses and was conducted into the ophthalmic ward. Afterwards they showed him the hydraulic lifts for raising and transporting critically ill patients. On entering Albert ward, he particularly noticed a little boy, whose leg had just been amputated close to the hip as a result of an accident. He saw the Chapel and visited the Victoria Ward for sick children.[21] St Thomas' Hospital had re-opened in 1871 at a new site at Westminster, opposite the Houses of Parliament. Its grand new buildings, built on the 'pavilion principle,' advocated by Florence Nightingale in her *Notes on Nursing*, represented the latest in modern hospital design and patient care. Dr Kirk hoped the Sultan would be inspired to build a public hospital for Zanzibar.

That evening the Sultan attended a state concert at Buckingham Palace, when a piece of music especially composed for his visit was played. He was so gratified that he adopted it as his own national anthem.

Thursday 24 June: The Lord Mayor received the Sultan at the Mansion House. He then visited the Bank, the Mint and the London Docks and in the evening dined at Fishmongers Hall.

Friday 25 June: At the Alexandra Hotel, the Sultan received a deputation from the Church Missionary Society, which presented him with an atlas and urged him to continue his work towards the abolition of the slave trade. In the afternoon he inspected Westminster Abbey and visited the Deanery. He attended the Countess of Derby's reception in the evening.

Saturday 26 June: He made numerous purchases of goods ordered and brought to the hotel.[22] Behind the scenes everything did not go entirely smoothly. Kirk kept a close eye on the events planned for the Sultan's entertainment and intervened if he thought they were inappropriate. On this day a reception to be given by Lady Stanley in Barghash's honour was cancelled at the last minute, when Kirk heard that her husband, Lord Stanley of Alderley, was planning to use the opportunity to ask Barghash to join his scheme for a pan-Islamic alliance. Lady Stanley was very annoyed, and the Sultan attended a reception given by the Marchioness of Salisbury instead.[23]

Sunday 27 June Sunday: He dined with Sassoon David Sassoon. Sassoon was a son of the enormously wealthy Bombay merchant David Sassoon. He was David's eldest son by his second wife and had come to England in 1858 and now lived at Ashley Park, Surrey. The family were Baghdadi Jews of Sephardic extraction, and Sassoon was the first of the family to settle in England. Their business had started in the Persian Gulf, where they had traded in cloth and hides, but by the 1870s their wealth came mainly from the export of raw cotton from India, and the trade in manufactured textiles and opium. During the nineteenth century the opium trade accounted for one-seventh of British income in India and the Sassoons eventually controlled 70 per cent of the trade.[24] Tharia Topan also traded in opium, as did British companies such as Jardine Matheson, who made large fortunes from exporting opium to the Far East.

Monday 28 June: The Sultan went in a special train with the Prince and Princess of Wales to see the review of the troops at Aldershot. In the evening he attended a meeting of the Royal Geographical Society at Burlington House where in a speech translated by Dr Badger he referred to the African explorers Burton, Speke, Grant, Livingstone, Stanley and Cameron and said that since his arrival in England he had become convinced of the truth of the statements made by several Arabian poets respecting the advantages of travel.

Tuesday 29 June: On a visit to Woolwich, the Sultan saw the 40-ton Nasmyth hammer in action after which he was quoted as saying, 'I have seen the gate of Hell.'[25] In the evening he dined with the Marquis and Marchioness of Salisbury. Disraeli described this banquet given in the Sultan's honour in a letter dated 30 June 1875 addressed to Lady Bradford. It was apparently a rather stiff affair, as the dinner guests were senior politicians, drawn from both sides of the house, who glowered at each other suspiciously across the table. The Sultan through his interpreters gave a speech praising the way political opponents in England were able to sit down together.

Wednesday 30 June: He went to the Opera at Convent Garden and saw *l'Africaine*.

Thursday 1 July: The Sultan travelled north to begin a tour of the industrial heartland in the Midlands and Lancashire, accompanied by his courtiers and twelve personal attendants – of which no doubt Peera Dewjee was one.

Friday 2 July – Sunday 4 July: The tour began in Birmingham, where the Sultan visited Osler's Glassworks, Birmingham Small Arms Company and a flower show of the Midland Horticultural Society and the next day went to Elkington's silver and electroplating works. After which he declared that Birmingham was 'truly a well of rare and wonderful things.'[26]

Monday 5 – Wednesday 7 July: The party were in Liverpool, where they visited the Liverpool docks and Laird's Shipbuilding Works and saw the launch of a steam yacht.

Thursday 8 – Saturday 10 July: It was the turn of Manchester, the cottonopolis of England. By this time the Sultan was becoming weary. He complained that he had walked more in Liverpool than he had done during five years in Zanzibar, and was not disposed or able to bear much fatigue.[27] The weather had taken a turn for the worse and it was pouring with rain, consequently the planned programme was shortened. First he was taken round Mr Richard Haworth's Egerton Mill in Salford and then to the print works of Messrs T Hoyle and Company in Mayfield, and thus saw how cotton goods were produced from the raw fibre right through to the finished item. This proved an eye opener to the Sultan and particularly interested one of his entourage who was described as 'a large cotton merchant in Zanzibar.'[28]

Lastly, he went to the cash and carry warehouse of Messrs Watts and Company in Portland Street. Standing six stories high with an enormous chandelier in the entrance hall, it was the last word in luxury and grandeur and the Sultan enjoyed himself looking at all the various goods for sale. He showed a keen interest and wanted to know the prices of several items, especially the embroidered work. The old Watts warehouse still exists and is now the Britannia Hotel. The grand entrance and open construction of the hall way is the same as when the Sultan visited. His visit to Manchester Town Hall was also a success. The Sultan was especially impressed by the clock tower, standing 285 feet high, and he paused several times to have another view as he was driven slowly round the building. He stayed at the Queens Hotel, Manchester.

Monday 12 July: He travelled back to London on the train. That afternoon he received an address from Corporation of London at the Guildhall when he was presented with a gold casket. Dr Badger acting as interpreter read a reply to this, in which the Sultan said he was not surprised that the subject of the slave trade should attract such attention in London seeing that it was costing England so much time and money to put an end to it. He then declared it was his highest desire that the interests of his own country and those of England should be identical. In the evening he was entertained by the Lord Mayor at a dinner at the Mansion House. In his address, translated again by Badger, he thanked the British press, especially the press of London, for the long and kindly accounts of his visit, which had already been translated into Arabic for a newspaper published at Constantinople and would be read with delight by Arabs everywhere. He also spoke of the cordiality with which he had been received by the Queen, by the heads of departments and various firms, which he would never forget. What he had seen of the liberty, industry and enterprise of this country would be a lesson to him, which he trusted would have some influence upon his own kingdom. By the help of God, without whom nothing is strong or great, he would do his best to abolish slavery and he hoped that ere long the freedom of the people within his territories would be like the freedom of the English.[29]

Tuesday 13 July: He received a deputation from the Bible Society and Lord Shaftesbury, who presented the Sultan with a handsome Bible translated into Arabic and asked the Sultan to do all in his power to circulate knowledge of the Bible amongst his people. Barghash replied, 'Inshallah! If it please God.' He said he was familiar with the words of Jesus and the writings of the Bible, which appear in the Koran.[30]

Wednesday 14 July: Packed! This must have been an extensive operation as both the Sultan and the members of his party had purchased large quantities of merchandise to take back to Zanzibar, for sale as well as for personal use.

Thursday 15 July: The Sultan left England for Paris.

The Sultan's ten-day visit to Paris was a more low-key affair, which did not receive the same attention and press coverage as the English tour. However, the French Government treated him as an official guest and the President held a dinner in his honour. Alfred Rabaud, an old friend from Zanzibar, travelled with him and oversaw the arrangements.[31] Seyyid Barghash stayed at the Hotel de Louvre in central Paris and visited the National Library, went to Versailles and attended a state performance at the Opera. This was apparently to see the ballet, *Coppelia*, which must have bored him, as he was caught yawning.

On his last day, Sunday 25 July, he received an official farewell visit at the Hotel du Louvre from President Mac Mahon and Duq D'Audiffret Pasquier.

Monday 26 July: The Sultan left Paris for Marseilles, where his ship waited for him.

Barghash and his entourage went on to Egypt. While in Cairo the Sultan and his councillors indulged in some luxury shopping and purchased eight Circassian slaves for their harems, six of whom were for the Sultan personally. In order not to arouse attention the slaves were sent on secretly to Jiddah to await shipment, but one of the girls, learning she was destined to be the concubine of the ancient councillor Hamud bin Mohammed, attempted to commit suicide by throwing herself from a high window into the street below. This caused something of a scandal.[32] The Sultan under the watchful eye of Kirk had created a good impression in England, and his intentions to suppress the slave trade in his country were believed to be genuine. Kirk feared his latest escapade could undo all the hard work of the last few months. Fortunately the news of the Sultan's latest slaving activities did not reach the general public in England.

The Sultan's visit to England had been an elaborate public relations exercise. He was paraded as a success story in England's fight against the slave trade. Here was a monarch who had seen the error of his ways and had shut his slave markets, of his own free will! For a whole month he was entertained by ambitious hostesses, taken to see the sights, and visited by the great and the good. The politicians fêted him, congratulating themselves on winning the war on slavery and claiming the moral high ground amongst nations. Fervent abolitionists rushed to see him and had no hesitation in pressing Bibles upon him while denouncing the evils of slavery. Senior clerics lectured him on the superior teachings of Christianity with little respect for his religious principles. Public bodies boasted and moralised and extolled the virtues and successes of free enterprise. Throughout these ordeals the Sultan remained dignified and polite, despite what he may have felt in private.

The endless press coverage promoted British interests, but it also gave Barghash the opportunity for press coverage in the Muslim countries of the East, which carried newspaper reports of his progress through Europe. One of the lessons he learnt from his European tour was the value of a favourable press and good publicity and he gave interviews to various Arabic journalists and writers based in England. The most famous of these was Louis Sabunji, who the Sultan first met in Manchester. Sabunji was a Syriac Catholic priest from Lebanon, who in 1875 was based in Manchester. Later he moved to London where he lived for 14 years. Barghash was so impressed with Sabunji that he employed him on a number of translation projects and provided sponsorship for his publications. He helped Sabunji revive his magazine *Al Nahla*, which appeared monthly from 1877 to 1880 and included many references to Barghash, who was portrayed as an enlightened Muslim ruler and reformer. Barghash employed Sabunji to compile the Arabic account of his European tour which was eventually printed in 1879 and to translate into Arabic all the written negotiations connected with Frere's mission and the closure of the slave markets.[33]

For Barghash the meetings with Queen Victoria and Edward, Prince of Wales, were the highlights of his trip. The friendly audience he received increased his prestige and status amongst his peers. Judging by the illustrations chosen for Sabunji's Arabic account of the trip, where the British royal family and their residences featured largely, the other most memorable moments for the Sultan were the visits to Brighton beach, Crystal Palace, the Houses of Parliament and the Ascot Races. He had been coached by Kirk and with the help of Badger's elegant translations made all the right noises to please the English public. When there were complaints that his speeches were always the same, he replied: 'How can I help it? It is the fault of the English people. You all welcome me; you all tell me I have done something for the abolition of the slave trade, and you hope I shall do more; what can I say but thank you, thank you, thank you.'[34]

There is no doubt Barghash derived considerable insight as well as personal satisfaction from the trip. He showed interest in all he saw, taking back modernising ideas with him to Zanzibar. He also gained a greater understanding of what his powerful ally expected from him.

His tour of the northern industrial towns and their factories, where he inspected the cotton goods, guns and various manufactured items destined as imports into Zanzibar was an enlightening and profitable experience. It was a business trip pure and simple, designed to market the wares of England.

His ten-day visit to France was different. Here he relaxed as no one was lecturing him on slavery or pushing Christianity at him. He enjoyed his stay in Paris, but saw that France was politically weak and could not be depended upon as an ally. There was plenty to see and buy as the style and elegance of French fashion was much in demand in Zanzibar.

During his time in France, Barghash was presented with a superb pair of Sevres vases and a tapestry chair cover embroidered by the Gobelins factory, but the visit he most enjoyed was to the *Jardin d'Acclimatation* where the gambols of the sea lions amused him.[35]

Barghash's return via Egypt demonstrated that his core beliefs had not changed. Despite the propaganda and determined proselytising of the English, he was still the same old Barghash. Two fingers up to the West, as he bought himself six beautiful slave girls for his harem.

---

1 This is Sir William Mackinnon successful businessman and founder of the British India Steam Navigation Company and Edward Dawes was his agent in London.

2 Durham University Library, WYL/43/16

3 Genesta Hamilton, *Princes of Zinj: The Rulers of Zanzibar,* London: Hutchinson, 1957, p 150

4 Robert Nunez Lyne, *Zanzibar in Contemporary Times*, London: Hurst & Blackett, 1905, p 92

5 Hamilton, *Princes of Zinj*, p 151

6 *ILN* Supplement, July 17, 1875. This shows the Sultan on a later visit to Manchester, when again he was fascinated by the lift.

7 The *Argus*, Melbourne, Australia, September 11, 1875, report from London, June 25.

8 See Alastair Hazell, *The Last Slave Market: Dr John Kirk and the Struggle to End the East African Slave Trade*, London: Constable & Robinson, 2011,

p 283-4, and the letters of Sir John Kirk held in the National Library of Scotland which contains a paper about *Bibi Salima*, which describes her as a lady 'of loose morals' and relates these events, Acc 9942/20.

9 *ILN*, June 19, 1875

10 Louis Sabunji, *Tanzih al-absar wa-al-afkar fi rihlat Sultan Zanjabar – The Recreation of the Sight and Mind; A Narrative of the Visit of His Highness the Sultan of Zanzibar,* 1879

11 This supplementary treaty was eventually signed on July 14 by Lord Derby and Nassir bin Said bin Abdullah.

12 *The Graphic,* June 19, 1875

13 *'More Slaveries than One!'* A cartoon which appeared in *Punch,* June 26, 1875. The caption beneath reads:
Right Hon B D: Now that your Highness has seen the blessings of Freedom I trust we may rely on your strenuous help in putting down Slavery!
Sultan Seyyid Barghash: Ah yes! Certainly! But remember oh Sheikh bin Dizzy, CONSERVATIVE PARTY VERY STRONG in Zanzibar

14 *Glasgow Herald,* June 14, 1875

15 Sir Arthur Hardinge in his book *A Diplomatist in the East,* London: Jonathan Cape, 1928, p 85-6, even goes as far as to write that after his European visit, Barghash was no longer addressed with his religious title, Seyyid, but merely as Sultan.

16 *The Graphic,* June 19, 1875

17 This incident was reported in the New Zealand newspaper, *Otago Daily Times,* September 3, 1875, page 3

18 *Glasgow Herald,* June 19, 1875

19 This was *Ya Fattah,* one of the titles of God in Islam meaning 'He that openeth the way,' which Barghash had chosen as his personal motto. He had it engraved in Arabic letters on a gold ring he wore on his little finger set with a turquoise, blue as the sea. Later on in his reign he changed this for a large diamond ring.

20 The *Argus,* Melbourne, Australia, September 11, 1875 – report from London dated June 25

21 *The British Medical Journal,* Vol 1, no 756 (June 26, 1875), p 863-4

22 *ILN*, July 3, 1875

23 Letters of Sir John Kirk, National Library of Scotland, Acc 9942/20

24 It was said that 'silver and gold, silks, gums and spices, opium and cotton, wool and wheat – whatever moves over sea or land feels the hand or bears the mark of Sassoon and Company.' Peter Stansky, *Sassoon; The Worlds of Philip and Sybil,* New Haven/London: Yale University Press, 2003, p 6

25 *The Times,* June 30, 1875

26 *ILN*, July 10, 1875

27 *Leeds Mercury*, July 10, 1875

28 *Manchester Times*, July 10, 1875. This was no doubt a reference to Tharia Topan.

29 *The Graphic*, July 17, 1875

30 *The Graphic*, July 17, 1875

31 Alfred Rabaud (d 1886) was a partner in the Marseilles shipping firm of Roux de Fraissinet, which had been established in Zanzibar since 1848. He later became president of the Marseilles Geographic Society of which Seyyid Barghash was a corresponding member.

32 Hazell, *Last Slave Market*, p 284

33 This extensive project was started in 1878 and not completed until 1881, and the original manuscript is kept in the rare books library of the University of Istanbul. It is thought that Sabunji never visited Zanzibar but worked from England with the assistance of Dr Badger. Information about Sabunji comes from R W Visser, 'Identities in early Arabic journalism: The case of Louis Ṣābūnjī,' PhD thesis, University of Amsterdam, 2014

34 Lyne, *Zanzibar in Contemporary Times*, p 94-95

35 *Appleton's Journal*: 'From Abroad; Our Paris Letter': July 28, 1875

Chapter Ten

A Time of Smoke and Mirrors

Following the return of the Sultan from Europe, Zanzibar settled into a period of deceptive calm and prosperity. Sir John Kirk's reputation rose to a new high in November 1875, when a British-led Egyptian expedition occupied the Somali towns of Brava and Kismayo. Kirk sprang to the defence of Barghash – it is said – literally jumping from his ship to swim ashore to personally negotiate the return of the two coastal towns. The seized ports were evacuated in January 1876, to the relief and gratitude of the Sultan. He feared Egypt's southward expansion into his territories, but had as yet no premonition of the far greater danger blowing in from Europe.

At the palace the balance of power had shifted decisively and Barghash listened to the advice of his Indian merchants and the British Consul, more than his Arab chiefs and holy men. The official photograph taken of Barghash and his councillors by Maull & Co in London in 1875 provides a graphic illustration of these changing demographics. Tharia Topan, the Ismaili merchant, stands in the centre of the picture directly behind the Sultan. The two Arabs standing beside him try to crowd him out, but they cannot; he keeps the central position. The Indian merchants were now the richest men in Zanzibar and their influence counted with the Sultan. Increasingly they were invited to drink coffee at the palace and attend the Sultan's *baraza* and foremost amongst the favourites was Peera Dewjee, known simply as 'the trusted one.'

While in Paris, Barghash had commissioned a French artist to paint a full length portrait of himself to hang next to his throne – an imposing icon for the increasingly autocratic nature of his reign. His father Seyyid Said had chosen to decorate his audience chamber with paintings of sea battles changing their position according to which nation had his favour. Barghash ignored the sensibilities of his most ardent Muslim subjects and put up an imposing picture of himself. H H Johnston describes seeing two identical portraits of the Sultan hanging on either side of the throne when he visited the Sultan in 1884, but he was probably mistaken. There is a large portrait of Majid in full Arab dress, in very similar format to the one ordered by Barghash, which still hangs in the Beit al-Ajaib and in dim light the two pictures look similar. The painting of Barghash is the poorer of the two, obviously done from a photograph to which the body was added.[1]

Consul Kirk continued to play a skilful diplomatic hand, allowing the Sultan to keep up an outward show of independent authority although increasingly power was being wielded elsewhere. Kirk did this by dropping a word of congratulation, or reproof, said in confidence, to one of the Sultan's assistants, which he knew would be reported straight back to the ear of the Sultan. 'One day he had to be congratulated and given credit, then he got a sharp word, but it had to be dropped outside to reach him from others, and I had to keep all this to myself. Even the assistants did not know the game...'[2]

Peera Dewjee would have been one of the main 'assistants' – and he quickly learnt the 'game' as later developments showed. In this way the Sultan kept up his pretence of power, which gained him respect from his Arabs, and the British Consul stayed in the background – an *éminence grise* behind the throne – or that is how Kirk liked to see himself. The process required great delicacy of touch as Barghash was both temperamental and difficult. He hated being manipulated, but he had no other choice if he wished to keep the sultanate. All the while Kirk kept up his relentless fight against the slave traffickers and pushed the Sultan to crack down on slave traders, even if it involved arresting and shaming his fellow Arabs and councillors.

Barghash continued in his daily programme of prayers and worship as a devout Ibadhi Muslim, held public *baraza* and settled disputes according to sharia law, but he was no longer under the thumb of his priests and counsillors. Wary of his Arab chiefs and always fearful of rebellion, he grew more and more ruthless, seizing property and casting suspects into prison at the merest whisper of treason. He singled out his younger brother Khalifa for particularly cruel treatment. Barghash held Khalifa in strict house confinement from 1872 and did not allow him to receive any significant visitors. His situation became so pitiful that in 1874 Turki of Muscat interceded on his behalf and wrote to the Government of British India to ask for assistance in releasing his brother from captivity. Khalifa was given the option of going to Muscat, but he refused as he wished to remain in Zanzibar. Captain W F Prideaux,[3] acting British Consul during Kirk's sick leave, reported meeting Khalifa when he was brought to the Sultan's palace in irons and he described him as looking miserable and squalid to an excessive degree. Khalifa feared worse treatment if he was moved to Muscat and he pleaded for British protection. Later Barghash informed Prideaux he still feared to release Khalifa, as he regarded him as a weakling destined to be used by enemies of his reign. Finally in 1876 Khalifa was released and allowed to leave Zanzibar for the Somali port of Merka. Although he was allowed to return to Zanzibar at a later date, he was not a factor in the political life of Zanzibar for the remainder of his brother Barghash's reign.[4]

Barghash had little time for any of his younger brothers whom he regarded as ignorant and unfit to rule. He told Kirk they had been spoilt by Majid and not been given the strict Omani Arab upbringing he had received from his father the great Seyyid Said. By the late 1870s of the more than thirty offspring who had inherited after Said's death in 1856, only fourteen were still alive. Healthy boys of the next generation were conspicuously absent. Barghash had daughters, but no sons and because of his medical condition he was thought unable to have further children. 'Elephantiasis has damaged him, there is no chance of any direct issue.'[5] But in 1876, to the surprise of many, Barghash fathered two sons. Seif died in infancy, but Khalid, born to one of his Circassian concubines, survived. It seemed Barghash's European tour had temporarily improved his health.

As Barghash's position as an independent sovereign grew weaker, he increasingly turned to displays of pomp and ceremony and lavish construction works to bolster his prestige in Zanzibar. He understood how to use outward show to keep up the appearance of power and impress his subjects. It helped him forget the fact that he was dependent on the goodwill of more powerful nations, bound to sign treaties and do as he was told. *Heshima*, that untranslatable Arabic concept, a mixture of honour, prestige and image, was always a major consideration for Barghash. He needed to feel like a sultan and maintain the appearance of a great and powerful man. The lavish public feasts and festivals and high profile modernisation schemes of the latter part of his reign not only kept the general populace on his side but also satisfied his own pride and *heshima*. But these grandiose projects left him perennially short of money and he was always looking for ways to increase his revenue.

Ivory and firearms by now had largely replaced slaves as the trade items of choice and proved just as lucrative, if not more so. There was an insatiable demand for ivory in Europe. It was used in the manufacture of all kinds of everyday items – piano keys, buttons, combs, knife handles, billiard balls, etc. No one asked what means were employed to get it, how many elephants were killed and lives ruined in the stampede for profit. British, American, French and German trading houses had agents based in Zanzibar and bidding was cut-throat at the ivory auctions, when the caravans came in. The Sultan was determined to share in the profit and collected tax on every *frasila* exported – the amount varying according to its quality. In 1877, in a surprise move, he declared a monopoly on firearms and gunpowder and signed a contract with the German company Hansing & Co, making them his main supplier. Now only the Sultan could buy and sell this valuable commodity – in the interests of national security and safety – or that was his excuse. He sold at considerable profit for himself and the former importers and dealers were not pleased. They accused Dr Kirk of masterminding the idea and enforcing the new regulation.[6] Barghash already charged 5 per cent export duty on hides and in August 1878 raised the tax on cloves to 2 per cent. But still he could not make ends meet. He was continuously overdrawn and searching for ways to make a profit.

Kirk assured Barghash that legitimate commerce was the way forward. The three Cs would do the trick. If only Africa could be opened up to Christianity, Commerce and Civilisation, then untold wealth would surely follow. It would become more like Europe – a tantalising vision! Livingstone had first developed the theory that legitimate trade would help create a free society. He had elevated commerce as the indispensable partner of Christianity and civilisation and in so doing had inadvertently provided an ethical basis for imperial expansion by linking moral fervour with right to power. Kirk agreed and thought European expansion into Africa would bring peace, stability and progress. Nowadays this is seen for what it was: exploitation and greed, thinly disguised as philanthropy. But at the time many prominent people sincerely believed this was the way both to improve living conditions in Africa and stop the age-old system of slavery. After his death, Livingstone was hailed as a modern day prophet and his admirers and former colleagues felt impelled to carry forward the great missionary's unfinished work in Africa. Kirk was one of the inner circle of believers, and he lost no opportunity in promoting this philosophy with the Sultan.

A first tentative step had been taken in September 1876 at the Belgian King Leopold II's Brussels Geographical Conference. A number of influential men including the businessman, Sir William Mackinnon, and Sir Bartle Frere gathered to discuss the feasibility of opening up the interior of Africa for better trade communications. Sir Bartle Frere, now Chairman of the Royal Geographic Society, favoured creating a line of stations along a route between the Swahili coast and Lake Tanganyika and called for the creation of an international organisation to be called the International African Association to co-ordinate similar initiatives by other nations.

Fired with enthusiasm, Mackinnon went back to Scotland and held meetings in Glasgow in November 1876 to set up a British committee of the International African Association, to fund two roads in East Africa – the first from the north end of Lake Nyasa to the south end of Lake Tanganyika and the second from a port on the Swahili Coast to the north end of Lake Nyasa.

The road party for the coastal road consisted of a former sergeant of the Royal Engineers named Mayes and two brothers from Edinburgh, Frederick and John Moir. They duly arrived in Zanzibar in June 1877 and began work on a road from Dar es Salaam. Mackinnon proposed renting Dar es Salaam from the Sultan as a base for his shipping operations on the East African mainland. But Mackinnon's scheme gradually expanded into a more ambitious proposal to lease the whole of the Sultan's mainland administration and use its customs revenues to create a development company, which would transform transport and communications between the coast and the interior.

British Consul General, Sir John Kirk, first put the idea to Barghash in April 1877 and to begin with the Sultan was enthusiastic. But almost at once the project began to unravel. In London, the RGS decided to sever ties from Brussels and Leopold's organisation and go it alone. Even Mackinnon's friends in Glasgow decided the International African Association gave too much influence to Leopold and the Roman Catholic powers. Mackinnon's British Committee of the International African Association closed. Funding became a problem when the City of Glasgow Bank collapsed and the English Government refused to back Mackinnon's African scheme.[7]

Mackinnon had overreached himself and as the extent of his proposals became known to the leading Arabs and Indians, they expressed serious doubts, fearing losses to their businesses if hinterland trade passed into Mackinnon's and British hands. In May 1878 Barghash, under pressure from local Arab and Indian interests, withdrew his support and made it clear he would not grant a lease of the whole of his mainland territories to Mackinnon. What had appeared at first glance to the Sultan to be an excellent moneymaking venture, on closer scrutiny was seen to be a bad idea. The Sultan felt he had been tricked by Kirk and Mackinnon into agreeing to a project, when the ramifications had not been properly explained to him. Reports of the drunken antics of the road building party and harassment of the local inhabitants further tarnished the project, and infuriated the Sultan. Then in June 1878 the *Glasgow*, the ship Barghash had ordered from England on the advice of Mackinnon, arrived in Zanzibar. The *Glasgow* was a severe disappointment to Barghash. He had expected something more magnificent. In a rage, he withdrew his business from Mackinnon's agency, Smith Mackenzie & Co. The Mackinnon-Kirk-Frere vision for commercial penetration of the Swahili coast was dead in the water.

Feelings ran high. Mackinnon, his BI ships and agent, Smith, Mackenzie & Co, who had seemed such a godsend to Zanzibar, were now reviled. Sir William Mackinnon, with the support of Sir Henry Bartle Frere, had been the architect of the mail steamship line, British India Steamship Navigation Company, BI for short, which first ran to India after the opening of the Suez Canal in 1869. In 1872 they extended the route to Aden and Zanzibar. In 1875 during his visit to England, probably in Liverpool, Barghash had met Sir William Mackinnon and agreed to put his personal business through the BI agency in Zanzibar. Two of Mackinnon's former employees from his Glasgow office, Archie Smith and Archie Brown, were sent out to Zanzibar as his representatives for the agency business. As a further token of friendship to set the seal on the close working relationship, Barghash on the recommendation of Mackinnon, had ordered himself an armed steam yacht to be called *Glasgow*, from the Denny yard at Dumbarton.

The *Glasgow* was built in 1878 as a royal yacht to replace the *Sea King*,[8] which had been destroyed in the disastrous hurricane in 1872. It was meant to resemble the flagship of the Royal Navy's East Indian Squadron, the screw frigate HMS *Glasgow*, which had impressed the Sultan during its visit to Zanzibar in 1873. On 17 April 1877 William Denny wrote to Barghash promising to build 'a vessel in every way a handsome and substantial piece of work' and on 14 May 1877 the ship was laid down. The vessel was constructed with an iron frame covered with teak planks and a keel made from rock elm. The hull was sheathed with Muntz metal below the waterline. It had three masts and a steam propulsion system with the special feature of a lifting propeller and was launched on 2 March 1878. It was 1,416 tons, 210 feet in length, had a 29-foot beam, 16-foot draft and a speed of 12 knots.

The *Glasgow* was fitted out with all modern conveniences. It had two state rooms, a luxurious main cabin, dining saloon, a bathroom and water closet for use by the Sultan. In all the vessel cost £32,735 and was fitted with an armament of nine muzzle loading cannon and a Gatling gun, the gift of Queen Victoria. It set sail for Zanzibar from Portsmouth on 17 April 1878 under the command of Captain Hand RN. Upon arrival in Zanzibar the Sultan inspected his new purchase and was not impressed. His *Glasgow* was considerably less imposing than its namesake, the British frigate, being over 40 feet shorter with two thirds the beam. The ship lay at anchor in harbour throughout the rest of the sultan's reign and was never used by Barghash or his three successors prior to 1896.[9]

Mackinnon and his steamships had proved a severe disappointment and worse followed. It is at this point that we have one of our earliest

The Sultan's ship 'The Glasgow'

152

recorded snapshots of Peera Dewjee from a letter written by the American merchant William Hathorne in November 1878. Infuriated with the Smith Mackenzie agent Archie Smith, who would not give him the Sultan's bill of lading immediately but told him to wait his turn, Peera grabbed him by the neck and shook him and the two men started to fight:

> Pera, the Sultan's man, went down to Smith's the day before yesterday for his B/L. Smith told him he would have to take his regular turn, then Pera had some words & Smith more, until P. got S. by the neck and shook him! Just fancy it! Instead of Smith taking a piece of board & 'busting' his head, he scrambled around awhile with Pera until some of the Hindis who were in the office interfered & separated them. Then Smith went to Kirk who told him he would have to get out a summons, which Smith declined, as he says, preferring to settle the matter himself in some other way.[10]

Smith changed his mind and did get out a summons and Peera was fined by the British consular court. Information about this can be read in a letter written by Kirk to Mackinnon dated 25 May 1879, which is amongst the Mackinnon Letters held in the SOAS library, London.

> The unfortunate dispute with one of the sultan's people I look on as of no consequence it was not his fault. Pira the man in question was sure about that time to have a quarrel with some white man – he is a clever but vulgar unscrupulous pushing fellow, most useful to the Sultan and a good servant to him although objectionable and underhand to everyone else, though being a thoroughly good servant and a perfect spy he has gained in influence and at that time he thought necessary to show it by insulting some white man, for a first offence he had a sharp punishment in this court but I suppose the Sultan paid the fine. I only mention his name in order to clear Smith in the affair because I know that Pira has found means since then to get a good deal of business transferred from Smith Mackenzie into his own hands or perhaps he had this in view from the first.[11]

Relations broke down completely and after this the Sultan started his own shipping line to compete with BI. The mail ships, though good for their British owners, were not proving popular with Indian and Arab shippers, who had to pay higher prices for transporting goods.

Interest in opening up the interior of Africa did not stop with Mackinnon's set-back. King Leopold in Belgium continued to support the International African Association, which held further well publicised meetings in Brussels, with the King in attendance. It purported to be a moral and beneficial organisation only interested in countering the evils of slavery, furthering Christianity and helping poor heathen Africa enjoy the benefits of westernisation. Instead it served as a smoke screen for the Belgian King. Jealous of his fellow kings of larger more powerful kingdoms, he was determined to stake his claim in Africa, have a share of African riches and his own colonies. He sent explorers out to discover the unknown areas and report back on mineral wealth and trade routes and suitable areas for European settlement and agriculture. This was the era of the discovery of gold and diamond mines in South Africa and there was a belief that unexpected sources of wealth would be discovered deep in Africa. King Leopold employed the explorer Henry M Stanley. Stanley's epic trans-Africa trek in 1874-77, when he crossed from East to West Africa had shown what was possible and helped fuel the ambitious dreams of the Belgian King for getting, as he famously wrote, 'a slice of this magnificent African cake.'[12]

Sultan Barghash continued to be quite relaxed about giving out his usual firmans (virtual passports), letters of safe passage and introductions to an increasing number of European 'explorers' and missionaries. European visitors were good for business as they employed porters and the shopkeepers benefited and the Sultan knew part of the profit would eventually come back to him. It is proof of the tolerant mindset that existed in Zanzibar that, despite the ever increasing visitors and settlers of every hue and creed, no attempts were made to stem the flow and all were made welcome. The Arabs stationed in the main interior trading depots like Tabora and Ujiji, men such as Tippu Tip, were instructed to give assistance to the European travellers. They duly fed and protected them, even nursed them back to health, on the strength of a short letter with the Sultan's seal. Often without Arab help the expeditions would have foundered and the leaders perished. It is a sad fact that many Europeans did not acknowledge their debt to these interior Arabs and played down their involvement once safety had been reached, and their audiences in the West often did not receive a true picture of conditions on the ground.

The Arabs based in the interior were not formally employed by the Sultan and they received no pay, but they recognised the Sultan in Zanzibar as their overlord. They funded themselves and made themselves comfortable settling down and often living for many years in their trading depots along the main caravan routes. They sent slaves and ivory down to the coast at irregular intervals to satisfy their creditors and hopefully turn in a profit. For security in the interior they surrounded themselves by armed retainers and domestic slaves and paid bribes and made alliances with the main African chiefs. There are descriptions of Arabs living to a high standard in Tabora, in houses filled with Persian carpets and with gardens full of vegetables and crops. They dressed in splendour in long white robes with magnificent jewelled swords and daggers in their belts and kept up their harems. The African tribesmen feared and respected them. It was hardly an empire, but a loose-knit area of control, based on alliances of mutual convenience, trade, and superior weaponry. In the late 1870s the claim that pipes played in Zanzibar could be heard in Uganda was not entirely far-fetched.

Barghash seems not to have suspected the ulterior motives and evil designs maturing in the brains of his European 'friends.' He had closed the slave market in Zanzibar in 1873 only under intense pressure and thought he had done enough to satisfy the anti-slavery agitators, who enjoyed such extraordinary (as he thought) popularity in the capitals of the West. He did not think his own realm was their next target. After all, he was repeatedly told that it was not, both by Badger and Kirk, the two Europeans he trusted most. Was he too trusting, over-confident and naive? Hampered because he only spoke Arabic, Hindustani and Swahili and did not understand the Western mind? Tharia Topan, his chief Indian advisor and customs master from 1876-9, spoke Hindustani, but only a smattering of English, and he too appears not to have read the warning signs. Or perhaps he was unconcerned as long as his business continued to flourish. He was one of a powerful group of Indian financiers who were turned (by self-interest) into instruments of British domination. Tharia Topan was close to Sir John Kirk, who relied on him for information, but it seems the information only went one way.

Perhaps as a result of the Mackinnon debacle, Barghash realised he needed better information about what his Western friends were up to. He needed sharp eyes and quick wits beside him to thwart foreign plots and schemes to steal his kingdom and his revenue. Peera Dewjee was his most trusted servant and evidence points that after returning from the Sultan's tour of Europe, Peera began to take on an increasingly important role as the Sultan's right hand man. After 1878 he began to organise a network of shopkeepers and servants, who reported back to him, so as to keep the Sultan better informed about what was afoot in Zanzibar and the wider world. As an Indian he was well placed to infiltrate all societies, and his love of gossip made him a natural candidate for information gathering or spying. Unlike the Omani Arab who was locked into a social framework, bound by religious practices and customs which prevented him mixing easily, the Ismaili Peera belonged to a much freer religion and stratum of society.

The Arabs and Europeans of this period mistrusted and misunderstood each other. The hospitality and courtly manners of the Arabs acted as a smokescreen to their true feelings. The tragedy of the Sultans of Zanzibar and their fellow Arabs, in part, stems from the cultural miscommunication. Often the European took the word of an Arab literally, while perhaps he just had the intention of doing what he said, if it were possible, or something else did not turn up first, or if he was just being polite. There was always that hint of uncertainty – *inshallah* – God willing – and quite often God wasn't. Europeans expected a definite 'yes' or 'no' and were infuriated when they did not get a straight answer. They didn't like the slower pace of the Arab – even time was calculated differently which made for more annoyance and missed appointments. Europeans accused Arabs of being devious and untrustworthy. They did not appreciate the importance of *heshima* to the Arab. Arabs, on their side, underestimated the Westerners, thinking them boorish, rude and stupid.

It is generally agreed that events following the death of Captain Brownrigg, the senior British Naval officer in Zanzibar, in a shoot-out with an Arab dhow in December 1881, completed the downfall of the Arab chiefs and set the stage for a European takeover. Barghash found the British obsession with suppressing the slave trade had unexpected benefits for him. As long as he gave the British a free hand to catch and punish slave traders and make anti-slavery laws, they did not interfere in other aspects of his rule. His Arab chiefs – over-mighty barons – had always been a thorn in his side and the British destruction of their main source of income, the slave trade, made his position, in the short term, easier, while saving him the trouble and the blame. The downside was that the Sultan of Zanzibar became increasingly divorced from his people, isolated and distant, free to do as he liked but with no real power beyond his palace gates. His traditional allies and former ruling class, the Zanzibari Arabs, were now reduced to a shadow of their former selves, impoverished and side-lined. His friends, the Indians, were motivated by profit only and had feet in two camps.

Based on Lyne's detailed and full account,[13] here is what happened. On 26 November 1881, Captain Brownrigg proceeded from Zanzibar to Pemba, a favourite haunt for illegal slave traders, on a visit of inspection. He was cruising in HMS *London*'s steam pinnace on the west side of Pemba island when they sighted two dhows. They were examined and allowed to pass, then a third came in sight. This small dhow flew French colours, which seemed suspicious. Brownrigg instructed his coxswain to stand ready with a boat hook and rope to board her, to see if she was carrying slaves. As the pinnace came alongside the dhow, the Arab captain waved his papers to indicate he was a legal trader, but the British noticed about eight Arabs crouching with rifles ready to repel boarders. Shots were fired and a fierce battle ensued between the two crews, which resulted in several deaths. Captain Brownrigg was killed along with another British sailor. The dhow sped away and landed her cargo of about 100 slaves at Wete and the British seamen limped back to Zanzibar.

A Muscat Arab, Hindi bin Khatim was the chief suspect. He was a notorious slave dealer who had just been released from prison having been acquitted for lack of evidence. Intent on revenge, General Mathews, with a force of 100 men accompanied by the British Consul Mr Holmwood[14] and the French Consul M Greffuhle, immediately set off in the Sultan's steamer *Star* to find the dhow. They found the dhow in Wete creek and confiscated it. But the slaves and Arabs had disappeared and no one divulged any information. In the end they took a relative of Hindi's called Suliman bin Abdullah and offered him money for information. He took the bribe but said he needed time. Mathews gave him a day and then, convinced he was playing false, seized his property and burnt his houses to the ground.

Eventually Mathews arrested Nasser bin Ali, the Arab chief of Wete, and took him aboard ship for interrogation. Terrified that his property too would be destroyed, he cracked and promised to show them where Hindi bin Khatim was hiding. At midnight Mathews and his men eventually discovered the hideout on the east coast of Pemba at a place called Chimba and surrounded the house, but the Arabs tried to break out and make a run for it. Another fierce fight erupted, but the Arabs were hopelessly outnumbered. Finally they captured the main culprit, Hindi, but he was so badly injured that after amputation of a hand and leg by the naval surgeon, he died of shock. Two of his fellow Arabs were captured alive and sentenced to death by hanging by the British consular court. Barghash petitioned this judgment and as a favour to the Sultan, the court commuted the death sentence to life imprisonment. The French Consul protested in vain at the violation of their flag by the Royal Navy, though it was alleged the dhow had not been properly registered. There is no mention as to what happened to the 100 slaves, if indeed there were any aboard. That fact had remained unproven.

Lieutenant Lloyd William Mathews of the British Navy Royal Marines, who led the attack, had been tasked in 1877 with forming a disciplined fighting force for the Sultan. Before this the Sultan's army was an undisciplined rabble, unreliable in battle and a danger to the townspeople. Lieutenant Mathews put the men in smart uniforms and drilled them and improved security on the island. To begin with he worked for the Royal Navy and he and his force of local soldiers hunted down suspected slavers and acted as a police force on the island. But after 1881 the Sultan employed Mathews directly and gave him the rank of General, although his core loyalties still lay with British interests.[15] A bluff, straightforward man, Mathews was happiest in the company of his soldiers and shunned European society. Mathews rose to become Chief Minister of Zanzibar. He married a local lady and became deeply attached to his adopted country and a permanent fixture in town. Honoured with a knighthood in 1894, he also received the order of Hamoudieh in 1897. He died in 1901 from malaria and overwork and a huge crowd turned out for his funeral procession.[16]

Lyne's frank account shows how brutal and ruthless the British had become in going after suspected slave traders. They were prepared to bribe and burn property and even ignore the flag of another nation in pursuit of their aim, while all the time hypocritically claiming the moral high ground and citing the rule of law. The fact that a senior naval officer had been killed made their response even fiercer. The young American businessman Edward D Ropes was not an admirer of the English. His description of Colonel S B Miles, Frederick Holmwood's superior, the acting British Consul General, shows how other nationalities viewed with dismay the rising British arrogance in Zanzibar:

> The 'Col' is you know one of the bloodiest of bloody Englishmen and is blind in one eye and very near sighted in the other and wears one eye glass. Zanzibar is as everybody knows a very stickler of a place for etiquette etc accounted for by the large number of English here. What do the English do here anyway? They do no business or anything else except play lawn tennis and catch a little dhow with a Capt or one of his own men as crew and call it putting down the slave trade. Glorious work for the

heroes(?) of Tel el Kebir! This noble work they are doing out here. Three thousand men, ten great men of war, iron clad with rifled cannon, yachts, steam-launches, hulks, stations – all work for a year and catch a 7 ton dhow and one little slave![17]

Initially the Arab owners of the clove plantations on Pemba had celebrated Brownrigg's death as an act of courage by Arabs standing up to the English bully, but after the terrifying reprisals they were cowed and Arabs in Zanzibar realised they could expect no protection from their Sultan. He no longer ruled as Arab leader of an Arab state, but as an isolated figurehead, reliant on his favourites and members of his immediate household, a Sultan in name only. When he remembered his boyhood and looked back to the era of his father, Barghash must have wondered at the change. How had it all come to this?

---

1 'The upper end of the room, where the "Sultan" ordinarily sits, has a large mirror in the centre, and on either side of the mirror is a full-length oil painting of Sayyid Barghash. These two paintings are identical in every detail. They were manufactured in Paris.' Apparently the top half was copied from a photograph Barghash had taken in London and the bottom half from another source altogether. They were combined to make a standing image. Harry H Johnston, *The Kilima-Njaro Expedition*, London: Kegan Paul, Trench & Co, 1886, p 32
2 Alistair Hazell, *The Last Slave Market: Dr John Kirk and the Struggle to End the East African Slave Trade*, London: Constable & Robinson, 2011, p 286 and letter from Kirk to Wylde, May 3, 1876 in the Kirk papers 9942/7
3 The elegantly insouciant and monocled Captain W F Prideaux, Kirk's deputy, was the kind of British officer who irritated the explorer, Stanley, extremely. But when Chuma and Susi with their porters reached Bagamoyo with Livingstone's body in February 1874, Prideaux paid off the sixty men from his own purse as he didn't want the Foreign Office to incur unnecessary expense – an honourable action which reflects well on his character.
4 Norman R Bennett, *A History of the Arab State of Zanzibar*, London: Methuen, 1978, p 103
5 Kirk to Wedderburn 1872, FO 84 1357

1. Khojas of Bombay, Nansi Parpia and family

2. General Sir Charles Napier

3. View of the waterfront c.1870

4. Salme in Arab dress wearing her jewellery

5. Sir Bartle Frere

6. Major Charles Bean Euan-Smith,
political officer and later British Consul in Zanzibar

7. Dr John Kirk, British Consul in Zanzibar

8. Carte de Visite for Barghash bin Said,
Sultan of Zanzibar

9. Staff of the British Agency, Dr Kirk, Mrs Kirk and daughter with Tharia Topan

10. *Group Portrait of Sultan Barghash and Entourage*

11. *Interior of the British Agency*

12. View of the waterfront showing the Sultan's Harem and clocktower

13. Beit al-Hukm with troops on parade

14. View of the Beit al-Ajaib with clocktower pre 1896

15. Sultan Ali bin Said

16. Sir William Mackinnon

17. The Sultan's Customs Officers, Mombasa c.1895

18. Door to the Customs House, Zanzibar

19. Porters carrying a package

20. Busy Zanzibar beachfront

*21. Peera Dewjee and his family in front of celebratory arch,
Queen Victoria's Golden Jubilee, 1887*

22. Sultan Hamed flanked by Arthur Hardinge and General Mathews, 1895

23. Destruction of Sultan's palace after the bombardment of 1896

24. Brilliant Star of Zanzibar, medal awarded to Peera Dewjee

25. Sultan Hamoud disembarking from the Royal barge with the Nyanza in the distance

26. Group of Prominent Citizens of Zanzibar

27. Rolling out the red carpet in Victoria Gardens
for the 1897 Diamond Jubilee Celebrations

28. Garden party in the Victoria Gardens

29. Portrait of Sewa Haji Paroo

30. Sultan Hamoud

31. Waterpots and Kangas

32. Fashionable lady of Zanzibar photographed by A C Gomes, 1890

33. Lamu interior decorated with plates

34. Plate imported by Peera Dewjee, which now hangs on the wall in the Zanzibar Serena Hotel

35. Zanzibar plate with clove decoration

36. Aga Khan III, HH Sir Sultan Mohammed Shah, photographed in London, 1902

*37. The British Residency, built in 1903, overlooking
Victoria Gardens with the Sultan's carriage in the foreground*

6 See Norman R Bennett, 'William H Hathorne: Merchant and Consul in Zanzibar,' *Essex Institute Historical Collections,* Vol 99, 1963, p 124 and 129. 'The Sultan some months since persuaded all the Hindi merchants, who have bought powder in years back to sign an agreement that they would buy no more from anybody; it is very doubtful if they would have done this, had they not been pushed to it by Dr Kirk, who takes a great interest in increasing the Sultan's revenue.' – letter dated March 6, 1878 to the American Arnold Hines & Co. 'Consequently Sultan Barghash with Kirk as his chief engineer is making $40,000 on powder annually.' – letter dated March 13, 1878 to the American Arnold Hines & Co.

7 There was to be a great deal of finger pointing over the failure of Mackinnon's 1877 project, as in future years regrets were expressed over the lost opportunity. Gladstone, who had succeeded Disraeli as prime minister, was against expansion into Africa and the expenditure needed. He is said to have communicated his lack of enthusiasm to Dr Badger, who was sent out to Zanzibar to translate the contractual terms for Barghash. Kirk then blamed Badger for upsetting Barghash and cited him as the chief architect of the disaster that followed. Badger the Arabic interpreter was a handy scapegoat, as in time-honoured custom it was the messenger who bore the blame.

8 The *Sea King* was one of Zanzibar's most famous ships. Built as a warship in 1863 in Glasgow, as the *Shenandoah*, it was the first composite auxiliary screw steamship in the world and took part in several sea battles during the American Civil War, fighting on the side of the Confederacy. At the end of the war, the captain, rather than surrender, sailed it to Liverpool and handed the ship over to the British Navy. It was bought by Sultan Majid in 1867 and renamed *Sea King*. Badly damaged in the hurricane, Barghash hoped it could be repaired. It set sail for Bombay with 130 passengers and crew. Leaking badly, it had to be abandoned and sank just outside the harbour, much to the chagrin of the Sultan who had been proud of his ship. Information from: Kevin Patience, *Shipwrecks and Salvage on the East African Coast,* 2006, p 145

9 It was brought out of retirement by the rebel Sultan Khalid, when she participated in the Anglo-Zanzibar War. Firing her guns on the British naval ships in harbour, she was promptly sunk by a flotilla of British ships on August 27, 1896. *Glasgow's* wreck remained in the harbour, her three masts and funnel projecting from the water, until 1912, when she was broken up for scrap. Her remains can still be found on the seabed and are a popular site for scuba divers. Information from Kevin Patience, *Shipwrecks and Salvage on the East African Coast,* 2006, p 148-9

10 Hathorne to Augustus Sparhawk, November 16, 1878. Norman R

Bennett, 'William H Hathorne; Merchant and Consul in Zanzibar,' in *Essex Institute Historical Collections*, Vol 99, 1963, p 136

11 Kirk to Mackinnon, May 25, 1879, Mackinnon Papers, 22 SOAS

12 Thomas Pakenham, *The Scramble for Africa*, London: Weidenfeld & Nicolson, 1991, p 22

13 Robert Nunez Lyne, *Zanzibar in Contemporary Times*, London: Hurst & Blackett, 1905, p 97-107. His detailed account reads as if he experienced the event first hand, or at least knew someone who had. Robert Nunez Lyne (1864-1961) was appointed Director of Agriculture for Zanzibar in 1896. He was awarded the Order of Hamoudieh 4th class on June 20, 1897.

14 Frederic Holmwood was one of those hard-working and underrated officials on which the success of the British Empire depended. Joining the staff of the British Consulate in Zanzibar c.1873, he rose steadily through the ranks. He was promoted to assistant political agent in 1876 and then vice-consul. He was made consul in 1880 and received a knighthood in 1887 before finally leaving Zanzibar in 1888. When Kirk, his high-flying boss, was away in Europe, Holmwood held the fort and ensured all ran smoothly for the replacement. At one point he upset the German Chancellor, Bismarck, by his keen promotion of a scheme to settle British Indian agriculturists on the mainland to improve commerce and extend British influence. He wrote articles about fish, most notably on the *remora* or sucking fish.

15 Lloyd William Mathews was born in Madeira in 1850, enlisting in the Royal Navy as a cadet in 1863. By the age of 31 he commanded the Sultan of Zanzibar's army, which due to his efforts, now consisted of 1,300 well-disciplined armed troops.

16 Robert Nunez Lyne was such an admirer of Mathews that he dedicated his book *Zanzibar in Contemporary Times* to his memory and wrote a fulsome biography about him entitled *An Apostle of Empire* (London: G. Allen & Unwin, 1936). Mathews was married to a Goan woman, who probably knew Lyne, who was also possibly part Goan.

17 *The Zanzibar letters of Edward D Ropes, Jr, 1882-1892*, Norman R Bennett, ed, Boston: African Studies Center, Boston University, 1973, p 26-27

Chapter Eleven

The Sultan's Right Hand Man

After 1878 documentary evidence for Peera Dewjee's role and actions occurs with increasing frequency. Often his name was misspelt or his presence was inferred rather than spelt out, with epithets such as 'the trusted one,' the 'Sultan's man' or 'assistant.' He was often described in unflattering terms because he stood up for the Sultan. The earliest contemporary account was of the fight he had with the Smith Mackenzie agent, who arrogantly told him to wait in line. It was a shocking event, which swiftly did the rounds of the island and delighted all those less than fond of the over-mighty English presence. Even more remarkably Peera got away lightly with a fine, which the Sultan paid, showing how important Peera had become and how favoured by the Sultan.[1]

By October 1879 Peera Dewjee had replaced Nassir bin Said bin Abdullah as the Sultan's chief minister. Proof of this appeared in a newspaper report of the visit of the Portuguese Governor of Mozambique to Zanzibar, which described Peera Dewjee as 'His Highness's private secretary and administrator general.' Peera Dewjee went on board the governor's ship, welcomed him to Zanzibar and arranged his audience with Sultan Barghash. Later Peera would often greet foreign dignitaries for the Sultan, but this was the earliest documented occasion. A magnificent banquet and display of fireworks followed and the Sultan presented medals to the Governor and his suite. There was good cause for celebration as the telegraph line between Mozambique and Zanzibar was formally opened.[2]

Peera Dewjee's unwavering loyalty and faithful friendship flattered and cheered Barghash when things went badly. Peera was amusing company and a persuasive talker, the perfect courtier, who did not disapprove and tell him what to do unlike Kirk and his stern holy men. Instead, Peera always came up with new ideas to keep his Sultan amused and in a good temper – he devised feasts, arranged concerts and even searched out the most beautiful concubines. He did not throw cold water on Barghash's ambitious modernisation schemes and building projects but gave encouragement and practical help to bring them to fruition. Barghash responded by giving his erstwhile barber and valet more responsibilities and favouring him above all others. As Barghash slowly withdrew from public life, harried by the English, disliked by his fellow Arabs, and troubled by illness, he became increasingly dependent on Peera.

Harry H Johnston who met Peera in 1884 gave this description in his article for the *Graphic Magazine*:

Any one visiting Sir John Kirk at home will hardly have set foot in his house many hours without remarking the arrival of an Indian gentleman in a suit of white clothes of half Asiatic, half European cut, with a magnificent gold-embroidered turban, a watch chain, a ring, and an umbrella. This is Pira Doji, incorrectly known on board the mail steamers as 'The Prime Minister of Zanzibar.' He is really an astute Indian trader, who by his capacity for business and exceptional talents as a *raconteur* has known how to obtain a very large share of the 'Sultan's' confidence and esteem. Pira Doji is a most useful man to Sayyid Barghash. Without in reality attaining the position of Prime Minister or Grand Vizier (the Sayyid has no Ministers, and therefore rules cheaply), he has yet become a sort of financial adviser to the Prince of Zanzibar, and is at the same time head-waiter at State dinners, man-of-business, negotiator in delicate matrimonial affairs, and the picker-up and retailer of the town news. If Sayyid Barghash is mentioned in the *Times*, Pira forthwith goes to the 'Sultan' with a copy of the passage scored round with red chalk. If a European resident in Zanzibar sprains his ankle, or beats his cook, the 'Sultan' likewise hears of it through the same source. Consequently all new arrivals at the Consulate become objects of interest to Pira, and as likely to furnish 'paragraphs' for his princely gossip. If ever a 'Society' paper is founded in Zanzibar, it will have Pira Doji for its editor.

His Highness Sayyid Barghash having then heard of your arrival and as much of your antecedents, present intentions and future plans as Pira can glean from the Consul's household, it becomes incumbent on you to present yourself, or get your Consul to present you, at one of the Sultan's Friday levées.[3]

Further on Johnston wrote how the Sultan liked to watch the comings and goings of Zanzibar from his palace window and even had a powerful telescope set up so he could see more exactly what was going on. He kept photo albums containing portraits of important political figures, which he studied before official engagements. These were probably the *cartes de visite* he had accumulated on his European visit and added to over the years. Whenever an important newcomer arrived in Zanzibar, Peera Dewjee made sure to get his card – an important element of his intelligence briefing for the Sultan.

Salme, the sultan's disgruntled and estranged sister had this to say in 1885, when she visited Zanzibar and saw how successful Peera had become:

This Pera Daudji, a very wily and cunning Hindoo,[4] has become the Sultan's jack-of-all-trades. The lamp cleaner of old now devotes his services to the sultan of Zanzibar in the highest and lowest positions. All diplomatic negotiations pass through his hands, but the same hands wait upon the guests of the Sultan's table. His salary, thirty dollars a month, everyone will admit is a low one, but I was told that he made it worth anyone's while to increase it. This omnipotent Pera Daudji is not above bartering his influence. Of course his thirty dollars, that does not even suffice to pay for his costly dresses, are replenished from other sources of revenue. The court jeweller who refused to give a certain percentage to the ex-lamp-cleaner lost his custom in consequence.'[5]

While the German Karl Wilhelm Schmidt writing in 1888 says this:

The master of all such festivities, the maître de plaisir, in short the factotum of the Sultan was and seems still to be Pira Dautji a Moslem Indian. He has a strange position between a servant and a personal adjutant. Whoever wants to achieve something at the court, is well advised to communicate with Pira beforehand. All possible positions are administered by him. For instance he is superintendent of the stables, it means he supervises the coaches and the horses of the sultan. Coaches almost all of good and new quality are approximately a hundred, horses three times as much. The latter are nothing special since they don't survive well in Zanzibar. Coaches as well as horses are always provided to the Europeans on request, in a real oriental gesture of generosity. The superintendent of course is the agent and gets at such an occasion, his commission.[6]

A significant upward step in the ladder of success for Peera Dewjee was when he started conducting business on behalf of the Sultan. In Zanzibar all the large European firms had a local agent to facilitate their business dealings and navigate the way through the maze of custom controls and port dues. In much the same way Peera Dewjee acted as personal agent for all the Sultan's business transactions. He was responsible for procuring the goods and making sure they were shipped and landed to the Sultan's satisfaction and what was ordered was received as specified. There had been a time when a European trader in Zanzibar just had to sit in his house and wait for merchants to come to him eager to buy his cottons and foreign goods for cash at whatever price he wished to name. Those easy times had gone. The telegraph cable connecting Zanzibar to the rest of the world, which opened in 1879, was one of the main factors which transformed business practice. Now Zanzibar merchants could order direct from London and other capitals of the West without relying on an intermediary. Local merchants became more adventurous and cut-throat. Cheaper goods flooded the market. American cottons were undercut by piece goods from Bombay and Manchester, and foreign businessmen had to work much harder to achieve reasonable profits. Even Tharia Topan, the richest merchant in Zanzibar, faced stiff competition from other Indian merchants who organised themselves as syndicates and rings to manipulate prices to their advantage and bid against him. Doing business in Zanzibar had become a minefield for the unwary.

Peera Dewjee was in the forefront of these changes in the market place. In 1879 he started ordering goods on behalf of the Sultan from an agency company based in London called Maclean, Marris & Co. He telegraphed his orders direct and grandly instructed them to send their bill to Tharia Topan for payment. But Barghash as usual wildly overspent his budget and Tharia Topan, his director of Customs and Finance, became so concerned that he sent two letters to Maclean, Marris advising them not to process or pay for the orders sent for the Sultan by Peera Dewjee.[7] Tharia Topan found his role fraught with difficulties as the Sultan constantly overdrew his balance. He resigned from the post in 1880 and with the retirement of Topan, Peera Dewjee's influence over the Sultan became more marked.[8]

Peera Dewjee was the driving force behind the Sultan's decision to start his own shipping line so he could purchase and ship goods whenever he wanted, without hindrance. In 1880 the Sultan with Peera's help went on a spending spree to acquire suitable ships. First he bought the *Akola*, a former BI ship,[9] and then, wanting something more prestigious, he sent an official delegation to England on a mission to buy the *Nyanza*, an enormous steamship he had seen in Zanzibar. The Sultan's envoys, Haji Mohammed, scribe and late secretary to the Sultan, Bakashmar, treasurer to the Sultan, Peera Dewjee, special advisor and negotiating expert, and Bomanjee Manockjee, chief engineer to the Sultan, duly arrived in London on 21 August 1880 and stayed once more at the Alexandra Hotel in Hyde Park Corner, where Barghash and his entourage had stayed in 1875. They had come with specific instructions to meet with Sir Benjamin Phillips, Chairman of the Union Steamship Company, and persuade him to sell the *Nyanza* to the Sultan. Whilst in London, the Sultan's men called on old friends. One of these was former Consul Rigby. Rigby's daughter in her memoirs of her father paints a delightful picture of their visit. As a small child, aged five years, she recalled that she liked Bakashmar best, whom she described as 'large, ample, bearded and patriarchal, with a benign expression and voluminous robes…it was very bliss to sit on the old rogue's knee and play with his huge diamond ring while I listened to the flow of Arabic conversation.'[10] Bomanjee, her second favourite, could speak English and admired her toys. Unfortunately, she makes no mention of Peera Dewjee. Her father had kept up a correspondence with Barghash, who bore him no resentment, and with Bakashmar, whom he had known well in Zanzibar.

The negotiations were successful, the price agreed and the ship was bought for the Sultan for the princely sum of 400,000 Rupees. Bakashmar was pleased and proudly invited the Rigby family aboard to view the Sultan's newest acquisition. But the smile was wiped off his face when Bomanjee the Parsee engineer came down the gangway to greet them with two white Pomeranian dogs he had just purchased. As a strict Muslim, Bakashmar lamented how the ship had been polluted. His religion did not approve of dogs or pigs. Despite his grumbles, the *Nyanza* sailed back to Zanzibar filled with trade goods and presumably the dogs. It had been a triumphant undertaking and the *Nyanza* became the Sultan's favourite ship making up for his disappointment over the *Glasgow*. With a tonnage of over 2,000, length of 327 feet, a beam of 36 feet and a service speed of 12 knots, she was an exceptionally fast and handsome ocean steamer with operating costs to match. Her elegant raked lines were unmistakeable as she hove into view on the horizon off Zanzibar in the final days of 1880.[11]

The Sultan expressed his appreciation for his new ship the *Nyanza* in a letter to Sir Benjamin Phillips dated 28 March 1882. He sent this together with a gift of two elephant tusks on board the ship, to be hand delivered by Peera Dewjee. 'Our steamer the Nyanza sails for your parts, having on board our friend Peera Dewjee. The rest you will learn from him. You will receive two tusks of ivory. Anything else that you may require, a hint thereof will suffice.' Peera Dewjee, the representative of the Sultan, accompanied by Sir John Kirk duly presented the letter and gifts to Sir Benjamin at his London residence, 46 Portman Square.[12]

He also carried other gifts from the Sultan, including a silver-gilt sherbet tray with goblets for the Rigbys.

Peera Dewjee and the Sultan's men had had a busy time in England during their 1880 visit. In addition to the *Nyanza* they purchased a newly built cargo ship in Newcastle, which with the Sultan's approval was named *Swordsman*.[13] The *Times of India* carried a report of its arrival in Zanzibar early in 1881. It was carrying rails, trucks and water pipes for the Sultan. It was due to sail next for Bombay and thence to Calcutta to pick up rice.[14]

Swordsman was considerably smaller than *Nyanza*, registered at just over 600 tons, but cost the Sultan £20,000 to buy.

By the end of 1882 the Sultan's shipping service was up and running and Peera was determined to give it as much publicity as possible. He sent an article to *The Times*, which would be sure to catch the eye and bring in business, even if the information was not strictly correct!

> STEAM TO ZANZIBAR: Peera Dewjee, in the service of His Highness the Sultan of Zanzibar, writes: "His Highness the Sultan of Zanzibar having heard with deep regret that the British Government has decided to withdraw its mail subsidy from the British India Steam Navigation Company, and fearing the great injury that the merchants must suffer by the withdrawal of the steamers of that company, has determined to organize a service of his own. He has already purchased six steamers for this purpose…I shall feel obliged if you will give publicity to these arrangements."[15]

A few days later the following response appeared:

> ZANZIBAR: With reference to the letter from Peera Dewjee… to *The Times* of the 30th ult. intimating that the British Government had withdrawn the subsidy from the mail steamers, we are requested by the British India Steam Navigation Company to state that their regular monthly mail service to Zanzibar is being continued under contract with the Government, without any interruption.[16]

Peera Dewjee was often on board the Sultan's ships and travelled to England and Europe on a number of further occasions,[17] bearing gifts and messages from the Sultan and purchasing items on his behalf, whilst carrying on his own trading as well. Peera's service with the Sultan made him an extremely wealthy and well-respected figure. On one of his European visits the President of France received him at the Elysée Palace and treated him like an ambassador for the Sultan.

Sea travel had its dangers and Peera had a near escape in a frightening storm in December 1882. The *Nyanza* had called in at Plymouth to purchase a number of cattle and sheep from a Glastonbury farmer called William Allen, which the Sultan wanted as breeding stock. Soon after leaving Southampton on the voyage back to Zanzibar the ship was caught in a severe gale and had to put in at Yarmouth, Isle of Wight, for repairs before it could continue.[18] The gale force winds were reported in all the newspapers and several ships were wrecked with all hands lost. *Nyanza* was lucky to escape with only minor damage to its machinery, but all the livestock on deck were swept overboard and none survived. Only a cheese sent as a present from farmer Allen to the Sultan reached Zanzibar. In May 1883 Mr Allen was surprised to receive by special delivery a personal letter of thanks from the Sultan for the cheese and a pair of gold bracelets.[19]

In all the Sultan eventually purchased six ships and by 1883 the *Akola, Nyanza, Avoca,*[20] *Swordsman, Malacca*[21] and *Merka* were all in operation. They were manned with German or Arab officers and Indian crew with Peera Dewjee in overall charge. In addition to these cargo steamers Barghash owned four armed vessels, the *Deerhound, Glasgow, Sultan* and *Star.*

The European shipping lines were not pleased with the Sultan's new ships, which competed with theirs and reduced their profits. He charged lower rates than they did and even accepted goods in exchange at a barter rate instead of coin. But local shippers liked the favourable business terms and used the Sultan's steamers whenever they could. The Sultan's ships were never profitable, but they served a need and presented a challenge for the European lines, which for the first time faced local competition. Their main drawback was that they were not reliable and did not run to a regular timetable as the European liners did. Often the Sultan commandeered them at short notice for his personal use, or to bring in equipment and construction material for his building projects. The ships ferried pilgrims on the Haj and provided private transportation for important visitors. On one occasion at least, they brought in extra rice and foodstuffs when there was an acute shortage on the island, staving off famine. They ran direct between Zanzibar and Bombay and other ports. They provided a service not exclusively for European benefit. The Sultan once more had his fleet and an independent maritime presence. His pride was restored, temporarily at least.

The Sultan also had a passion for carriages and horses. Barghash viewed horses and carriages rather like sports cars of today. He collected them, the more the better, of all kinds and different types and makes.

He liked to drive out in state surrounded by his clattering Persian guard with Peera Dewjee seated beside him. Often he gave a horse as a present to a guest or loaned out one of his coaches for the day. This was a great treat as only the Sultan and the richest Indians could afford to own a carriage or maintain stables. Sometimes Peera Dewjee arranged tours for visitors or accompanied them on trips to the country and entertained them for the Sultan. The island had few roads, but Barghash soon built them so he could reach his main palaces by a road of sorts and the ladies of his harem could be transported more quickly, enclosed discreetly in a coach.

There is evidence Peera Dewjee was directly involved in the purchase of at least two of the royal carriages as a letter surviving in the Studebaker archives proves.

> On [July 20] 1880, the Studebaker Brothers, South Bend, [Indiana, U.S.A.], received a letter from Zanzibar. The letter read in part 'Gentlemen I hereby beg to address you these few lines and am glad to say that I have seen your illustrated catalogue of carriages sent by one of my friends from England [from which I chose two for His Highness.]…I wrote to my agent but did not receive from them any information till this date.
>
> I therefore request you kindly to inform me whether my said agents ever ordered from you such carriages. Please send me a reply as His Highness is anxious to have the carriages at once.
>
> My address is as follows: Peera Dewjee in h.h. The Sultan's Service, Zanzibar, Africa.[22]

The Studebaker Company had exhibited its carriages at the Paris Exhibition in 1878 and won a silver medal for excellence and the Sultan desperately wanted to buy a couple to add to his growing collection. Prompted by this letter from Peera Dewjee, a French carriage and a landau were sent out. They met with royal approval and in the end a total of ten Studebaker carriages were sent to Zanzibar.

Perhaps one of them was this barouche described by Edward D Ropes in May 1883.

> Last Sunday we got a team from H H and sallied forth to see the

island. It was the first time in my life that I had ever been in a barouche and I tell you it was a swell one, regular "West-Beach" style with gold trimmings inside and lined with green morocco and silver trimmings, large and roomy with splendid soft springs and a pair of great Australian horses in a magnificent gold mounted harness.

The coachman was a very tiny Goan with mutton chop whiskers, wearing a beaver hat, buff and gold livery and top boots, while the footman was Persian, dressed in the Sultan's military undress uniform with a fez cap. They drove out to the Sultan's *shamba* at Chukwani, six miles to the south of Zanzibar Town, over one of the Sultan's new but as yet unfinished roads – rough coral stones.

The palace at Chukwani had been built by Barghash as a holiday resort. It was situated on a promontory with a sandy beach below and the uninhabited Chumbe Island just opposite. It had a magnificent view of the sea and the shipping lanes, and even the mainland on a clear day

> His shamba is of course very large and covered with trees but not at all laid out. The house is a large roomy affair and like all Arab houses is rather dirty and in need of repairs. Out at one side he has a set of flying horses and a fandango!! Whether he has ever amused himself by taking a ride we could not find out but it's a favourite sport of his harem.[23]

The young American Ropes was thrilled by his excursion and he felt very grand to be driven out in a Sultan's coach. His experience contrasts with a similar expedition described a few years later in 1887 by Sir John Christopher Willoughby, guardsman and friend of the Prince of Wales.[24] By this time coaches, uniforms and the fairground equipment had suffered considerably from wear and tear.

> The following day, at the invitation of the Sultan, we drove out with Mr Holmwood and Mr Drummond to Chugnani [Chukwani], to which royal palace we were conveyed in royal carriages driven by vassals in royal livery. The carriages were very shaky old 'rattle traps' and the horses anything but high steppers, while the livery consisted of a dirty red coat and a white garment which looked like a cross between a pair of Turkish trousers and an English petticoat.
> …The building, as I have said was delightfully situated but to my

unarchitectural eye represented a builder's blot. The ground floor consisted, first of two large unfurnished rooms with floors and ceiling divided by a few trumpery chandeliers, and walls displaying cheap Paris mirrors and a few coloured prints from English Christmas periodicals. Then came something really attractive in the shape of a set of swimming and Turkish baths. A mean set of wooden stairs led to the first floor, where two rooms, corresponding in size with those below, were adorned by more chandeliers and mirrors and a few old chairs, which were put to shame by a really good carpet. These rooms and a cool balcony, also carpeted, formed the quarters of the Sultan's hundred wives, and were occupied by them whenever their lord and master could tear himself away from the grave affairs of state to spend a happy day at Chugnani. On such occasions all the ladies were packed into carriages at Zanzibar and safely delivered at the country palace, the Sultan bringing up the rear alone in his own carriage like an old ram.[25]

Then follows a marvellous description of a meal laid on by Peera Dewjee for the Sultan's distinguished guests. The tableware of mismatched cutlery and crockery, the wonderful flower arrangements and array of endless dishes of delicious food – and this was just breakfast! – brings to life this shabby-chic Zanzibar style feast.

On the balcony overlooking the sea a most sumptuous breakfast had been prepared for us, with Pira, the Sultan's factotum in attendance... Under his superintendence the table had been decorated with tropical flowers, oleanders, hibiscus, marigolds, double jasmine and crotons of lovely hues; and the royal electro-plate, consisting of odd sets of assorted patterns, had been carefully served out. The feast lasted for an hour and a half and the number of courses seemed endless. We had fish, beef, mutton, chickens, omelettes, and curries and finished up with jams, mangoes, bananas, and other fruits, all excellent. The crockery matched the electro-plate as it comprised the cracked remnants of a number of odd sets. We had brought our own wine, for it is contrary to the Sultan's creed to furnish anything but a sickly kind of sherbet to which we had not yet accustomed our digestions.

How to kill time after breakfast was a difficult problem as we had exhausted the attractions of the palace at a single glance and the garden was barren with the exception of a few oleanders and palm trees. Pira, however, pointed out with pride two attractions it possessed of more importance in the Sultan's eyes than mere beds of flowers. The first was a large steam merry-go-round, which had unfortunately 'stopped short never to go again'…The second was a big revolving wheel with cradles in perfect working order, but hardly represented a healthy form of recreation immediately after such a breakfast as we had finished.

The guests decided instead to sleep off breakfast on the balcony, but within an hour Peera announced that a 'slight lunch' was just served. This was another enormous meal, even by Edwardian standards, consisting of soup, mutton, pigeons, ducks, curried prawns, and iced puddings.

> We all ate until we were absolutely stuffed, and had no sooner finished than Pira desired to know at what time we should be prepared for dinner. I thought about that day week at the same hour might do, but the others made excuses for returning to Zanzibar at once, declaring another such gorge even a week hence might be dangerous.

The journey back also proved hazardous as a wheel came off one of the carriages, and when all five men squeezed into the other one, the extra weight proved too much for the unfortunate horses, which needed to rest every half mile. Finally on reaching the outskirts of town, a collision with a bullock cart in a narrow street, put an end to their transport altogether. They completed the journey on foot.

Construction and modern gadgets fascinated the Sultan. If he saw something he wanted, he had to have it however unsuitable for the climate of Africa and incongruous in Zanzibar. He wanted his kingdom to be impressive and look like the western capitals he had seen on his travels, with all the latest fashion items on show – clock towers, lifts and electric lights. His chief builder and engineer, Manockjee Bomanjee, was a genius, who worked ceaselessly to please his royal master. Soon there would be piped water for the townspeople, a clock tower on the seafront (a cross between Big Ben and the clock he had seen on Manchester Town Hall), street lights and even a small railway.[26] The town palace Beit al Sahel was cleverly extended to accommodate the royal wives and a cistern for fresh water supply placed nearby. The scientific discoveries of Dr Christie had ensured there would be no more cholera epidemics in Zanzibar as the importance of clean drinking water was at last established. His country palaces at Chuini, Chukwani and Marahubi all had ingenious fresh water supplies, while Marahubi, built in 1882 with domes and classical pillars, had its swimming pools set in a European styled garden. Victoria Gardens opened in 1887 in honour of Queen Victoria's Golden Jubilee was Zanzibar's first municipal park, a flowery retreat – built to emulate the great parks of London. It was Peera Dewjee's pet project. He had a house built overlooking the gardens, not far from the new British Residence, which would later be built there as well. Here ladies could take the air and out-door garden parties and entertainments could be enjoyed in the town without the inconvenience of travelling to the countryside.

Sultan Barghash's most ambitious project was the House of Wonders – Beit al-Ajaib – his new ceremonial palace. Built in a central position on the waterfront on the site of the former Portuguese palace of Queen Fatuma, it contained all the latest gadgets from Europe and was encased in three tiers of open work balconies, an airy façade supported by tall cast iron pillars tied in with iron girders. The use of construction material was typically Victorian industrial. The grand entrance and wedding cake style recalled the warehouses of Manchester, but the interior layout followed traditional Arab lines, with a large central courtyard off which the many rooms, balconies and galleries led. The top floor was fitted out as the royal apartments and panelled in dark wood. On the two upper floors passages linked the adjoining palaces. The front balcony had a splendid view of the waterfront and the Sultan used it as a vantage point to sight the moon at the start and end of Ramadhan. Work started on this influential building in 1883. It was completed by 1886 and remains a landmark in the town to this day. Meanwhile the Sultan continued to live at the old Beit al-Sahel palace and use the next door palace Beit al-Hukm for his official business.

The Sultan enjoyed music and feasting and Peera Dewjee played an important part in providing both. He organised the feasts on Muslim holy days and dinners laid on for important royal guests. He provided elaborate dishes and tempting new menus to beguile Barghash, who with his ailments and increasing disappointments, found food offered one of the few pleasures that remained. As he took virtually no exercise, he became markedly fat in his later years and judging from the few pictures we have of him, Peera too developed a somewhat sturdy physique to match his royal patron.

The Sultan was a talented musician who enjoyed listening to all kinds of music. Even before he visited Europe he had been familiar with Western music and he could play the piano. He purchased a mechanical piano or pianola in Paris in 1875 and surprised onlookers by giving a performance in the shop.[27] He had a genuine love of music and eagerly acquired new score sheets and listened to new tunes. When he visited Liverpool in 1875 and a 'Zanzibar March' composed in his honour welcomed him to the town, his immediate reaction was to request a copy of the score, so his own musicians could learn to play it for him. When the Sultan was seriously ill in 1888, Edward Ropes the American merchant sent him a score of 'Marching thro' Georgia' hoping to cheer him up.

By 1882 Barghash gave concerts every Wednesday evening. Chairs would be set up in the palace square, where those who wished might listen to operatic selections and Arabic airs. His orchestra consisted of 35 Goan musicians conducted by a German bandmaster and he mixed the music from Arabia, India and Europe.[28] Peera Dewjee is often cited as the master of ceremonies and the organiser of all public concerts and entertainments. One German source described how he brought in troupes of travelling entertainers, jugglers and acrobats from Arabia, India and Egypt who performed in the evening on the square in front of the veranda of the palace by torchlight.[29] It was a fantastical sight as the figures danced and leaped, lit by the flickering lights of flares against the dark background of night.

On Fridays the Sultan's troops paraded along the waterfront and through the narrow streets of the town led by a brass band, which also played on ceremonial occasions and had an extensive repertoire of national anthems and popular marches. If the Sultan paid a formal visit to someone in the town, he would be preceded by his Persian guard on horseback and his brass band. The business community found these parades disruptive, but the common man enjoyed the opportunity to down tools and watch the colourful spectacle. At times there were weddings, when the incessant noise and din of the celebrations consisting of African dancing and beating of drums lasted late into the night. Zanzibar was a noisy and vibrant town which never slept.

At the Sultan's side throughout all this incessant activity was Peera Dewjee. He had risen so far and fast that his influence was now all pervasive. He had become as Salme says 'omnipotent' and 'a jack of all trades' to the Sultan. In later years he was sometimes known as the Sultan's Chief Steward, but during Barghash's lifetime, his role and position was never clearly defined. On at least one occasion Barghash refers to him as 'our friend Peera Dewjee,'[30] which suggests a person of equal rather than lower standing and certainly not a servant. When Peera Dewjee sent a communiqué to *The Times* he grandly referred to himself as being 'in the service of His Highness the Sultan of Zanzibar'[31] as if he was a high ranking official.

In the Turkish Empire of the Ottomans, the *ustadar* or steward was an important post in charge of state politics but Peera Dewjee combined a diplomatic and political role together with the western interpretation of a steward's post, a kind of upper servant, responsible for the day-to-day running of a grand household. Stewards often appear in Arab literature, and one famous tale from the *Arabian Nights* gave a portrayal, which may have struck close to the mark. The story of the Sultan's Steward tells the tale of a young man, the son of a merchant who was addicted to wine and playing the lute and on his death left nothing but debts. The son had to work hard to pay them off, which he did and became a successful cloth merchant. One day a lady from the palace of the Sultan came to his shop to buy fabrics. He fell deeply in love and was so enamoured he forgot to ask her for payment. She returned his love and came often to buy more. In the end they agreed to marry and she arranged to smuggle him into the palace past the guards inside a chest full of fabrics. The ruse succeeded, but when the marriage feast was put before him he ate without washing his hands. This offended her and she called her servants who whipped him and tied him up and cut off his thumbs and big toes. He promised always to wash his hands before a meal, and she was appeased and they married and she gave him money to buy a fine house and live well. This young man became the Sultan's Steward.

It is a strange story with no proven parallels to be drawn with Peera's life, but the tales of the *Arabian Nights* were very popular in Zanzibar. They were a mixture of fantasy and a satiric commentary on everyday life. It is possible that Peera could have had an affair with one of the palace ladies, which helped him achieve his position of special trust, which others from his background did not. With his elegant clothes and easy manners, one can imagine him being a ladies' man. However, nothing at all is known about Peera's private life and whatever might have gone on, or not, behind the closed doors of the female quarters of Barghash's household remains a well-kept secret. In Arab polite society of that era, even to mention the name of a female relative in general conversation was considered extremely rude. The name of Peera's wife has never been recorded, nor when he married. All we know is the names of his children and the approximate dates of their birth. His eldest son Abdulhussein was born about 1878.

The energy and determination of both the Sultan and Peera, as they worked together to modernise and bring western improvements to Zanzibar, was impressive and left behind a legacy of material benefit for the town. But Barghash failed to consolidate his position or strengthen his administration.

---

1 Usually an assault on a European would have been dealt with most severely. The first Parsee to settle in Zanzibar c.1850, Manockjee Aspondiarji Nanabhai Mistry, had to flee Bombay to save his life, because he had argued with and punched his European overseer, who died as a result of the blow. As a carpenter and construction engineer, he was a most useful addition

to Zanzibar society. He had formerly been one of the supervisors of works on the Victoria Terminus station and its railway bridges, before misfortune befell him. Information from 'Parsee Lustre on the Emerald Isle of Zanzibar', unpublished MS by Hasheng H Kashed. It is likely the Sultan's chief engineer Bomanji Manockjee, was either the son or at least a relative of this individual.

2 *Times of India*, November 26, 1879

3 *The Graphic*, May 1885, p 469 -472, 'Sir John Kirk at Home' by H H Johnston

4 Peera Dewjee was of course Muslim, but in Zanzibar the common term at that time for an Indian Muslim merchant was Hindoo, or Hindi, while the Hindu merchants were known as Banyans.

5 Emily Ruete, *Memoirs of an Arabian Princess*, G S P Freeman-Grenville, ed, London and the Hague, East-West Publications, 1994, p 193

6 Karl Wilhelm Schmidt, *Sansibar, ein Ostafrikanisches Culturbild*, Leipzig: F A Brockhaus, 1888 (translation by Prof Erich Meffert)

7 Norman R Bennett, ed, 'William H. Hathorne Merchant and Consul in Zanzibar,' *Essex Historical Collections*, Vol 99, 1963, p 137-8. The two letters reproduced were sent secretly by a third party as Tharia did not want the Sultan to blame him for withdrawing his credit.

8 The post of Chief of Customs was taken up again by the Hindu company of Jairam Sewji.

9 Built in 1875 and scrapped in 1889.

10 Mrs Charles E B Russell, *General Rigby, Zanzibar, and the Slave Trade*, London: Allen & Unwin, 1935, p 309-10

11 The *Nyanza* was originally built in 1864 as a paddle steamer for the P & O's Southampton to Alexandria service, and was sold to the Union Steamship Company in 1873. They immediately refitted the ship with a two-cylinder compound engine driving a single screw to cut down on its heavy consumption of coal. Performance was much improved and she became renowned as one of the fastest ships of her era. In 1880 she spent a short time on the monthly Zanzibar service, before being sold to the Sultan of Zanzibar as his private yacht. When not required by the Sultan, she traded between Zanzibar and Bombay. In 1889 after a collision in the Suez Canal, she was acquired by Mahallah & Co of Zanzibar and operated by them for the Sultan, who could not afford the repairs or running costs of the vessel. She was broken up in June 1904.

12 *The Times*, June 30, 1882

13 Built in 1880 as a cargo ship, it was wrecked in 1893.

14 *Times of India*, February 4, 1881, 'Notes from Zanzibar (from our own Correspondent)'

15 *The Times*, November 30, 1882

16 *The Times*, December 11, 1882. The original contract with the government had been for ten years from 1872, ending in 1882. The subsidy was renewed but the sum reduced.

17 One German reference goes so far to name him as admiral of the Sultan's fleet! Oscar Baumann, *In Deutsch-Ostafrika während des Aufstandes*, Wien und Olmütz: Eduard Hölzel, 1890, p 22

18 *Daily News,* December 4, 1882. 'Wrecks and Casualties: Steamer Nyanza from Southampton to Zanzibar, with passengers and cargo, has anchored in Yarmouth (I W) Roads with machinery slightly damaged. Will repair and proceed.'

19 *Western Gazette*, May 25, 1883

20 *Avoca* was built in 1866 for P&O and was bought by the Sultan for £12,943 in 1882. In 1896 it was sold to Haji Kassim Jusab of Bombay.

21 *Malacca*, originally called *King of the Greeks* was built for a Greek shipping company in 1865, but was renamed and bought by P&O in 1866. They sold it to the Sultan of Zanzibar in 1882 for £14,916. It was sold on in 1892 to a shipping company in Manchester and broken up in 1894.

22 *Arizona Republic*, July 20, 1967: 'On this day' by Estey I Reed

23 *The Zanzibar letters of Edward D Ropes, Jr, 1882-1892*, Norman R Bennett, ed, Boston: African Studies Center, Boston University, 1973, p 26

24 John Christopher Willoughby, *East Africa and its Big Game: The Narrative of a Sporting Trip from Zanzibar to the Borders of the Masai*, London: Longmans, Green, 1889, p 11-14

25 Chukwani Palace was completely demolished and little remains today but a few ruins of its elaborate bathing system. Originally intended as a health spa for his wives, water for the various baths was pumped up by means of steam power from a natural cave well half a mile away. The water was stored in large outside tanks, connected by channels to the baths and ready for use where needed. The baths were last used during WWII by the Royal Air Force who were stationed at Chukwani.

26 An order was placed with W G Bagnall of Stafford for a tiny four-wheel tank engine, which was to become the first in East Africa. Named the *Sultanee* it arrived in February 1881 and was intended to run on a track from the town palace to Chukwani, but the line was never completed. At one point the Sultan asked the King of the Belgiums to pay for a railway in Zanzibar but his request was turned down and Zanzibar had to wait until 1905 for an American company to construct the Bububu railway. Kevin Patience, *Zanzibar and the Bububu Railway*, 1995

27 'The surprise will be much greater when we reveal the Barghash bin Said…is a skilled pianist! We ask our readers to believe that this is not a joke. In the shops of M Laeape, where he went shopping for a mechanical piano (pianola) the Sultan had the pleasure of amazing his hosts by performing on an ordinary piano, you can almost say as a virtuoso, the great Fantaisie of Thalberg.' *Revue et Gazette Musicale de Paris*, No 51, August 1, 1875

28 This was probably the origin of the fashion for *Taarab* music, famous in Zanzibar.

29 C Falkenhorst, *Schwarze Fürsten: Bilder aus der geschichte des dunkeln Welteils*, Leipzig: Ferdinand Hirt & Sohn, 1892, p 39

30 See letter sent to Sir Benjamin Phillips, chairman of the Union Steamship Company.

31 See announcement in *The Times*, November 30, 1882, about the Sultan's Steamers.

Chapter Twelve

The Fall of the Arab East African Empire and Death of Barghash

Then he said to me: 'Hamed be not angry with me, I want to have no
more to do with the mainland. The Europeans want to take Zanzibar here
from me; how should I be able to keep the mainland? Happy are those who
did not live to see the present state of affairs...'

When I heard those words I knew it was all up for us.[1]

*Tippu Tip's account of his interview
with Sultan Barghash in 1886.*

In 1883, just three years before, Barghash had seemed on top of the
world enjoying an improved financial position and the freedom to
indulge in his costly building projects. A high point came in October
1883 when the Sultan was invested with the Grand Cross of the Order
of St Michael and St George. Eight British men-of-war commanded
by Admiral Sir William Hewett, flying ensign and pennants, came
into Zanzibar harbour to present the Sultan with his medal. It was
a grand show. There was a dinner at the palace and then another on
board the Royal Navy flagship for the Sultan. Peera Dewjee arranged
the Sultan's dinner. In honour of the British guests the menu included
'roast beef with radish sauces' and ice puddings 'à la Victoria, à la
Gladstone, and à la Prince of Wales.' It was a memorable occasion.[2]

That same year Barghash, looking for ways to increase his revenues
and secure his position, believing that a British takeover was inevitable
sooner rather than later, made an offer to Sir John Kirk. He said he
was prepared to put Zanzibar and all his territories formally under
British Protection in return for a guarantee that his young son Khalid
be appointed Sultan after his death. This may have been prompted
by a letter sent to him by Salme warning him of British intent which

was written in 1883, when she was still putting her case in the royal courts of Germany and Britain and trying to regain favour with her brother. Kirk transmitted the proposal to Whitehall, but they turned the offer down. The Gladstone administration, wrestling with more pressing problems, had no interest in acquiring additional land holdings or new colonies in Africa. The situation in Zanzibar, in the opinion of Gladstone and his Foreign Secretary, Lord Granville, was perfectly satisfactory. There was no need for change. The system of 'informal empire,' was cheap and simple, an exercise of power without responsibility.

One more attempt to place the region more securely under British control came in September 1884. Harry Johnston travelled in the Kilimanjaro area, ostensibly looking for botanical species. He signed various friendship treaties with local chiefs with the idea of establishing a British trading base in the interior. This scheme had the support of several businessmen in England, notably Sir William Mackinnon and James Hutton, leader of a group of Manchester capitalists,[3] but when the Foreign Office wrote to Kirk, asking for his expert opinion about the proposal, he was less than enthusiastic. He pointed out that a trade concession without the inclusion of a coastal port was unworkable, and questioned the legality of such a project, bringing up the Anglo-French declaration of 1862 guaranteeing the independence of Zanzibar. Gladstone, troubled with problems in Sudan, rather tetchily washed his hands of the whole project in December 1884, famously saying he failed to see the point of doing anything with 'the mountain country behind Zanzibar with an unrememberable name.'

The Johnston scheme had been hatched up in haste to forestall possible German moves in the region, as he and his supporters feared Germany's increasingly imperialistic policies could pose a threat. The German Chancellor, Bismarck, bowing to popular opinion in Germany, had begun aggressively acquiring colonies and protectorates in South West and West Africa and was known to be keen to acquire more. When it was heard the explorer Gerhard Rohlfs was to be sent to Zanzibar as the next German Consul General, anxiety grew that East Africa was Germany's next target. Rohlfs had strongly imperialistic views and believed the acquisition of colonies added to national greatness. As an interim safeguard, Kirk persuaded Barghash to promise he would accept no protectorate from a European nation, nor cede any of his sovereign rights without prior British consent.

No one noticed when a small party of young Germans landed in Saadani and headed for the interior in November 1884. Their leader was Dr Carl Peters, a young history professor and co-founder of the German Colonization Society, an unofficial and as yet unknown organisation. He and his companions, Dr Carl Lucas, Karl Juhlke and Graf Joachim von Pfeil, were on a mission to grab another slice of Africa for Germany. Their first attempt to land at Lamu had been foiled as the amount of firearms and ammunition they carried aroused suspicions. But on arriving at Saadani, a small port just to the north of Bagamoyo close to Zanzibar, they managed to sneak ashore without being noticed. They hastened to the Kilimanjaro region, which lay along the caravan route to the Great Lakes, and had been identified as a prime area for European settlement. Peters signed up ten chiefs in three weeks and then hurried back to Berlin with his treaties, handing them over to the German government in early February 1885.

History writers have remained amazed at the boldness and simplicity of Peters's plan and the openly deceptive means of obtaining his so called 'treaties' from the African chiefs and village headmen. On arriving in the territories of a chief, Peters first sent ahead a messenger with presents and a request to set up camp. When this was granted, he invited the chief to dine with him and plied him with drink and food. During the evening entertainment Peters produced a document and suggested the chief sign it to show his friendship with the German Empire. The chief, primed with bribes and relaxed after enjoying a good dinner, made no objection. Then Peters read out the document in German, which the chief could not understand, and asked him to put his cross at the bottom of the paper. The African chief, unaware of the significance of his action, did so and, lo and behold, Germany had acquired a new protectorate. Peters shook his victim heartily by the hand, ran up the German flag and fired a salute. More drink flowed and Peters hurried on to perform the same ceremony at the next village.

While Peters was still on his way back to Germany, Dr Rohlfs, the new German Consul, arrived in Zanzibar. His arrival on 27 January 1885 on board the German battleship *Gneisenau* created a stir in town.

Peera Dewjee was the first on board to greet him and arrange for the customary audience with the Sultan. A letter written by one of the junior officers on board the *Gneisenau* gives a contemporary eyewitness account of this audience which took place on January 30.[4] He wrote how the meeting was stiff and awkward and the tense atmosphere increased when the Sultan produced a newspaper cutting, which reported Germany intended to annex Zanzibar.[5] The Sultan did not trust his German visitors and an invitation from Captain Valois to watch some naval shooting exercises on board the *Gneisenau*, scheduled for 6 February, added to his alarm and suspicion. Barghash did not attend, nor did he send his representative. Nevertheless, the initial meeting proceeded with the usual refreshments of coffee and sherbet and concluded with the requisite formalities of smiles and handshakes. The Sultan was well

The German Battleship, Gneisenau

informed of German intentions but it seems unlikely Rohlfs had pre-knowledge of developments about to unfold or that his arrival was part of a coordinated move by Germany.

The German chancellor Bismarck was impressed by Peters's initiative and, unlike Britain, had no qualms about legalities. He approved the treaties in mid-February and on 3 March 1885 awarded an imperial charter and complete control of the claimed territories to Peters and his Society, which was re-formed as the German East Africa Company (*Deutsch-Ostafrikanische Gesellschaft*) on 2 April with Peters as director. Events had moved at lightning speed and secrecy, and four named provinces – Usagara, Ungulu, Uzigua and Ukami – were now declared protectorates of the German Empire.

If Kirk was badly shaken at how easily the Germans had slipped through the net right under his nose and stolen a march on him, he was yet more dismayed by the supine reaction of the Foreign Office. They made no attempt to deny the legitimacy of the treaties but accepted them as a *fait accompli* asking only that Zanzibar be left in peace and free trade be allowed to continue unhindered. The 1862 Anglo-French treaty was apparently a dead letter and the Sultan's territories there for the taking. Barghash was understandably devastated and wanted to go to Germany immediately and protest in person, but he was dissuaded. At the stroke of a pen he had lost control of a number of strategic centres on the mainland. His only hope lay in his British allies, but they had deserted him, more interested in appeasing Germany than in supporting the territorial claims of Zanzibar.

Barghash tried to recover the situation by sending General Mathews with troops to the Kilimanjaro region to reinforce his claims and undo the treaties, but his small army was not up to the job and the Sultan's authority in the hinterland was too weak. Lucas and Juhlke, who had been left by Peters in Africa to continue collecting treaties, followed behind Mathews. As soon as Mathews persuaded the chiefs of the Chagga tribe to swear loyalty to Zanzibar, the German envoys converted them back for Germany. The African chiefs viewed it as a game and were more interested in the flags and gifts and the attention they received, as they played one foreigner off against another. One incident cited by Genesta Hamilton illustrated this well:

> Mandara, the Chief of Moshi, having just put his mark to a treaty with Juhlke, then revealed to him the real desire of his heart. 'I beg thee,' he said, 'to bring with thee a better flagstaff than General Mathews brought with him.'[6]

The German Consul Rohlfs became increasingly arrogant and impolite in his treatment of the Sultan, as he adopted a bullying tone and demanded he recognise the treaties, which the Sultan steadfastly refused to do.[7] Tensions rose in Zanzibar and then ratcheted up another notch when on 7 August Commodore Carl Paschen steamed into harbour at the head of five German warships, and three days later issued an ultimatum ordering Barghash to withdraw his objections to Peters's Treaties. In Paschen's memoirs he described his first audience with Barghash, with Peera Dewjee acting as translator and advisor:

> The Sultan was surrounded by his entire court; Mr Tekely, an Austrian, was translator on our side, and on the Sultan's Pira Daudji, his Chamberlain, valet, barber and advisor in all affairs of state. After I had taken my place near the throne, and after having been introduced by Consul-General Travers, I read an address to the Sultan with at the end a request for a further audience, in order to inform him of the wishes of the German Government with regard to the mainland territory.
> The audience took place the following day, without any honorific formalities, the throne-room having been rearranged as an office. The Sultan was alone with his translator, on my side only Travers and our translator.[8]

This is the first time Peera Dewjee is documented in the role of translator. The term may mean interpreter of information rather than translator from one language to another, as it is unlikely Peera spoke fluent German. But Tekely could speak English, and it is probable the German demands were translated into English, and then transmitted by Peera to the Sultan. Barghash could speak Arabic, Swahili and Hindustani and a few words of English.

With the German fleet blockading the port and their guns trained on the palace, Kirk had the unenviable task of telling Barghash to enter into negotiations with the Germans. The Foreign Office had instructed Kirk to advise Barghash to submit to German demands as Britain would not support him against their German friends. It must have been an unpleasant task, as Barghash saw his kingmaker eat humble pie. The British Empire was no longer supreme. Kirk was yesterday's man and the Sultan, an insignificant pawn in a new game being played out by the international powers – the scramble for Africa.

Rear Admiral Knorr arrived soon afterwards to take control of negotiations for Germany. As an added weapon in his armoury, he had brought with him Princess Salme and her three children, who arrived in Zanzibar in convoy with the German warships. Presumably, they intended to put her young son forward as the German candidate for the Sultanate, if Barghash proved recalcitrant. But the Germans didn't need Salme as Barghash had already caved in and agreed to come to the negotiating table and start talks about recognising a German Protectorate over the regions covered by Peters's treaties. The free use of Dar es Salaam port by Germany was also up for discussion.

Kirk found he could deal with Admiral Knorr and the new German consul, who had more diplomatic finesse than Rohlfs, and seemed friendly to Britain. They listened to Kirk and respected his expertise on Zanzibar affairs. When he suggested it would be best not to humiliate and infuriate Barghash further by pushing his sister's claims, they followed his recommendation. Salme came ashore, but her visit was handled discreetly and she did not meet with her brother or regain her lost inheritance. Barghash is said to have sent her a small gift of money, but he refused to see her or her son. Salme returned to Germany bitterly disappointed. She was particularly angry with Peera Dewjee, whom she blamed for blocking her access to her brother, and she vented her displeasure by writing a particularly unflattering description of him in her memoirs. She accused him of spying on her and having his agents keep an eye on her. She was very well aware how powerful he had become.

Of course we were well set around with spies, mostly Hindoos, but to their great disgust we only conversed in German. Even on the night preceding our departure two of my friends (who had come on board to bid me goodbye under the cover of darkness) called my attention to the dusky figure of a man, who had often honoured our ship with his presence in the guise of a hawker and who in truth was a very active and clever tool employed by the now influential but former lamp-cleaner and court barber Madolji, Pera Daudji.[9]

Kirk, who had worked so hard to suppress the slave trade and ensure British influence was paramount in Zanzibar, now saw his life's work slipping away as the Germans moved swiftly ahead to strip the Sultan of his mainland territories, while Britain stood by and did nothing. All he could do was play for time and hope for a change of policy. This came when the Liberal Government headed by Gladstone fell in June and was replaced by a Tory Government with Lord Salisbury as Prime Minister and Percy Anderson in the Foreign Office. Belatedly the cabinet re-discovered an interest in Africa and an appetite for colonial expansion. They realised the German intervention had put an end to the comfortable system of informal empire that had worked so well in the past, and that a new strategy was needed to prevent Germany from taking over the whole of East Africa.

They settled on a scheme to partition the mainland between Germany and Britain. In December 1885, Britain, Germany and France formed a commission to determine the precise limits of the Sultan's authority. As Bartle Frere had done before in 1873, the commissioners visited the more important ports along the East African coast gathering information in each to ascertain the nature of its ties to Zanzibar. Barghash tried to defend his interests by sending one of his vessels in advance of the Europeans to ensure that his presence at each port was impressive.[10] Almost certainly Peera Dewjee was in charge of this move and he would have primed the Arab officials to make sure they turned out to best advantage and demonstrated the strength of their allegiance to the Sultan in Zanzibar. The Europeans bickered for almost a year unable to determine the exact nature and extent of the Sultan's authority along the Coast – the Germans wanting it to be less and the British more.

Bismarck was impatient; he wanted to resolve the East African impasse (unlike the British who wanted to prolong negotiations as long as possible) and in October 1886 an agreement was finally reached. The Sultan was awarded full sovereign rights over Zanzibar, Pemba and Mafia islands as well as over a ten-mile coastal strip extending from the Minigani River in the south to the port of Kipini in the north. The agreement also recognised his rights over the Somali ports of Kismayu, Brava, Merka, Mogadishu and Warshaykh. The British agreed to support a lease of the customs houses of Dar es Salaam and Pangani to the German East Africa Company. The Sultan's former possessions in the hinterland, where his authority was not clearly present, were to be divided into British and German spheres, in the north and south respectively. A dividing line began at the Umba River inland to Lake Jipe and on to where the first south latitude met at Lake Victoria. Germany was also awarded a protectorate over Witu, a small strip of land on the northern coast near Lamu.[11] France agreed to go along with the British and German division of the spoils, as long as they were given the Comoro Islands. With a heavy heart, but faced with no other alternative, Barghash eventually signed the agreement in December 1886.

At the end of 1886 the softly-spoken German consul Travers was replaced by Arendt, a more confrontational style of diplomat. He and Dr Lucas, the resident Director of the German East Africa Company, made themselves unpopular by continually trying to extend their territorial claims and harassing the ailing Sultan with their demands. The sailors of the German Navy made a nuisance of themselves as they roistered drunkenly in the streets of Zanzibar and there were frequent complaints of assault. The situation in Zanzibar deteriorated and business suffered. To add to Zanzibar's woes, the chief of Customs resigned, and no successor could be found. No one wanted the position as it was no longer profitable. In the end the Sultan took it over and had it managed jointly by Nasser Lillani and Peera Dewjee. Nasser Lillani was one of the richest merchants in the kingdom, who agreed to take on the post as a personal favour to the Sultan. In an effort to raise more revenue, the Sultan's customs officials not only increased export and import taxes but also resorted to secret bidding rings to force up the price of ivory, Zanzibar's most valuable commodity. In 1887 Ropes, the American ivory trader, complained bitterly that business had gone rotten. He railed against the Zanzibar cutthroats: 'P Dossa, Nassir Lila, Salie Jacksie, Peera Dewjie, Seewar Hadjie & Musa...all a set of rushing, failing, cheating, swindling gamblers, buying anything & everything for luck.'[12]

Barghash, seeing his revenues fall away so alarmingly, listened to the recommendations of the new British Consul Holmwood[13] and agreed to approach the Mackinnon consortium and ask them to undertake the economic direction of his territories placed within the British sphere by the 1886 agreement. They agreed. Finally, after many disappointments and false starts, Mackinnon had his trading concession in East Africa and the opportunity to develop the area for commerce. In May 1887 the group now calling itself the British East African Association was awarded 50 years full political and judicial rights in return for revenues equal to existing customs collections. The Association was renamed the Imperial British East Africa Company (IBEACo).

Also in May 1887, Dr Peters, who had been in Germany busily fund-raising and recruiting personnel for the German East Africa Company, returned to Zanzibar to take overall charge. He brought with him a group of keen new officials eager to start work and develop the German sector. Consul Arendt by this time had arranged the lease of the ports of Pangani and Dar es Salaam to the German Company and when Peters and his colleagues wanted to go on a tour of inspection to check the facilities of the ports and familiarise themselves with the coastline, the Sultan sent Peera Dewjee to host Peters and his party on board one of the His Highness' steamers. [14]

Despite the Sultan's hospitality and compliance with German demands, trouble soon brewed in the German sector. Peters, who now had the title of Reich Commissar, upset the resident Arabs with his aggressive manner and habit of treating them as if they were his inferiors to be ordered about. The semi-independent subjects and officials of the Sultan were not used to such harsh behaviour and disrespect and resented it deeply. They complained and Peters had to come in person and apologise to Barghash. He put the blame on Arendt for not smoothing the way beforehand and Arendt as a result was recalled to Berlin in disgrace.

Arendt was furious and in turn pointed the finger at the British Consul Holmwood, claiming he had inflamed local opinion against Germany and had not behaved as a friend and ally should do. He was particularly annoyed that Holmwood had gone ahead without informing him and had persuaded the Sultan to give the British more favourable concessions in their sector than the Germans had in theirs. He insisted Holmwood should be recalled as well. In July Arendt was replaced by Michahelles, who was told to start negotiations for a concession similar to the British one. Discussions dragged on during the latter part of the year. Peters, puffed up with his own success, pressed for the inclusion of Zanzibar and Pemba within the German sector. This proved a step too far and the distraught Sultan became angry and obstinate. Fed up with all the complaints about Peters, Berlin became disenchanted with their man. They told Peters to stop his aggressive and over-ambitious demands and recalled him to Germany in December 1887. The more conciliatory Michahelles concluded an agreement with the Sultan under the original terms.

Barghash's health worsened during 1887 and he became increasingly bitter and reclusive, no longer going on his walk-abouts in town or appearing to his people. He stayed holed up in his palace, sitting for long periods in his long narrow reception room with its hanging chandeliers, oriental carpets and gilt wood chairs upholstered in red velvet. Round the walls were ranged a medley of kitchen clocks, ormolu time-pieces, barometers, telescopes, opera glasses, musical boxes and what nots, collected in happier times. The endless demands of the Germans and British had sapped his energies and his will to live. By now he hated the sight of the Europeans, who had stolen his dominions and had lured him with their false promises of a better future. The fortunes of the Sultanate of Zanzibar sagged, Barghash's building works stalled and his palaces fell into disrepair.

Seeing the Sultan's weakness, the Portuguese to the south took their opportunity and settled the on-going boundary dispute by attacking and taking Miningani and Tunghi. To the north the Italians eyed Somalia with covetous eyes, while Belgium claimed the Congo. Barghash washed his hands in despair and referred all mainland disputes to the Anglo-German Boundary Commission.

In addition to all his other duties, Peera Dewjee had become Barghash's chief political advisor and minister of foreign affairs. He was present at all official audiences and whenever international agreements were signed. He also acted as the Sultan's representative attending official functions and entertaining visiting VIPs. Despite their lacklustre performance as allies, Britain still retained their special relationship and this well-established tie was strengthened by Peera Dewjee's natural allegiance to Britain. Barghash found the German officials difficult to deal with, and the high turn-over of consuls cannot have helped. He was more comfortable with the British, and especially the long-serving consular staff, with whom he had built up trust over the years.

Exactly how much influence Peera Dewjee had on the momentous events of the final years of Barghash's reign is difficult to judge, as we have to rely on European accounts, which of course only tell their side of the story. Nevertheless, the peaceful takeover of the mainland by Germany and Britain must have been helped by Peera Dewjee's good relations with the European officials and his ability to restrain Barghash. Without his emollient presence at the Sultan's side, there might well have been violence and bloodshed in Zanzibar. Peera Dewjee worked together with both Kirk and then Holmwood to keep the situation calm and allow business to continue, which was, as he well knew, the lifeblood of Zanzibar. He made an effort to be on friendly terms with the Germans and he hosted Dr Peters and sweet-talked his mistress, Baroness Frieda von Bülow, on board the Sultan's steamer. He had considerable diplomatic skill, which was tested to the full at this time, his main concerns being to ensure a smooth take-over and limit the damage to Zanzibar and his Sultan.

It was no doubt due to Peera Dewjee's guiding influence that Barghash kept up a public face of pride and dignity and gave way gracefully to the German demands, and then to the carve-up of his territories, despite what he might have felt and said in private. There had been a real danger in 1885 that had he remained obdurate, he might have lost his throne, possibly to Salme's son. Thanks to his good sense in listening to the advice of cooler heads this was averted. Contrary to what is written, the presence of the Indian merchants was an important factor in the successful partitioning of the Sultan's territories, as it was in their interest to conserve a peaceful environment for commerce.

Early in February 1888, Barghash, under doctor's orders, went on a sea voyage on board the *Nyanza*, to recover from a severe chest infection, which had been troubling him for some months. He got as far as Mogadishu, where he stayed for a few days, but feeling much better he returned to Zanzibar sooner than expected. However, he suffered a relapse in March and became dangerously ill again. On a sudden whim, he decided to try the sulphur baths in Baushar, near Muscat, to see if they would cure him. He set off again on the *Nyanza* taking with him his wife,[15] Peera Dewjee, 150 regular soldiers and three lakhs of rupees. The doctor in Zanzibar had advised him against the baths but to no avail; the Sultan did as he wished. After the first bath he felt better, but he grew worse after the second bath and even worse after the third. He was so ill that the doctor from the British Agency in Muscat was summoned and he advised Peera Dewjee to take the Sultan back to Zanzibar immediately as his condition had become critical. The Sultan begged Peera Dewjee to tell him the truth and tell him how long he had to live. Realising he only had a few days, Sultan Barghash gave the orders to return to Zanzibar at once. He wished to die amongst his people and family. He fainted three times during the return voyage and everyone thought he had died. But three times he revived. He could not face food and ate only a little fruit.

The *Nyanza* arrived in Zanzibar in the early morning of 27 March, but Barghash wanted to avoid arriving in daylight in his city as he did not want people to see the deplorable state of his health. The ship made a secret landing at Mkokotoni to the north of Zanzibar. That evening at nightfall the *Nyanza* steamed majestically into Zanzibar harbour without rousing any suspicion that their Sultan was near death. The surroundings of the palace were cleared of all the curious crowd come to welcome back their Sultan, leaving the palace square strangely deserted with only the ticking of the clock in the tower to break the unusual silence. A few women from the harem could be glimpsed peeping anxiously through the shutters of the windows overlooking the front. General Mathews stood alone at the end of the landing pier waiting to greet the Sultan. Carried on a chair, Barghash was transferred from the steamship into a launch with ten oarsmen who rowed him ashore. But once on land, he refused any help and walked unaided across the deserted square, which led to his palace where he laid on his bed, this time never to get up again.

He refused to see anybody, neither his brothers, nor his relatives, nor the councillors. His breathing became more difficult. For a few more hours he remained lucid and then feeling he was nearing the end, he gave a few orders. Then his agony started, a short agony, painful, tearing, and at midnight, the screams of the women from the harem informed the people of Zanzibar that Sultan Barghash, their ruler for nearly eighteen years, was dead.[16]

The role Peera Dewjee played during the final days of Barghash's life demonstrates how extremely close a friend and confidant he had become. Though unreported, it was almost certainly Peera who would have been at the death bed to take the final orders, when his Arab councillors, holy men and relatives were sent away. The orchestration of the discreet arrival of the dying sultan was also surely Peera Dewjee's doing. He made contact with General Mathews[17] to allow him to clear the palace area and prevent any public disturbance. The death of the Sultan in his own bed in the middle of the night was perfectly timed to minimise alarm, in fact so perfectly timed one cannot help wondering if the Sultan had in fact died previously and the whole charade was stage-managed by Peera Dewjee as part of a pre-arranged plan to forestall trouble and ensure a smooth transition to the next Sultan.

As Barghash's death was not unexpected, precautions had already been taken by the Consuls of England and Germany. They had reached a joint decision to both support the claim of Khalifa, the eldest surviving brother, rather than Khalid, Barghash's young son, who was favoured by some of the Arabs. Once the signal of death was heard, at midnight both Consuls went to the palace square and ordered General Mathews to proclaim Khalifa Sultan of Zanzibar. As Khalifa was the legal heir according to customary Muslim law, the majority in Zanzibar accepted this announcement and the fears of unrest proved groundless.[18]

Barghash's character was a strange mixture. He was vain, fickle and unpredictable, but he was a man of undoubted intelligence, energy and ambition. Like his father before him, he presented a generous and affable face to the Europeans he came in contact with but was cruel and ruthless to his own people. He was feared and hated by the Arabs who saw him as a capricious despot. He had little love or compassion for his fellow man. He made his slaves run at the double carrying heavy building materials on their heads to speed up his building projects and was unmoved when they fell from the scaffolding or suffered terrible injuries, crushed under collapsing masonry. He whipped his wives at the slightest provocation and his sisters also received harsh punishment if they displeased him. In the words of Salme: 'His bowels of mercy are closed alike against subject and relation.'[19] Barghash was by all accounts avaricious and grasping. He levied taxes on everything. Sometimes strange fancies went through his head. On one occasion he sacked all the captains of his fleet; another time he purchased compulsorily, at a quarter of the price, a house already contracted for sale to someone else. He started the construction of a railway, laid seven or eight miles of track, but then abandoned it suddenly and left the engine to rust in a siding. He bought expensive clocks from a European trader, always by the dozen, because he liked the sound of the ticking. He was pious and dignified with a regal presence and had the respect if not the love of the populace of Zanzibar.

Peera Dewjee's influence over Barghash was largely beneficial. He was the mover and fixer behind the scenes. He tempered the wilder flights of fancy and kept the Sultan anchored in reality.

Without Peera Dewjee at his side, it is doubtful Barghash would have weathered the storms of his eventful reign. Barghash was fortunate to have such a faithful and able man as Peera in whom to place his trust. He also showed foresight in recognising the abilities and potential of the former lamp cleaner and barber and giving him the chance to show his worth. Peera Dewjee's weakest area was in the financial management of the Sultan's affairs. He did not succeed in curbing the Sultan's extravagant spending habits and the Sultan's shipping line was a disastrous business venture, which lost money continually. Peera Dewjee undoubtedly enriched himself at the Sultan's expense, but this was expected in a society where there were no salaried civil servants, nor a structured workforce. The close working partnership lasted for almost thirty years and gave the Sultan continuity and stability in a period of unsettling change.

As Bennett points out, if Barghash had died in 1884 he would have gone down in history as a worthy successor to his father Seyyid Said, and been remembered as a reformer and energetic builder who oversaw the economic expansion and modernisation of Zanzibar. It was the final four years which fatally damaged his reputation as a great Arab ruler. [20]

---

1 *Tippoo Tib: The Story of his Career in Central Africa*, narrated from his own accounts by Dr Heinrich Brode and translated by H Havelock, London: Edward Arnold, 1907, p 181
2 *The Times*, October 11, 1883
3 Both men were involved with Leopold's International African Association projects for the opening up Africa. As astute businessmen they were wary about financing the Johnston project and wanted backing from the British Government before committing themselves.

4 'Gneisenau in Sansibar: Bericht eines Augenzeuges', *Schorers Familienblatt*, 1885. (Translated by Margaret Marks) http://www.jadu.de/jaduland/kolonien/afrika/tanzania/text/gneisenau.html, accessed Dec 3, 2014.

5 This may have been one of Henri Blowitz's famous articles written for *The Times* newspaper. He had been reporting on the West African conference being held in Paris and speculating on Bismarck's next moves.

6 Genesta Hamilton, *Princes of Zinj: The Rulers of Zanzibar*, London: Hutchinson, 1957, p 167

7 Rohlfs, whose blunt manner had upset the Sultan and caused unnecessary tensions, left on July 18 and was replaced by a professional diplomat called Travers. The Sultan had refused to see him off and sent Peera, who behaved very coldly towards him.

8 Carl Paschen, *Aus der Werdezeit zweier Marinen*, Berlin: Mittler, 1908, p 249-50. Translated for the author by David Paisey.

9 Emily Said-Ruete *Memoirs of an Arabian Princess*, G S P Freeman-Grenville, ed, London & The Hague, East-West Publications, 1994, p 193

10 Norman R Bennett, *A History of the Arab State of Zanzibar*, London: Methuen, 1978, p 131

11 Two German brothers named Denhardt had been trading in Lamu and the Tana River district since 1878. Like Peters they wanted East Africa to belong to Germany and early in 1885 the younger brother Clemens went to the district of Witu to see if he could do the same there as Peters. He persuaded the chief Ahmed Fumo Luti, nicknamed Simba (the lion), to sign a treaty in April 1885. This chief, although he knew well enough that his overlord was the Sultan of Zanzibar, agreed to put Witu and the neighbouring Swahili lands under the protection of Germany. Barghash was furious and the British did not like it either as Witu district lay within the northern sector claimed by Britain. In the British-German Treaty of 1890, Germany ceded it to Britain.

12 *The Zanzibar Letters of Edward D Ropes, Jr, 1882-1892*, Norman R Bennett, ed, Boston: African Studies Center, Boston University, 1973, p 76-7

13 During 1887 Holmwood replaced Kirk as Barghash's most trusted foreign advisor. Holmwood's long experience in Zanzibar and sympathetic understanding gave his words added weight with the Sultan and Peera Dewjee, both of whom he had known for many years. His contribution to the stability of Zanzibar during this troubled period has been overlooked. Sir John Kirk left Zanzibar at the end of 1886.

14 The presence of Peera Dewjee can be inferred from the letters of

Frieda von Bülow. In August 1887 she went on another voyage down the coast with Dr Peters in the Sultan's steamer *Barawa*. Dr Peters's lover and ardent supporter of his colonial ambitions, she had come out to build a hospital in Dar es Salaam sponsored by the German National Women's League and was now looking to find further sites for hospitals. She wrote that Peera Dewjee was on board and provided lavish catering for the special passengers, which included the Governor of Kilwa and his family. There was a whole array of provisions, silver cutlery, porcelain tableware, and Goan waiters to serve at table. She had various conversations with Peera, who told her how he too had become a passionate admirer of Dr Peters since going with him on a previous trip to Dar-es-Salaam. Ulrich van der Heyden, ed, *Kolonialer Alltag in Deutsch-Ostafrika in Dokumenten*, Berlin: Trafo, 2009, p 160. Translated for the author by David Paisey.

15 This was possibly Sayyida Moza bint Hamad Al-Busaid, who died in 1918 and was the daughter of the Wali of Musnah, rather than one of his concubines.

16 This detailed description of Barghash's death comes from an account written by Etienne Marras, a French trader resident in Zanzibar, for the *Bulletin de Geographie d'Aix-Marseilles*, Vol 12, 1888, p 264-69. Translated by Marie-Paule Nicholson.

17 General Mathews had been left in charge during the absence of Barghash.

18 Letter from Etienne Marras, *Bulletin de Geographie d'Aix-Marseilles*, Vol 12

19 *Memoirs of an Arabian Princess*, p 197

20 Bennett, *History of the Arab State of Zanzibar*, p 137

Chapter Thirteen

Sultan Khalifa

W hen Khalifa was suddenly pulled from his bed in the middle of the night, he was ill with a fever and could not believe his brother was really dead and he was now Sultan. For over an hour Khalifa categorically refused to come to town thinking it was a plot to have him assassinated. Only after he was given assurances by the foreign envoys did he agree to leave. He had been living quietly under house arrest in the countryside since his return from Merka, on a meagre monthly allowance. Forbidden to see visitors, he only came into town under supervision on the days of the public *baraza*, which he was obliged to attend with his brother Ali. When he arrived at the palace at 3 am on the morning of 28 March 1888, suspicious and bewildered, he was mobbed by those who wanted to congratulate him. Only then did Khalifa truly believe he was Sultan.

After seeing the body of his brother, he went to pray for over an hour in the mosque close to the palace. At 5.30 am the funeral ceremony began. The whole populace of Zanzibar turned out and, in keeping with Muslim traditions, everyone wanted to touch the bier and pay their last respects as the body of their Sultan was carried out for burial. It took over an hour-and-a-half to cover the short distance to the graveyard next to the palace because of the crowd of people. At 8 am Khalifa was formally proclaimed Sultan by all the Arabs and influential Swahili in a public reception that lasted two hours. In a spirit of thanksgiving and as a sign of a new beginning, Khalifa announced that all prisoners, except murderers, should be set free. Three hundred and fifty emaciated and ragged individuals emerged from prison.

For two days the town was in mourning, the flags of the consulates and ships remained at half-mast and all trade ceased. On Friday the period of official mourning ended, normal activity resumed, the boats and consulates raised their best flags and the Italian naval cruiser, *Staffetta*, was the first to greet the new Sultan with a 21-gun salute, which echoed around the waterfront. At a great public *baraza* Khalifa received loyal tributes and congratulations from his people. Finally all the Europeans of Zanzibar, preceded by their respective consuls, came in turn to congratulate the new Sultan.

According to an eye-witness description, Khalifa cut a poor figure compared with his brother Barghash. He was small and short sighted with a dark complexion.

> He is horribly pock-marked and his face is scattered by scant and patchy thick hairs. He is of smaller size and his manners are coarser. It is said that he will reform a lot of the things his brother had introduced in the State. He is apparently very generous but intellectually weak. The future will tell if his two advisors, Seyyid Ali and Mohamed bin Suliman, of whom great things are said, will lead him on the right path.[1]

The one known engraving of Khalifa shows him in Arab dress wearing glasses with a distinctly aquiline nose. Like Barghash, his mother had been Ethiopian. He was aged around 36 at the time of his accession.

Khalifa's reign started well. Humbly admitting to his ignorance of public affairs and unfamiliarity with the conduct of his office, he listened to his advisors and followed the guidance of the new British Consul General, Charles Euan-Smith, who had arrived to take over from Holmwood just a few days before Barghash's death. He gave out generous gifts and arranged for Barghash's wives to be sent back to Arabia. According to one German report Khalifa often took the air in his carriage with Peera Dewjee on the box seat.[2] Initially the populace were enthusiastic and thought him an improvement on the old Sultan.

On 28 April he signed an agreement with Germany, which gave the German East Africa Company (DOAG) the right to administer, under the Sultan's authority and flag, the coastal territory located between the Umba and Ruvuma Rivers. This concession had been under discussion previously, but the final paperwork had stalled due to Barghash's last illness. The Germans wanted an arrangement similar to that in the British sector and Khalifa gave in without much pressure. But showing his displeasure, he is said to have informed the coastal Arabs he had done so against his will, and that if they could in any way thwart the German enterprise on the mainland such action on their part would afford him satisfaction.[3]

Peera Dewjee's expertise was still needed at the palace and as the political situation became more complex and dangerous, his knowledge of the European mindset and ability to talk with European officials became ever more useful. Khalifa, unlike Barghash, had little previous exposure to Europeans nor did his Arab mentors have a thorough understanding of western politics and they quickly floundered. Peera Dewjee became the new Sultan's chief diplomatic advisor.

Although there is no definite record of this, it is probable Peera also oversaw customs collection in Zanzibar, the chief revenue of the state. Barghash had taken over the responsibility of the Customs in 1886, handing over the day-to-day management jointly to Nasser Lillani and Peera Dewjee, but Lillani died in 1888 presumably leaving Peera in sole charge. The revenues from import and export taxes had fallen considerably as the British and Germans oversaw the customs collection in their own sectors. In 1888 the Germans also established a separate customs system in Zanzibar for goods coming from or destined for the German coast. This ate into the Sultan's revenues yet further and his income continued to decline as trading ships began to bypass Zanzibar, calling in at Dar es Salaam or Mombasa instead. The Sultan's steamers, operating at heavy losses, had to be gradually sold off or scrapped as part of the cost-cutting exercise. Barghash had left all his personal properties and fortune to his son Khalid and although a large stash of rupees was found in the harem, this did not nearly cover the debts he owed. After an initial period of euphoria, Khalifa found his coffers empty, his credit finished and his income stream much diminished. Unlike his brother, he could not afford lavish building projects or a large harem. Fortunately his tastes were simple and he was used to living on a shoestring.

In May Ernst Vohsen arrived to replace Dr Peters as resident director of the German East Africa Company. He had commercial experience in West Africa, but he was unfamiliar with East Africa. His overriding aim was to bring in a profit as fast as possible. He brought with him about 60 officials to provide administrators for the Company's new territories at the coast and he arranged with the Sultan that Germany would assume control over the concession on 15 August 1888.

In preparation for installing the new administration in the German sector, Vohsen issued a series of proclamations. Trade in future had to flow through seven designated ports: Tanga, Pangani, Bagamoyo, Dar es Salaam, Kilwa, Lindi and Mkindani, each of which would become an administrative centre for a district, where a German agent and his staff would be posted to supervise the Arab and indigenous officials. Land ownership was to be registered within six months and judicial courts under the authority of the company agents were to be created in the designated ports.

The population of the German coastline was nervous and confused by the prospect of the changes about to be enforced upon them, but they remained peaceful. However, on transfer day, 15 August, resentment flared to the surface over the seemingly trivial but extremely emotive subject of flags. The German Company officials insisted the company flag should fly – alongside the Sultan's flag – before each town's headquarters,[4] but the Arab officials had not been told to do this. The Liwali (the Sultan's appointed Governor) in Bagamoyo refused to move his flagstaff from his residence without prior instructions from Zanzibar, but the armed German sailors simply cut it down and replaced it in front of their headquarters. The Liwali, Amir bin Suleiman Lemki, fled the town in alarm. The situation in the other ports was no better as the heavily armed Germans moved in to take possession, interfering with the Sultan's flag and forcing the Arab officials to submit to their demands. A storm of complaints followed – Said bin Hamadi had been knocked down and kicked because he refused to rent his house to a German, while at Pangani German officers violated a mosque by walking inside with dogs at their heels and loudly demanding the whereabouts of the Liwali. By the end of August the entire coast was in uproar; rumours indicated a general uprising was imminent.[5]

The Germans had behaved with appalling arrogance. They had walked in like freebooting pirates and conquerors, rather than paying guests or leaseholders. Having dreamt up a wonderful new system for efficient administration, they had ignored the feelings of the residents and had failed to factor in a small point that struck at the heart of the matter – the Sultan's flagstaff. Michahelles, the consul, tried to distance the German Government from the rapidly disintegrating situation, describing the company officials' actions as 'unjustifiable and reprehensible' and expressing his regret to Khalifa, but it was too late for diplomacy – the damage had been done.

The German Navy stationed at Zanzibar under Rear Admiral Deinhard at first refused to become involved in the Company's problems, brought on by their foolishness, so Vohsen turned to Sultan Khalifa to restore order. There now followed an unedifying period when all sides tried to point the finger of blame and the wrangling served only to inflame the situation. Under pressure from the Europeans and alarmed for the security of his subjects, the Sultan did try to restore calm in the coastal towns by placing 200 of his armed forces at the disposal of the German Company, at their request. When this failed to work – because many of the Sultan's soldiers sympathised with the locals – he then sent a small force to Pangani, but the Sultan's troops led by General Mathews had to withdraw such was the anger against the Germans.

The so-called Bushiri Uprising had started. It was named after Abushiri bin Salim, one of the disaffected residents of Pangani and its most notorious and successful leader. The German company agents were besieged in their centres by angry rebels, only hanging on to coastal positions when eventually assisted by the German Navy. It was not an organised or full-scale uprising but rather an intermittent guerrilla war of protest, which was disruptive and left the Germans unsure as to where it might flare up next and what the next target might be. Dar es Salaam was left largely unaffected, but a major battle with the Bushiri rebels in Bagamoyo on 22 September destroyed much of the town. More than 4,000 inhabitants sought refuge at the Catholic mission.

The mood in Zanzibar was fraught and Khalifa became increasingly angry and frightened as a flurry of letters came from Bismarck trying to exonerate Germany by saying the uprising was directed as much against the Sultan's authority as against the Company and Arab opposition to the German actions to end the slave trade had been a principal cause for the disorder. Khalifa wrote back sending unusually frank replies and refused to accept any of the blame. In one letter after listing the Company's misdeeds, he awarded full responsibility to it for the war saying simply, 'We gave the towns in peace, but the German Company has given us war.' The Arabs had wanted peace, instead the Germans 'spat on our flag everywhere and said we were no longer the Sultan but that they…were the Sultan.'[6]

The Germans, meanwhile, demanded stronger measures to contain the unrest and shore up their position. As the Sultan had so far failed to quell the unrest, the Germans proposed to blockade the coast themselves and cut off the rebels' supply of ammunitions. The British objected and insisted on joining the blockade as well, if it was to go ahead, and the French and Italians too wanted to take part. All feared Germany taking unilateral action. In the end the Europeans each agreed to blockade that part of the coast of interest to them. In Europe the proposed multi-national blockade was presented as a humanitarian anti-slavery measure, rather than the purely military operation it really was. Khalifa, with Peera Dewjee, delayed the formation of the blockade as long as they could, knowing how unpopular it would be, citing illness and any other excuse that could be dreamt up.

Khalifa was disillusioned by his European 'friends' and in a state of panic as he watched the collapse of his authority on the mainland and saw his sources of income vanish. On 18 November, ill with anxiety and depression, he withdrew to his country residence, leaving the affairs of state in the hands of his two most trusted subordinates, Peera Dewjee and Mohammed Bakashmar. He had a telephone installed and received daily updates on the situation, but refused to see or talk to any European – the cause of all the trouble.

The fate of Zanzibar now rested solely with Peera Dewjee. Bakashmar was so furiously anti-European that he refused to deal directly with their officials. Peera Dewjee had to handle the political situation at a particularly dangerous time for Zanzibar. Feelings against Germany ran high and the German residents of Zanzibar feared for their lives.

The British sector remained peaceful during this period only because the IBEACo was less efficient than the German Company and had not yet started their operations. Seeing the problems experienced by their German allies, they decided to proceed very cautiously and slowly indeed.[7] Other than the German company agents, the other Europeans affected by the Bushiri rebellion were the missionaries, living in remote out stations. They experienced fear but little actual harm, apart from a few isolated incidents. It was the local residents and the Indian businessmen of the coastal towns who suffered the most as trade was disrupted.

The fragile situation was not helped by the personalities involved. Vohsen had shown disastrous incompetence, while the Sultan had not given clear instructions to his coastal officials, nor taken a firm hand, either because he was too weak or because he did not wish the German

Company to succeed. His natural leanings and those of Peera Dewjee, his chief minister, were towards the British, who had nurtured Zanzibar under their patronage and system of indirect empire. Perhaps he and Peera at this stage hoped the Germans would give up and go away and leave Zanzibar to carry on as before. But this was not going to happen: there was too much German prestige at stake. They could not be seen to fail and had no intention of allowing their British rivals to gain the upper hand.

The English position was even more complicated. The Consul General, Colonel Charles Euan-Smith, Bartle Frere's favourite and former secretary, had orders from Whitehall instructing him to support the German position according to the agreements signed, but also to uphold British interests in the region, especially those involving the British East Africa Company. 'Tea Party Smith,' as he had been known in India, needed great skill to navigate his way through the conflicting loyalties and agendas of his brief. His life was further complicated by delusions of grandeur, which left him heavily in debt. He lived a lie; continually teetering on the edge of bankruptcy and for many years had been in the pay of Sir William Mackinnon, who provided him with funds.[8] He played a double, if not a triple, game as he supported Germany, while keeping an eye on British interests and scheming behind the scenes on Mackinnon's behalf. To add to the toxic mix of politics and personalities, Peera Dewjee and the new British Consul disliked each other. Peera saw through the façade and knew all about Colonel Smith. They had both known each other in humbler circumstances and both had risen from modest beginnings to their present elevated positions through an ability to flatter and achieve favoured status. Of the two, Peera Dewjee was probably the more intelligent and able. The unfortunate Khalifa, a nervous and not overly intelligent man, was caught between the two protagonists. The imperious manner of the magnificent British Consul intimidated Sultan Khalifa and to begin with he agreed to all the Consul said. Then, on the advice of Peera Dewjee, he had to go back on his word.

The Germans and their British allies became impatient and could wait no longer:

Colonel Euan-Smith to the Sultan of Zanzibar
Zanzibar, November 30, 1888
(Translation)

Your Highness,

Her Majesty's government having heard with extreme regret that your Highness' illness has so far incapacitated you from the dispatch of business as to prevent your issuing the Proclamation concerning the blockade which you promised to issue in your letter of the 8th November, has agreed with the German Government that the Proclamation shall, pending your Highness' hoped-for recovery, and in view of the fact that your Highness had verbally given your full consent to the blockade, be issued in your Highness' name, and that the blockade shall commence to be in force from the 2nd December at noon.[9]

With or without the Sultan's agreement the blockade was going ahead, at the say-so of Germany and Britain.

Adding to the dangerous political build-up, a certain unwelcome visitor was also in Zanzibar, hoping to take advantage of Germany's influential position to press her claims. Princess Salme had arrived in Zanzibar in May 1888 with the expectation that, with German support, Khalifa would show more generosity than Barghash had. However, her attempts to regain her inheritance and position within the Sultan's family once again proved fruitless. She wrote begging letters which were not answered. When she went to the Palace and asked to see Khalifa, Peera Dewjee met her and said he was unavailable and would not see her. She then tried her youngest brother Ali, and approached the British Consul for help but all to no avail. She remained in Zanzibar until November 1888. Only then did she leave, dismayed perhaps by the prospect of war, and by a final realisation that there was no inheritance or future for her or her children in Zanzibar. Disappointed and tired of life in Europe, she went to live in Beirut.

Another visitor to Zanzibar was Sir John Kirk, who came with his daughter Dolly in late November 1888 and left at the end of February 1889. He came to close his bank accounts and sell his property in Mbweni to Elizabeth Thackeray for her missionary work. He stayed at the British consulate as a guest of Colonel Euan-Smith and was horrified by the situation. He had arrived at a particularly tricky time and Colonel Euan-Smith asked him to keep a low profile as he did not want hopes to be raised in Zanzibar that Kirk had come to put things right. He made Kirk promise not to interfere politically in any way. Consequently, Kirk did not go to the palace to see Khalifa or Peera Dewjee and he avoided his old Indian friends. Instead, he went on a trip up the coast and visited Mombasa and saw the missionaries at Freretown. On his return to Zanzibar, he found the situation had deteriorated further. The final letters he wrote back to his wife, on Consular headed note-paper, betrayed his agonised state of mind, and what he thought of Euan-Smith – his 'shameful behaviour' and the mess he was making of affairs in Zanzibar.

Khalifa by now had become obstinate and refused to see the British Consul. He 'is a tool in the hands of the sharia law men of which Peera is one,' wrote Kirk. Colonel Euan-Smith blamed Peera Dewjee for his loss of influence over the Sultan. The two diplomats discussed the options and when Euan-Smith said he thought the solution was to remove Peera Dewjee, Kirk said it would certainly shock the Sultan. However, he confided to his wife that he thought Euan-Smith was making a mistake and taking the wrong approach. He wrote with disapproval about Euan-Smith's lifestyle saying how 'he must be making a pot of money and spends nothing' (inferring he was accepting gifts and bribes) and said he had not enjoyed staying with Euan-Smith, despite the lavish hospitality. He saw how unpopular the British Consul was in Zanzibar and wrote that he was even afraid to go to church 'lest he be insulted.' In one of his last letters written in February, Kirk lamented: 'We have no influence. Poor Zanzibar is a changed place. The Indians are despairing and listless, the Arabs sulking.'[10]

Things had indeed gone from bad to worse in Zanzibar. The entire coast was now blockaded by foreign warships, there was a virtual shut down on all trading and the cost of food and everyday items in Zanzibar had soared. Further down the coast people rioted when the mail steamers were prevented from landing at Kilwa and Lindi.

Suddenly on 18 December Khalifa returned to Zanzibar from his country villa. He called a public *baraza* to declare he had decided to govern by sharia law and uphold the tenets of his religion as his father would have done. He showed he meant business by ordering the prisoners held in the fort under sentence of death be executed without further delay. Four prisoners duly had their heads chopped off in the fruit market in front of a large crowd. Horrified by such a barbaric display – the sword used was blunt and the executioner inept – European officials protested strongly, but Khalifa would not listen and chopped off another four heads the next day. The awful spectacle of the executioner inexpertly hacking off the heads of his victims in front of an enthusiastic crowd drove the Indian community to protest as well. A further delegation of Europeans and Indians eventually persuaded the Sultan to stop the grisly spectacle. Euan-Smith, the British Consul, took the lead in giving him a good telling off and Khalifa, chastened but unrepentant, reluctantly stopped the executions.

Colonel Euan-Smith to the Marquis of Salisbury

Zanzibar December 22, 1888, 4.40 pm
(Telegraphic)

I HAD early this morning prolonged interview with Sultan, who ultimately accepted unreservedly the views of Her Majesty's Government, and countermanded all executions recently ordered, including that of five people fixed for 10 a.m. to-day. I informed His Highness that Her Majesty's Government had no intention of interfering with his just sovereign rights in respect of capital punishment, which were in principle approved by the Her Majesty's Government. This should, however, according to Mahommedan law only take place after public judgement, and within reasonable time from committal of crime.

His Highness implied that he had acted hastily, and promised that any future execution should be carried out with strict attention to decency and order.

The French Consul accorded me his hearty non-official support. The German Consul replied that, having no instructions, he must inquire into the circumstances before taking any action. The entirely satisfactory results of my interview, which have much strengthened His Highness' position, and which have given undisguised public satisfaction, rendered this co-operation unnecessary.[11]

There was much speculation as to what had spurred Khalifa to start the beheadings. Some thought he hoped to frighten the Europeans so they would go away and that it was part of a superstitious rite to propitiate the spirits, to bring him good fortune and defeat his enemies. Others thought he wanted to strengthen his authority by returning to the precepts of the Koran as practised by his father and hoped God might as a result look more kindly upon him. Euan-Smith had a poor opinion of Khalifa whom he thought had a weak disposition and was abnormally ignorant of the affairs of the world.[12] Others went further and thought his mind had been permanently unhinged by his brother's cruel treatment. Salme alleges that both her younger brothers Khalifa and Ali were addicted to drink and opium, which might explain his sometimes erratic behaviour.[13]

The naval blockade failed to make any difference to the coastal disturbances. The ships were too thinly spread to prevent supplies getting through to the rebels.[14] Four German naval ships monitored the coast from Rovuma to Tanga. Britain also had four ships employed in the north, from Tanga to Lamu, and an additional one, HMS *Agamemnon,* acted as a guard-ship to watch over European and British interests in Zanzibar. The blockade was ineffective and unpopular with everyone, even the naval personnel, many of whom fell sick. Nevertheless, Rear-Admiral Deinhard received orders from Germany to continue the blockade of the coast for a further six months. What did eventually make the difference was the decision to send in German troops under the command of Hermann Wissmann to fight the rebels on land. The German Military Expedition arrived in Zanzibar on 31 March 1889.

The atmosphere in Zanzibar had become despondent and a poisonous breeding ground for treason and intrigue. Khalifa had lost control of the situation. Certain factions thought him unfit to rule, and wanted his brother Ali to be Sultan. Ali had allied himself to the pro-British camp and Euan-Smith, who by now loathed Khalifa, joined the conspirators and tried to depose him in favour of Ali. He wrote to Lord Salisbury with this proposal in February 1889, but Salisbury firmly quashed the idea.[15] Ali was warned that if he continued to intrigue against his brother he might jeopardise his own future and so he postponed his scheming for the time being.

The complicated diplomatic game of playing off the Sultan, Germany and England and trying to keep the advantage took its toll on Euan-Smith. He had showed signs of stress in December and this got steadily worse over the next two months. The German Consul, Michahelles, an affable and jovial man, gained in influence and disturbing rumours hinted that the Sultan was thinking of putting Zanzibar under French protection in return for Pemba. Euan-Smith's enormous numbers of dispatches and telegraphic reports make tedious reading and he seemed to be driving himself towards a nervous breakdown. His relations with the Sultan had reached a low point and he desperately looked for ways to reassert his influence. If he could not remove the Sultan, then Peera Dewjee, the British Indian and closest adviser to the Sultan, was an obvious target. Peera Dewjee had become too powerful. He was in charge of the Sultan's appointments and could decide who saw the Sultan and who did not. He was not intimidated and had dared to turn the British Consul away, while giving the German Consul preference. Beneath the smooth excuses of an experienced courtier, the Colonel had detected a hint of scorn and even mischievous enjoyment. Peera Dewjee had to go!

Euan-Smith began to write secret dispatches to London, smearing the character of Peera Dewjee, which became increasingly virulent and unbalanced. Here is an early one dated 24 December 1888.

> The second point is as to the position of the man Peera Dewji with regard to Zanzibar politics. This man may be briefly described as a low-

212

born but extremely clever, capable and unscrupulous adventurer. I am convinced that the unwholesome influence he exercises over the Sultan's indolent mind is not exaggerated by the Arabs, but they imply that nothing can be done to counteract his influence because he is a British Indian Subject under English protection. I am convinced that this man represents a standing danger to the best interests of the Sultan and of Zanzibar. I consider therefore that His Highness should either be pressed in a friendly manner to dismiss him from his service and deport him from Zanzibar or that I myself in the case of grave necessity should be empowered to take this step.[16]

While in this one dated 27 February 1889 he has become almost frantic with his wild accusations against Peera.

In continuation of my telegram no. 68 Secret of the 20th instant, I have the honour to submit the following report to your Lordship.

The character and conduct of the man Peera Dewji, there in referred to, at the present moment one of two principal advisers of H.H. the Sultan… repeatedly has been animadverted upon by me in my dispatches to Your Lordship. I have known that for some months past he has been actively intriguing against British interests and against this Agency. Substantial proof as to such intrigues it would not be possible for me to produce, but the consensus of opinion on this head, collected from all quarters, and from people of all classes leaves in my mind no doubt whatever that, in the person Peera Dewji English interests at Zanzibar and in East Africa, and especially the Imperial British East Africa Company, have an active and uncompromising enemy. Arabs and Europeans of all classes have warned me of this and the Sultan himself has more than half confessed as much to me. The most conclusive proof of all is to be found in His Highness' recent actions and present attitude in which the evil influence of Peera Dewji is to be distinctly traced. Latterly I have been aware that this man was looking forward to the arrival of Lieutenant Wissman to aggrandize himself by alliance with the Germans in open hostility to the English. I have received information from sources that are beyond suspicion that he has made direct overtures to the German authorities here, asking for their support and protection, assuring them that his influence with the Sultan is paramount and promising them that he would obtain from His Highness everything that they could wish for. He has also been making inquiries as to the possibility of changing his nationality and becoming a German subject, and being, as I am informed, greatly in debt to British subjects, he has lodged all his valuables and securities in German hands.

Before dispatching to your lordship the telegram, above noted, I took advantage of the presence of Sir John Kirk in Zanzibar and laid before him all the information that was at my command regarding Peera Dewji.[17]

What Lord Salisbury thought of such a report full of unsubstantiated hearsay and anti-German sentiment is not reported, but Euan-Smith did get permission to remove Peera under an order in Council dated 2 March 1889. This gave the British Consul-General the power to deport any British subject whose conduct was dangerous to the peace and good order of Zanzibar for a period of up to two years.

On Saturday 9 March Colonel Euan-Smith called Peera into his office to inform him that he had received a telegram from London with an order to deport him from Zanzibar within 24 hours, but he was prepared to give him three weeks grace to sort out his affairs. Peera Dewjee described this interview and subsequent events in his own words in a letter he sent to William Mackinnon dated 2 April 1889.

> At this unexpected announcement I was very much astonished and bewildered however I demanded the reason of his dealing me in this manner, but he would give me no other reason than to say I am doing good to the Sultan and not to himself, he also said that I was good to him only for six months and after that I did bad to the British Government. I urged him to show me the bad I have done to our government, to which he said that he heard from other people that I am doing bad. I told him that what other people told him was through malice and cannot be accredited. I then asked him to try me before a court of inquiry and I am in a position to prove that the charges he brings against me are groundless, but he refused all my pleadings. I reminded him the good I have done him, which he did not deny, but he was determined to have his instructions carried into effects. I told him he was doing a great wrong to me and my family and exercising absolute despotism. I shall have a great loss in my business and my debtors both English and German will be greatly effected by this rash proceeding of the Consul General against an innocent man.
>
> All the above has passed between us in close doors, and he told me that it was strictly private but no sooner I came out people [k]new what had passed between us.[18]

Peera immediately afterwards went to the Sultan and then sent a telegraph to James Hutton and William Mackinnon to ask for their help.

Previously, on 20 March he had written Mackinnon an extraordinary letter explaining exactly what Euan-Smith had been up to in Zanzibar. British consular officials were not supposed to receive gifts or favours, which could be construed as bribes, but Euan-Smith apparently had no such scruples. He had been receiving and demanding a great many gifts from the Sultan and the British Indian residents in order to refurnish the Consulate to his taste and kit himself out in grand style. Hundreds of yards of carpets, hanging lamps, Japanese flower pots, Chinese vases with trees in them; if he saw something he liked in the Palace or in an Indian house, he asked Peera to get it for him.

> On one occasion, when Col Smith came to visit His Highness he saw in the Visiting Room of the Palace, large Japanese flower Pots, on which he had his eyes upon them and he called Peera Dewjee to tell [His] Highness that he wanted them, and they were given to him and he placed them in his visiting Room. It was known to the Public of other nations and they all laughed and joked on the subject.

The Sultan gave him the use of two carriages and when these broke down and the horses died, he demanded another two from British Indian merchants and so the list went on. It was all done in an underhand way. When Khalifa openly sent Mrs Smith a present of jewellery, it was returned, as he said that it would be noticed. 'His Highness was very much annoyed and said he ought not to have accepted so many things taken privately. Perhaps Col Smith does not like to have what is given him but to have the meanness to ask for things.'

> Col Smith wishing to have a new Veranda and Balcony to the house communicated the matter to His Highness and requested him to give him workmen and all necessary materials and the whole house was changed and it cost His Highness about two thousand pounds Sterling. Col Smith was telling other people that he was spending his own money for the house, but people soon came to know the real truth.

Peera also complained about Euan-Smith's attitude to Indians and noted their response.

> Col Smith when seeing a British Indian Subject not saluting him he calls him in his house and orders him to come to his house to salute him every day, and great many other injustice is practised by him to the British Indian Subjects. It would [be] to much if everything is enumerated. Sewjee Hadjee, a British Indian Subject who undertakes to convey goods to the interior of Africa of all nation – got into his displeasure and he was finding an opportunity to Chastise him, but he being a sharp fellow, he made his way to Bombay before the Consul could get hold of him…News have been spread the Col Smith is going Home for three months and the British Indian Subjects say Praise be God that he may not come back. [19]

No doubt Peera's complaints about the British Consul were justified as they are borne out by Kirk's earlier comments in his letter to his wife. Mackinnon did not take the matter further, but probably had a private word with his protégé, Euan-Smith, on his return to England. The two letters remained unnoticed in Mackinnon's general correspondence until recently.

When Khalifa heard the news that Peera was to be sent away, he was very upset and refused to let him go, saying he had given entire satisfaction to his late brother and to himself. Euan-Smith tried to force the Sultan by his old tactic of smearing Peera's character, and adding in a charge of gun running.[20] The Sultan was very surprised by what he heard, but didn't believe him. On 1 April the Sultan still refused to release Peera, saying the British Consul wanted to take away his faithful servant 'without the least cause and against his wishes.' The next day Euan-Smith told Peera to ask for his release from the Sultan and said if he didn't get it he would make sure he was banished for longer.[21]

Euan-Smith left for England soon afterwards on sick leave and Khalifa was so angry with him that he refused to grant him the customary farewell audience and asked that he not come back. The deputy consul Hawes had to draw up an official order to deport Peera Dewjee, which he did on 7 April. Peera Dewjee finally left for Bombay on 9 April.

Ironically, when this deportation order was later examined in

London, it was found not to be in the correct legal format, so the deportation in fact was null and void. No one blamed Hawes, who had drawn up the form to the best of his ability, but the Foreign Office helpfully sent out a set of pre-worded forms, for 'order of prohibition' and 'order of removal' for use on future occasions.[22]

Salme described Peera Dewjee as Madolji Peera Dewjee. The term Madolji is is a mystery. It's possible it was used as a pejorative meaning little drummer or one who stirs up and spreads gossip. Madol is the term for a small Indian drum. Peera Dewjee was certainly a past master in the Swahili art of *fitina* or intrigue and knew how to use it to his advantage. Zanzibar, a small island, was a hotbed for rumour and gossip and Peera was the most expert of the rumour mongers. Kirk called him 'a perfect spy,'[23] while a German source commented how his channels of communication were never clogged. Peera always knew the latest news before anyone else and was extraordinarily well informed about all aspects of Zanzibar and its residents.[24] Following Kirk's example before him, he would drop a word here and there and the next thing it would be all round the island, or in a national newspaper. With the advent of the telegraph, news could swirl round the world and be on the desk at Whitehall in a few hours.

An example of this is can be seen from two reports in *The Standard* newspaper for April 1889. The first is dated 25 April and is 'from our correspondent in Berlin:'

> Colonel Euan-Smith, the English Consul General in Zanzibar, is reported to have recently fined the Sultan's steward Peera Dewjee, who is an Indian merchant and a British subject, the sum of one thousand rupees, for importing arms, and has, for political reasons, expelled him from Zanzibar. Peera has gone straight to England to appeal against the action of the British Consul…If unsuccessful, Peera intends to become a German subject, and that many other Indians of position in Zanzibar will follow his example.

The second, which appeared in *The Standard* for 27 April 1889, was from 'Our Correspondent, Paris, Friday night:'

> I am asked to state that the Berlin telegram in *The Standard* yesterday respecting a fine alleged to have been imposed…is not quite correct. Peera Dewjee was fined, not one thousand rupees, but two hundred, and not by Colonel Euan-Smith, but by Mr Berkeley, the Acting Judge of the Consular Court. My informant assures me, moreover, that he has Peera's authority for denying the report of his intention to become a German subject – a report he believes to have been fabricated with a view to injure him.

Peera is up to the old trick of playing the German and French card to upset the English, and it certainly worked. One can just imagine him being interviewed and then denying all. By this time all kinds of exaggerated reports have been circulated and the diplomats are left with egg all over their face and in a tizz. The threat of the Indian merchants becoming German nationals and taking their money out of British banks was no doubt worrying.

The British Consul's allegations against Peera contained truth. His worry about Germany's increasing influence in Zanzibar and amongst the Indian merchants was genuine, but with the changing political landscape it was inevitable this would happen. As the Sultan's chief advisor, Peera Dewjee's main concern had to be for the peace and security of the realm and by early 1889 Germany was more proactive in this than Britain, which offered kind words but no more. As a businessman it made economic sense for Peera to have a good relationship with Germany when he did business within the German sector. Sewa Haji, his colleague based at Bagamoyo, the centre of the ivory trade, worked closely with Germany. Peera steered the Sultan towards Germany because it benefited Zanzibar to have a closer relationship. Euan-Smith naturally wanted to restore Britain's influence, but he chose a petty and vindictive course, more like a personal vendetta than the reasoned policy judgement of a senior diplomat.

When Euan-Smith's temporary replacement, Gerald Portal, arrived, the consular reports had a much calmer tone and relations with the Sultan improved. Euan-Smith's personal feud with Peera had fuelled much of the problem. With his removal diplomatic relations returned to normal without the clash between the personalities of

Peera and Euan-Smith. Tea Party Smith had created a storm in a teacup! But, however trivial the incident was, it provides insight into the workings of the palace of Zanzibar at the time.

---

1 *Bulletin de Géographie d' Aix-Marseille*, Vol 12, 1888, p 269. This concludes the account of Etienne Marras, describing the death of Barghash and succession of Khalifa as Sultan. Translated by Marie-Paule Nicholson.

2 Oscar Baumann, In Deutsch-Ostafrika wahrend des Aufstandes, [In German East Africa During the Uprising] Vien und Olmütz; Eduard Hölzel, 1890, p 22

3 Norman R Bennett, *A History of the Arab State of Zanzibar*, London: Methuen, 1978, p 140. This was contained in a report from Euan-Smith to Lord Salisbury. Euan-Smith concluded that in his opinion Khalifa was too timid to have said such a thing and there was no danger of unrest. Famous last words!

4 The company flag was a Southern Cross superimposed over German national colours. The Sultan's was a plain red flag.

5 Norman R Bennett, *Arab versus European: Diplomacy and War in Nineteenth-Century East Central Africa,* New York: Africana Publishing Co, 1986, p 149

6 *Ibid*, p 153

7 The IBEACo agreement was only concluded on September 3, 1888 when it received a Royal Charter to open up the British sphere of influence to legitimate trade and this was officially endorsed by Khalifa on October 9, 1886. The IBEACo made its capital at Mombasa and opened its first inland station at Machakos in 1889.

8 John S Galbraith, *Mackinnon & East Africa 1878-1895: A study in the New Imperialism*, London: Cambridge University Press, 1972, p 33. Galbraith explains that Mackinnon and Euan-Smith had been friends for many years. Euan-Smith, a prodigal spender, was perpetually in debt and had the practice of over 20 years of asking MacKinnon for loans, which he gave freely. Apparently Euan-Smith had a standing authorization from Mackinnon to draw on him for funds. Although Galbraith says that despite the loans Euan-Smith did not support Mackinnon's ventures, this is not the case. Smith shared Mackinnon's anti-German sentiments and furthered his interests whenever possible.

9 British Parliamentary Paper: *Further Correspondence Respecting Germany and Zanzibar*, C.5822, Africa No 1 (1889) no 20

10 Kirk Letters, National Library of Scotland, Acc 9942/11. The information has been taken from letters dated November 21, 1888; February 17, 1889; and the last one, written off Cape Delgado, dated February 25, 1889, which contained the most explicit information.

11 British Parliamentary Paper: *Further Correspondence respecting Germany and Zanzibar*, C.5822, No 17

12 FO 84/ 1906 & 1907

13 This was suggested in a letter to her children probably written in 1888, which is mentioned in the introduction by Evan Donzel to *An Arabian Princess Between Two Worlds: Memoirs, Letters Home, Sequels to the Memoirs, Syrian Customs and Usages*, Leiden: E J Brill, 1993, p 88

14 There were rumours that British Indians were helping the rebels by smuggling arms and ammunition in their dhows concealed in bales of cloth and kerosene tins.

15 FO 84/ 1977 p 61-73 No 113, Euan-Smith to Salisbury, Secret proposal to deport Seyyid Khalifa

16 FO 84/ 1911 no. 300, Confidential, Zanzibar December 24, 1888

17 FO 84 /1977 no 104, Secret

18 [55] Mackinnon Papers, SOAS: Letters from H M Stanley, General correspondence Box 55, folder 218

19 Dewjee to Mackinnon, March 20, 1889, SOAS, Mackinnon Papers, 218

20 March 28, 1889, Euan-Smith made a last attempt to persuade the Sultan to send Peera away, to avoid the necessity of deporting him officially. FO 84 /1977, p 427- 429, no 69

21 [55] Dewjee to Mackinnon, April 2, 1889, SOAS, Mackinnon Papers, 218

22 FO 84/ 1973, p 327, no 166

23 [42] Kirk to Mackinnon, May 5, 1879, SOAS Mackinnon Papers, 22

24 Hermann Schreiber, *Denhardts Griff nach Afrika: Die Geschichte einer Deutschen Kolonialerwerbung*, Berlin: Scherl, 1938, p 165. 'The versatile and well-informed Indian Peera Dewjee got to know through channels that God knows are never clogged that Gerhard Rohlfs has been recalled.' Translation from the German.

Chapter 14

The End Game: Peera leaves the Service of the Sultan

The road to the fall of the Arab State of Zanzibar was a long and winding one, with a totally unforeseen endgame. The crescendo of increasingly rapid implosions which took place in the six years 1884-1890 shocked the bewildered inhabitants of the island. In a few short years the Sultan of Zanzibar lost his former dominions in the East African hinterland and all but lost Zanzibar, which became a British Protectorate, with a Sultan in name only. The old slave markets were closed and the slave trade extinguished. The West introduced their ideologies and administrative systems and British and Indian civil servants replaced the Sultan's holy men, chiefs and favourites. Bureaucracy trumped word of mouth as new government ministries sprang up with paperwork and accountants. Efficiency and accountability were the new watchwords, concepts previously unknown in the former palace regime of the Sultan.

Peera Dewjee arrived in Bombay aboard the BISNCo's steamer *Mecca* at the end of April. He had been escorted on board on 9 April with instructions being given to the captain that while he was to allow Peera to have full liberty, he was not to let him leave the vessel till she arrived in Bombay. Peera, who received a first class passage, did not attempt to defy this order.[1] In Bombay, by instruction of the British Government, he was kept under police surveillance. However, the exile conditions were not adhered to severely and he had access to his friends and continued to conduct his business.

Mackinnon successfully interceded on his behalf with Euan-Smith and they reduced his deportation term to six months. Peera wrote a number of letters to Mackinnon during his exile in Bombay, which have survived and are amongst the Mackinnon Papers in SOAS, University of London.

The earliest of the letters is dated 25 June 1889. It reads in part:

Dear Sir,

Your kind and sympathetic note of the 7th just came to hand yesterday and once more I have to thank you from the bottom of my heart for all that you have done for my humble self. I took the liberty of again communicating my thanks to you by wire yesterday.

Your sentiments about H.H. the Sultan are also worthy of the goodness of your heart and I will not fail to apprise him of them as soon as I get back there. As regards this and my future relations towards Col. Smith, you may depend upon my following your sound and disinterested advice. At present a sort of anarchy prevails at Zanzibar and matters are pretty much as they have been since some time past but they may take a turn to the better before long, which will be a regular boon to us all.

From private accounts received by me, it seems that Bakashmar has acquired the greatest influence at the Zanzibar Court at present, but he is far from being popular.

Perhaps you will know this officer if I recall to your mind the part he played at the time of Sir Bartle Frere's Mission to Zanzibar as well as Dr Badger. Had it not been for the difficulties he then created perhaps the present trouble from the Germans would never have come. Syed Burgash knew all this and had seen fit to put him down and it was during his degradation that the late Mr. Mackenzie was able to conclude his business in Mombasa.[2] Perhaps you will mention all this to Col. Smith for his information and guidance.

General Mathews also privately writes to me to say that he has got a C.M.G. for which are all very glad but he also complains of Bakashmar's ill will towards him.

I shall write to you from time to time and keep you posted up to all the passing events.

Meanwhile believe me to remain always at your service.

The next letter is dated 4 October and is headed 'Samuel Street, Khoja Moholla, Bombay.' In it Peera thanked Mackinnon most effusively for his letter dated 4 September, which contained the news of his imminent release. He said he had already been in touch with his wife by telegraph, informing her he was coming home soon. This is one of the rare hints of domesticity from Peera Dewjee: to mention his wife in writing was unusual in the Muslim society he frequented.

He devoted the rest of the letter to shipping news and gossip. He professed himself glad to hear the BI line was proposing a direct mail service link between Zanzibar and Bombay, but warned that the Germans were also thinking of opening a direct mail service. He said he had learnt this from a Mr Wolff of the German East Africa Company who had visited Bombay on the ship *Harmonic*.[3] He had offered Peera employment, but he had turned it down. The captain of the *Harmonic*, a friend formerly in the service of the Sultan, had given him the interesting news that Sewa Haji had visited Berlin and Hamburg to ask for an Africa-based shipping line and the Germans were now thinking about it.[4]

Peera then wrote about the Sultan's steamers: how both the SS *Murka* and *Malacca* were soon to be condemned leaving only the *Avoca* and *Swordsman* fit for service, the *Kilwa* and *Barawa* being too small for the Bombay to Zanzibar run, while the *Nyanza* was the Sultan's fancy boat remaining always in Zanzibar harbour. The Sultan's ships needed replacing and updating with new technology and he had recently seen Haji Bakashmar in Bombay, trying to buy a new steamer for the Sultan. He gave assurances to Mackinnon that, if on his return he got his old job back as agent for the Sultan's Shipping office, he would work quite in harmony with Mr Nicol, Mackinnon's agent in Zanzibar. He said he was right now helping the BI line by filling it up with his own cargo and that of his friends, and was worried that if the Sultan got wind of this, as his steamers ran in competition with the BI Line, he might not get his job back.[5]

On 29 October 1889 the Secretary of State for Foreign affairs wrote to the Government of Bombay requesting that Peera Dewjee be released from police surveillance and granted permission to return to Zanzibar after November 30.[6]

After this news Peera wrote one final letter to Mr Mackinnon just before leaving for Zanzibar dated 15 November 1889.

> I was very anxious to meet Mr Mackenzie[7] and Col Euan-Smith at Aden and I am as yet without any reply thereto although I have this afternoon received Mr Mackenzie's telegram informing me that instructions were

wired to the Bombay Govt for my early departure. But these instructions are too late as the mail leaves at 5 pm today...I have therefore resolved to start by the SS Avoca (of the Sultan line) leaving here about the 23rd Inst for Zanzibar direct, and I have this day written to Mr Mackenzie to make arrangement to take me to Col Euan-Smith for an interview on the same day I land on the shores of Zanzibar. And you will also be good enough to request him by telegram to kindly make this arrangement. I have again to repeat my heartfelt thanks at all the troubles you have taken and are still taking in my interest.

Peera's true character shines through in these letters, especially his energy and enthusiasm. He is a natural intelligence agent, eager to give out information and gather news. First he tells Mackinnon how he has turned down an offer of German employment and then indulges in a spot of industrial espionage, giving his benefactor the inside track on German intentions to start a new shipping line. He asked for an interview with Euan-Smith immediately on his return to Zanzibar, presumably to patch up hard feelings and reassure the British Consul he was now prepared to work with him. He even promised to cooperate with Smith Mackenzie's agent in Zanzibar, should he get his old job back. He promises to work for the English. Banishment to Bombay seemed to have worked its magic!

Meanwhile in Zanzibar, Major Wissmann had been having success in containing the mainland rebels and after fierce battles on the outskirts of Bagamoyo and Dar es Salaam, Abushiri was defeated and went on the run in July. The naval blockade was lifted and the Europeans decided to celebrate their success with an additional tightening of the rules regarding slavery. But Khalifa protested that a general abolition might cause unrest to break out again. Germany didn't want this, so they watered down the proposed measures with an announcement that all slaves brought to the islands after 1 November 1889 were henceforth free.

In August the Acting British Consul General, Gerald Portal, had organised the deportation of Bakashmar. The pious elderly Arab, now chief advisor to the Sultan, was accused of advising the Sultan to resist the anti-slavery measures and of assisting the rebels on the mainland.

He went without fuss, relief almost, taking all his family and valuables back to the Yemen. The charming and courteous Arab, who had been so friendly with Rigby and Playfair in the earlier days, had become increasingly angry and extreme in his Muslim views, hating all Europeans and the changes they had brought in the region. But he, like Peera, would soon return to Zanzibar.[8]

December 1889 saw the return to Zanzibar of both Peera Dewjee and the British Consul General Euan-Smith. Peera arrived on 6 December[9] and Col Smith a few days earlier. In his luggage, Euan-Smith had brought with him a present from Queen Victoria to the Sultan; the insignia of the Commander of St Michael and St George. The medal was conferred on the Sultan in a ceremony in front of the English and German naval commanders, a large crowd of Europeans and all the Arab nobles and Indian grandees. Khalifa was much gratified. Indeed, as the Consul noted he had never seen him so 'genuinely pleased.' Relations between the two were more cordial for a while.

Euan-Smith attributed the improved relations

> entirely to the removal of Peera Dewjee and Bakashmar and to the certainty which HH feels that he must rely entirely on England…Peera Dewjee has returned to Zanzibar. He is much subdued and there is I think, for the present, little chance that he will succeed in regaining, or indeed that he will endeavour to regain, his former position of confidence with the Sultan.[10]

Having lost his two most trusted advisors, Khalifa now relied on the judgement of Sheikh Abdulaziz b. Abdulghany, former *Khadi* of Zanzibar under Barghash, who had become his closest personal friend. He signed and wrote most of the letters from Sultan Khalifa to the British Consul Euan-Smith after the fall of Peera Dewjee and Bakashmar. But Euan-Smith soon saw him as an enemy and wanted to remove him. He accused him of reporting all the daily correspondence between the Sultan and the British agency to the Germans and said he had been the chief architect behind the notorious public executions and now stood in the way of anti-slavery reforms.

The rapprochement between Khalifa and Euan-Smith was short lived. As soon as the Consul started pushing for more slavery regulations, relations cooled. The British wanted a law awarding freedom to all slave children born in Zanzibar after 1 January 1890, but Khalifa pointed out that, if it was enforced, the children would be abandoned by their owners. He warned that if the British forced a total abolition of slavery, the Arabs would send all their slaves to the English officials in Zanzibar leaving them to provide the freemen with support and employment. Khalifa dug his heels in, became stubborn and refused to agree to any more reforms. In frustration Euan-Smith adopted his bullying, hectoring tone once more. The intrigues started up again as supporters of Seyyid Ali and Suleiman bin Hamid, his uncle (who had been to England with Barghash), schemed with the British Consul hoping to overthrow the unpopular Khalifa.

The Bushiri rebellion on the mainland was crushed when Abushiri was captured and hanged on 15 December at Bagamoyo. Whilst being interrogated by his German captors before he was hanged, the doomed Arab said Sultan Khalifa had encouraged his resistance and had promised to recognize him as governor of all the mainland territories if he achieved victory over the Germans. There was also a mysterious box containing documents of a treasonable nature, which was captured with him. In it were letters from Mackinnon and his agent W J Nicol addressed to H M Stanley indicating an acute hostility to Germany and a plan to shut off the Germans from the interior, showing that IBEACo did not act always in accordance with the friendly professions of the home government.[11] The British and German governments made a pact to keep the contents of Abushiri's box and his last confessions secret so as not to stir up renewed trouble in the region.

Khalifa's unexpected death came on 13 February 1890. He had gone to Chukwani Palace a few days earlier for a rest and some shooting, but on his return to town he suddenly ran a high temperature and appeared to be suffering from heat-stroke and died.[12] His death certainly sounds suspicious, but at the time no questions were asked and his brother Ali succeeded him quickly and quietly.

Euan-Smith reported Khalifa's death was 'unregretted by all.' Khalifa has received a bad press from most historians, probably due to their overwhelmingly Western bias. Although not an attractive or strong figure, he appears to have done his best to withstand the tide from Europe sweeping over his former territories and to uphold his Muslim principles.

Ali was the last surviving son of Seyyid Said. He had been born in Muscat just before the death of his father and was aged about 36 years old when he succeeded Khalifa. If anything, he had an even weaker character than his brother and accepted the status quo and did whatever the British Consul, Euan-Smith, told him. He made very little attempt to stand up to European demands and appeared fatalistic in his acceptance of a greater force.

Perpetually harried by the European powers demanding more and more treaties to extend their power and restrict slavery, Ali grew tired and dispirited and lost favour with his subjects. The Germans wished to buy their sphere of influence outright and stop paying rent based on the customs duties they received. When they offered the paltry sum of £100,000, Ali asked the German consul if he thought the Sultan's domains were like a camel to be bought and sold in a few minutes. But then, with typical resignation, Sultan Ali said: 'I am in the hands of God. If it is to be that the great Emperor of Germany will take my dominions from me, I am weak, and cannot help myself.' The British interceded on his behalf and the Germans made a final offer of £200,000 and with that Ali had to be content.[13] A grief-stricken Ali poured out his woes to Euan-Smith, who by now had complete control over him, and used the opportunity to suggest he put himself and what was left of his Kingdom under British protection. Ali agreed saying if God and the English deserted him all was lost.[14] A British protectorate over Zanzibar was declared on 7 November 1890.

Succumbing to the overpowering European presence, Sultan Ali no longer bothered to consult, even as a formality, with his Arab chiefs. The leading Arabs became increasingly annoyed about the sweeping changes being put in place by the English and Germans, without their consent, and they began to murmur and plot. Arendt, the German consul, who had returned after an absence of two years, terrified the Sultan, while Euan-Smith bludgeoned him into submission. He weakly acceded to all their demands. Ali, who had seemed intelligent and active before becoming Sultan, was reported, according to the *Times of India*, to be looking 'a little aged and much careworn.'

> His chief pleasure seems to be to enlarge the domain of his harem, and people it with as many Georgian and Circassian girls as he possibly can collect together. Even very recently a batch of some half a dozen such girls was reported as being brought from Jeddah or some such place. There is no wonder, then that he should not have that sprightliness about him that he had in his hard times. It is said that he has already pledged himself to the English government for the total abolition of slavery in the town and island of Zanzibar at least and it now remains to be seen when a final blow is dealt to this nefarious traffic here.[15] There is another thing which may be mentioned against the Sultan and that is that he has now turned adrift his former friends and adherents – men who stood faithful by him and did him yeoman's service at a time when he sorely stood in need of it. But gratitude is an element in human character that is conspicuous in these days by its almost entire absence, and the Arab character is no exception.[16]

Peera Dewjee does not seem to have had a close relationship with Ali, who distanced himself from his brother's former advisors and friends and had little interest in business. The Sultan's steamers lay rotting in the harbour while Ali, already suffering from signs of tuberculosis, abandoned himself to pleasure and oblivion. His favourite companion was Chatubhai, the son of Ibji Sewji, one of the rich Hindu merchants of Zanzibar,[17] while his chief advisor was his uncle Suleiman bin Hamid, a corrupt and grasping individual.[18] Peera Dewjee kept a low profile, avoiding the British Consul Euan-Smith whose influence now reigned supreme at the palace.

The port and customs management were now so chaotic that, as a measure to stem the exodus of merchants and trade from Zanzibar to the new mainland ports under European control, it was suggested Zanzibar be made a duty-free zone. Only with the attraction of being a free port could Zanzibar continue to profit as a transit and collection point and take advantage of the infrastructure already in place. British personnel were hired to oversee port operations and in October 1890, H Robertson took over the reorganisation of the customs administration. Zanzibar was duly declared a free port on 1 February 1892 and the economy started to improve. At the ceremony, which the Sultan did not attend, only the British flag flew and not the Zanzibari flag: a sign of how times had changed.

Charles Bean Euan-Smith, the almost exact contemporary of Peera Dewjee,[19] left Zanzibar in 1891 and was replaced by Gerald Portal, who arrived in August. After Dr Kirk, Colonel Euan-Smith was the most influential and effective British Consul of the period. He completed the work started by Bartle Frere and Kirk, pushing through important measures to end slavery and presiding over the formation of a British Protectorate of Zanzibar. He also oversaw the final break-up of the mainland territories of the Sultan, which were shared out amongst the major European powers. His proudest moment was the decree of August 1890, masterminded by himself, which he claimed settled the whole question of slavery in the Zanzibar dominions.[20] This he counted as a personal triumph.

'Tea Party' Smith, Euan-Smith was an ambitious social climber, with a penchant for luxurious living and splendour. Originally plain Mr Smith, he added Euan to his name to make it sound more distinguished. With his military training and background in India, he was used to giving orders and got his way by bulldozing his opponents into agreement, rather than by more subtle diplomatic tactics. His imperious and bullying manner made many enemies, but he served British interests well and achieved what he set out to do. Zanzibar proved to be the pinnacle of his career and his next posting ended in failure. Appointed ambassador to Morocco, he was relieved of his post in 1893, having upset the King of Morocco badly with his arrogant behaviour. He had treated the King as if he were just a vassal Indian princeling to be ordered about at will. A photograph taken in 1893 shows him in full court dress, his chest plastered with glittering medals. Peera Dewjee, no doubt, felt vindicated when he heard how

Euan-Smith had met his just deserts, and must have reflected on how the man's overweening pride and conceit had led to his downfall.

Unpopular though he was, nevertheless the name of the British Consul remained indelibly imprinted upon Zanzibar with the foundation of the Euan-Smith Madrassa. This school aimed to provide a modern system of education for Muslim children and opened on 1 January 1891 under the direction of an Indian headmaster trained at Bombay University. There were already several missionary-run schools catering to Christians, but none for Muslims. The principle donors were Tharia Topan, the Aga Khan, and Seyyid Ali, while local Indian merchants funded the remainder of the costs. It was named after the Consul in recognition of the leading role he had taken in stimulating the Indian merchants to give donations for the school! During the early years of its existence most of the pupils came from the Ismaili Khoja community, which was the first Muslim community in Zanzibar to appreciate the advantages of a western style education. The Madrassa offered four years of instruction. In the first two years classes were taught in English and Gujarati and during the final two, all classes were in English. The teachers reported that the children, mostly born in Zanzibar, had difficulty with both languages since they normally spoke only Swahili at home and at play.[21]

With Gerald Herbert Portal,[22] the successor to Euan-Smith, a new era dawned and Zanzibar learned what it was to be a British Protectorate. Fired by his experience in the strict bureaucracy of Cromer's Egyptian service, Portal oversaw a massive assault on the existing Arab system of government, which he described as hardly a government at all but 'an embodiment of all the worst and most barbarous characteristics of a primitive Arab despotism.'[23] In a far-reaching programme of reorganisation, he dismissed all the palace hangers-on and Arab officials and set up new departments of administration headed by Britons and British Indians. Gone was the old casual financial management of the palace, where the Sultan kept the treasury of the kingdom under his bed and government wages were paid out in embroidered shawls, jewels and favourable business contracts. Sultan Ali was now awarded a fixed annual sum, amounting to about one third of the state's total revenues for the expenses of his household. All other revenues went into the British-supervised treasury. Sultan Ali regretted his lost independence. But Portal's timely and energetic intervention came just in time as Zanzibar's economic survival hung in the balance, as trade migrated to the European controlled mainland ports. His overhaul of government administration and creation of a free port ensured the island sultanate remained a profitable and sustainable enterprise for years to come. However, his policy of utilizing Western-educated members of the Indian community, while neglecting the Swahili and other African inhabitants, sowed the seeds of trouble for the future.

----

1 *Times of India*, May 11, 1889, article entitled 'The Zanzibar Intrigues'
2 This refers to E N Mackenzie, who with Archibald Smith formed the agency Smith, Mackenzie & Co, in Zanzibar in 1877. They were agents for Mackinnon's British India Steamship Navigation Co and were thus closely involved with the formation of the British East Africa Company. After Archibald Smith's death in 1882, Mackenzie headed the company. He died from malaria in Zanzibar in 1888, soon after returning from a trip with General Mathews to reconnoitre the country behind Mombasa. His deputy J W Buchanan then took over and was sent from Zanzibar to set up a base in Mombasa and he and his young assistant W J W Nicol took turns on Mombasa Island, each for a month at a time.
3 I cannot find a reference to this ship. Usually ships with names ending in 'ic' were White Star Line.
4 DOAL, Deutsch Ost-Afrika Linie, was formed April 19, 1890. It was a joint venture of the companies C Woermann, F Laeisz, August Bolten and Hansing & Co. The first weekly trips to Bombay and Zanzibar started in 1892. The company still operates in East Africa today.
5 Mackinnon papers, SOAS
6 IOR/L/PJ/6/263 file 1934, 'Return to Zanzibar of BI subject deported to Bombay last April'
7 This is George S Mackenzie, chief administrator of the Imperial British East Africa Company.
8 Mohammed Mohammed Bakashmar's long career with the Sultans

of Zanzibar started under Seyyid Said. Originally from Yemen, he first of all worked in the service of Thuweini, who because of his usefulness recommended him to his father Seyyid Said, under whose service he first came to Zanzibar. He looked after court finances for Majid, Barghash and Khalifa and became a very wealthy man in his own right. While in exile in Eastern Arabia, he found solace in the reform movement coming out of Egypt and Syria, which was introducing new modes of Islamic ideology in response to the intellectual challenges posed by the Christian West. He came back to Zanzibar and began to teach and introduce these ideas helping to modernise the beliefs of the next generation of Sunni Muslims in East Africa and give them tools to withstand the onward march of Christianity in the region. Randall L Pouwels, *Horn & Crescent: Cultural Change and Traditional Islam on the East African Coast, 800-1900*, Cambridge: Cambridge University Press, 2002, p 169-171

9 *Birmingham Daily Post*, December 7, 1889: 'Zanzibar, December 6 – Peera Dewjee who was ordered to leave Zanzibar at the beginning of last April, and to remain for a certain time in Bombay for intriguing against the authorities, returned here today on board the Sultan's steamer *Avoca*.'

10 FO 84/1982, p 143-46

11 FO 244/470, 244/471

12 Genesta Hamilton, *Princes of Zinj: The Rulers of Zanzibar,* London: Hutchinson, 1957, p 204

13 This offer was agreed on September 25, 1890

14 Hamilton, *Princes of Zinj*, p 205-6

15 Announced in the decree of August 1, 1890

16 *Times of India*, July 9, 1890, 'Zanzibar notes (from a Correspondent) Zanzibar June 28'

17 *Samachar* Newspaper, 1929, Jubilee edition

18 According to Genesta Hamilton, *Princes of Zinj*, p 230

19 He was born in 1842 and died in 1910.

20 It prohibited altogether the buying and selling of slaves and gave slaves the right to buy their freedom at a fair price without the necessity of receiving their owners consent. Unsurprisingly the decree proved controversial and its contents were largely ignored, but the onward march towards total abolition gathered pace as the impoverished Zanzibar Arabs could no longer afford the luxury of slaves and economic necessity forced them to reduce their reliance upon slave labour.

21 Norman R Bennett, *A History of the Arab State of Zanzibar*, London: Methuen, p 172

22 Gerald Portal born in 1858 was Consul in Zanzibar from 1891-3. He left in January 1893 on a mission to Buganda for the Foreign Office and died in England in 1894 at the early age of 36 from an illness contracted on the Uganda expedition. His papers are preserved in Rhodes House Library in Oxford.

23 Bennett, *A History of the Arab State of Zanzibar*, p 167-8

Chapter Fifteen

The Return of Peera

On his return Peera found Zanzibar a changed place. Adapting to circumstances, at the age of almost 50 he found himself working for an English company.

W J W Nicol writing to Sir William Mackinnon in a letter dated 22 February 1892 reported that 'Peera Dewjee joined Forwood Bros, under pressure from Colonel Euan-Smith in 1890 and now works entirely for them and practically manages their business here now that Mr Robertson has gone home.'[1]

Forwood Bros & Co was a Liverpool shipping and trading company headed by two brothers, Arthur and William Forwood (after 1885 two more brothers and a nephew joined). They were an extremely successful family of merchants and ship owners, who had offices in London, New York, New Orleans and Bombay and also owned the Morocco quay in London, where some of their sailings terminated. They had originally made their money from the cotton trade. When the American Civil War disrupted the cotton trade, the brothers made a fortune, first from wartime speculation and blockade running, and then from exploiting telegraph and cotton futures.

Sir Arthur Bower Forwood (1836-1898) the elder brother became a politician and was appointed financial secretary to the Admiralty, a post he held from 1887-92. He was the first commercial ship owner to become an Admiralty minister. The younger brother Sir William Bower Forwood (1840-1928) devoted himself to civic affairs becoming a Liverpool city councillor, Mayor of Liverpool and eventually High Sheriff of Lancashire. He was also a director of the Cunard Line from 1888. Both brothers had retired from direct involvement in trade by 1890, when Peera Dewjee became an employee, though they retained important business interests.

Arthur and William Forwood were managing directors of the West India and Pacific Steamship Company and of a line of mail steamers known as the Atlas Steamship Company. They were also involved in the coal bunkering trade and owned the Mersey Steamship Company, which operated out of Dartmouth. Coal was an essential commodity for Zanzibar, as they did not produce their own. Aden was the nearest coaling station and Sultan Barghash had his own storage facility in Zanzibar as he needed huge amounts of coal for running his steamships and operating his various mechanical gadgets. The Royal Naval ships also depended on a regular supply of coal.

Both Forwood brothers were resolute champions of the Empire and keen to exploit new business opportunities in British overseas territories. In 1890 the Forwoods, at the request of the Sultan, took on a contract to re-organise the Customs House and Port in Zanzibar and sent out their man, Hugh C Robertson to head the project.[2]Robertson became Director of the Port and Customs in 1890, once the British Protectorate was formally declared. He also started a Zanzibar agency for Forwood Bros & Co, with the assistance of two other employees Roland Thomas and Francis Campin. Peera Dewjee was assigned to Forwoods to work with Robertson and help him sort out the management and operations of the port to make it a more profitable and efficient enterprise. Peera, who knew the ins and outs of the port and customs in Zanzibar like the back of his hand, was the ideal man for the job and his expertise was invaluable. When Zanzibar became a free port in 1892, it injected new life into the declining economy of the island.[3]

Forwood Bros & Co also founded a local newspaper for Zanzibar, the *Gazette for Zanzibar and East Africa*, usually referred to as the *Zanzibar Gazette*. The first edition came out on 1 February 1892, the same day as the Free Port declaration, and was priced at one anna. It was the first newspaper to be produced in East Africa. The British Consul Gerald Portal gave it his enthusiastic support and one cannot help suspecting Peera Dewjee had a hand in its production. With his keen interest in communication and newspapers it was, quite possibly, his idea. It came out on a weekly basis, every Wednesday, and had articles and advertisements in Gujarati and Arabic as well as in English. When Forwood Bros closed their Zanzibar office,[4] the Zanzibar Government took over the *Gazette* on 22 October 1894 and it became the first official gazette to be published in the East African territories. The *Zanzibar Gazette* served as a mouthpiece for the government and it publicised government announcements and legal notices.

It was printed on sheets of poor quality paper measuring roughly 12 x 9 inches and illustrations were rare. The advertisement section contained announcements by shipping lines, merchants, insurance agencies, safari outfitters as well as descriptions of proprietary brands of imported food, drink, clothing and medicaments. The Bombay-recruited staff printed the paper with creditable regularity despite the frequent mechanical hitches of the printing presses and the multiplicity of languages.

The first editor of the *Gazette* was Francis Campin, the managing director of Forwood Bros in Zanzibar and sponsor of the paper. He was followed in May 1894 by his colleague Arthur Marsden, and from October 1894 onwards by a succession of government officials. Simon Figueira maintained continuity when he took over the production management of the *Gazette* from Campin in 1893. Trade reports, statistics and prospects occupied a prominent place in the newspaper as one of its main functions was to promote business in Zanzibar and to provide trading companies with a medium for advertising their wares.[5]

The *Zanzibar Gazette* is also a marvellous source of information about life in Zanzibar at the end of the nineteenth century. As a prominent Indian grandee and citizen of Zanzibar, Peera Dewjee is often mentioned and the newspaper provides a wealth of documentary evidence for Peera Dewjee's later life.

For instance, in August 1892 we hear Peera's eldest son Abdulhussein Peera was sent to boarding school in England. He was the first Zanzibari to receive an education in England and set a precedent for others to follow. Sultan Hamoud sent his son Ali to Harrow School a few years later.

> Khoja Peera Dewjee (who was for many years in the service of HH
> Sayid Bargash) in sending his eldest son Abdulhussein to England to be
> educated has set an example, which would be to the benefit of Zanzibar if
> followed by other leading British Indian residents...Abdulhussein Peera is
> the first Indian youth sent from Zanzibar to England for his education: he
> enters Sir Anthony Browne's School at Brentwood (Essex).[6]

Abdulhussein went to England in the charge of Roland Thomas, the retiring representative of Forwoods, leaving Zanzibar on 3 August 1892, and travelling by the French Messageries Maritime Ship, SS *Amazone*. Not surprisingly, Peera Dewjee did not subscribe to the Euan-Smith Madrassa School, when there was a funds drive that August. In an article dated 24 August in the *Zanzibar Gazette* it described teething problems at the school, as boys were withdrawn to help in their fathers' shops and missed school on feast days and so got no opportunity to learn. There was a plea to give the teachers more cooperation.

According to the records of the Sir Anthony Browne's school (now called Brentwood School), Abdulhussein attended for just over two years from September 1892 until the end of 1894. In July 1893 he was awarded a special prize for boys above average age of form and he played in the 1894 school football and cricket teams. There is a photograph of the cricket XI of 1894, which shows him seated next to the captain and wearing a striped blazer and cap. He looks to be about 14 or 15 years of age. He is last mentioned in school records as being in the Christmas play, for December 1894, when he was cast as the tinker, Tom Snout, in Shakespeare's *A Midsummer Night's Dream*.[7]

Whether or not Forwood Bros, or even Sir William Mackinnon himself helped with school fees, is unknown, but it is a possibility, especially as Peera Dewjee had cash flow problems. Where Abdulhussein stayed during school holidays is also unknown, but a German source records that Peera Dewjee sent his eldest son to school in England and to be trained in business with the Manchester merchant William Birch junior.[8] In 1894 Peera Dewjee founded the family firm of Abdool

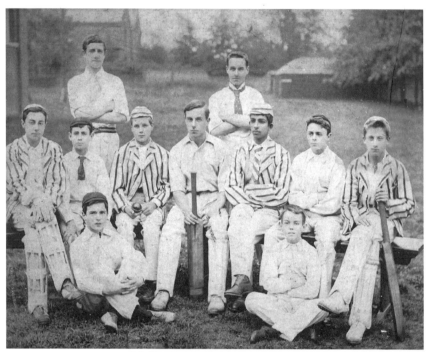
Abdulhussein Peera on the cricket team

Hoossein Bros & Co.[9] It operated as a commission agency, imported cotton goods and general merchandise from Manchester, London and Europe, and exported African produce. The first business they represented was the Manchester Shipping Company of William Birch Jr & Co Ltd.[10]

Peera Dewjee's new career with Forwoods, though it started promisingly, did not last long. Roland Thomas, who headed the Forwoods agency in Zanzibar, had been sympathetic to Peera and recognised how important the Indian merchants were for Zanzibar. He helped set up the Zanzibar Chamber of Commerce in 1892 and recommended Indian merchants should be represented on the main committee, which was duly done. But after his departure his colleagues, Campin and Marsden, quickly fell out with Peera.

In December 1892 Peera's younger brother, Rashid, was declared bankrupt.[11] In January 1893 the Clan Line ship SS *Clan Macleod* docked with 320 tons of iron water pipes to improve the water supply in Zanzibar town. These were under the agency of Forwood Bros and the pipes were discharged in record time. It was reported that Khoja Peera Dewjee and the Sultan were amongst the guests entertained on board. It was a moment of success for Peera but the next month disturbing notices appeared in the *Gazette*. Peera Dewjee had been sacked and his connection with Forwoods abruptly ended.

The first notice dated 15 February read:

> The connection hitherto existing between ourselves and Khoja Peera Dewjee ceases from this date. Khoja Peera Dewjee is no longer authorised to transact business or to receive money on behalf of our firm Forwood Bros. & Co.

A second dated 22 February read:

> We hearby give notice that in regard to any money due on goods sold by Peera Dewjee during the last two years, we hold the debtors liable to ourselves. Any payments made after this date to Peera Dewjee will be made at the debtor's risk.

Campin accused Peera Dewjee of misappropriation of company funds and his trial by the Consular Court in Zanzibar began on May before Judge de Sausmarez. In the *Zanzibar Gazette* issue for 31 May 1893 there was a full account of the court case *Forwood Bros & Co v Peera Dewjee*, which attracted a great deal of interest from local merchants. Campin gave evidence that he had found his account book short of Rs 160.12.0 and accused Peera of fiddling the books. There was then some confusion as Peera's clerk Dewji Canji first said he had collected the money and handed it over to Peera and then denied doing so. Peera employed Canji to collect money in the bazaar and he relied on Canji to account for it, first of all in a rough ledger and then written up as a fair copy – all in Gujarati. He, Peera, then used to take the fair copy to Campin in his office, with the cash and translate the list of collections into English for him. On this particular occasion the cash did not tally with the collections listed. Under further questioning the clerk Canji then admitted that Peera was in the habit of borrowing money from the collections temporarily and then paying it back (Thomas the former rep had allowed him to do this). Peera defended himself by saying that Campin too had manipulated the books on a number of occasions. The final judgement of the court was that Peera had no right to retain monies of the firm even temporarily to suit his convenience and he was ordered to pay back the amount claimed with costs.

The amount of money involved was not large, but the point of principle was clear. The case is interesting as it illustrates how business was done in Zanzibar at this date. Peera, with his background of service with the Sultan, was accustomed to more flexible accounting practices and a less rigid attention to exactitude; while the Englishman Campin expected a degree of subservience and obedience from a company employee, which Peera found intolerable. Working for a European did not suit him, as he had been used to running his own business and enjoying a far greater amount of independence. Campin's lawsuit brought against Peera revealed that their working relationship had broken down and that there was animosity between the two men. It is another example of Peera's feisty character and his refusal to be cowed by those in authority.

The fall out with Forwoods did not hinder Peera as he quickly found employment elsewhere, which was more to his liking. In April 1893 the new Sultan Hamed asked Peera to be his shipping agent in charge of the Sultan's steamers. He had his old job back and a Sultan he could work with once more.

Sultan Ali had died on 5 March 1893 at the age of 38, according to the report in the *Zanzibar Gazette*, as a result of diseases of the liver, dropsy and general debility, leaving no will and having made no provision for his children. He was the last of the sons of Said to rule in Zanzibar and as he lay dying there was a resurgence of plots and counter-plots as three claimants made a bid for the Sultanate. The English favoured Seyyid Hamed bin Thuweini, a son of Said's eldest son. He had been banished to India after an unsuccessful attempt to usurp his uncle Turki as Sultan of Oman. He was also forced to divorce his wife, the Seyyida Turkiyeh, the daughter of Turki, who was then married off to another of her cousins. Hamed, after a suitable period of exile in Bombay, was allowed to settle in Zanzibar and married Barghash's eldest daughter, Nunu, as his second wife. In 1893, he was aged about 40, a seemingly mature and intelligent man, who in the opinion of the British was the most suitable candidate. Khalid, Barghash's son also wanted to be Sultan. He was aged about 16 at this time, but was discounted as an immature and unruly teenager. The third claimant was Hamoud bin Mohammed, a nephew of Thuweini, but he was unambitious and content to abide by the decision of the British who duly proclaimed Hamed bin Thuweini Sultan of Zanzibar.

Like his father before him, young Khalid bin Barghash had a fiery temperament and he tried to stage a *coup d'état* and seize the palace. One of the princesses, who supported his claim, opened a back door to let him in with his followers, but General Mathews had been pre-warned and was prepared for trouble. Within an hour Mr Rennell Rodd, the British Consul, and Captain Campbell RN came marching into the square at the head of 160 sailors and marines from the ships *Philomel* and *Blanche.* They mounted a machine-gun outside the palace and summoned the young prince to surrender and leave the palace. Khalid accepted his defeat and was put under house arrest. No-one took the attempted coup seriously and within two days he was restored to his place in Sultan Hamed's court.[12]

It is likely Peera Dewjee supported Hamed's claim. Certainly he was quickly rewarded with the return of his old job and a position at court.

> H.H. the Sultan of Zanzibar's ship SS Avoca will sail for Muscat calling at the Benadir Coast. For cargo and passengers apply to Peera Dewjee, Agent H.H. Sultan of Zanzibar.[13]

Sultan Hamed's brief reign (1893-1896) is chiefly remembered for the collapse of the Imperial British East Africa Company (IBEACo), and its buy-out by the British Government using money originally paid to the Sultan. In 1890 when the Germans took over the sector of the coast allotted to them, they had paid Sultan Ali £200,000. This money was invested in British Government bonds and after Ali's death and the declaration of the British Protectorate, the stock was transferred from the ownership of the Sultan to that of the Government of Zanzibar (its treasury department now manned by British officials). In March 1894 the Foreign Office proposed that this money be used to compensate the shareholders of the IBEACo, who had suffered heavy losses, and buy the company out as it evidently was not fit for purpose. In May 1894 Arthur Hardinge, the newly arrived British Consul, was instructed to tell the Sultan that the British Government wished the Zanzibar Government to re-purchase IBEACo for the sum of £150,000 – and also buy the Company's buildings, ships, etc. for the remaining £50,000. General Mathews, now First Minister for Zanzibar, and Consul Hardinge assumed this meant the British administered coastal belt would revert to being part of Zanzibar. Seyyid Hamed was delighted with the prospect of regaining a portion of his former dominions and nobody regretted parting with Zanzibar's nest-egg of £200,000. But then the news came back from the Foreign Office that this transaction did not mean the coastal strip had been returned to Zanzibar, but instead that it would now be administered by the British Government directly.

Despite protests and letters to point out that the Zanzibar Government might well have preferred to use their money for public works on the island rather than bailing out a private company, which would give no benefit whatsoever to Zanzibar, the Foreign Office remained adamant in its decision. Consul Hardinge had the unpleasant task of breaking the news to Sultan Hamed who in reply uttered his famous words of helpless defeat. 'So be it! I am merely a little bird in the claws of an eagle.'

The British now had the Sultan's coast and the money as well. As a sop to his wounded pride, Sultan Hamed asked that his monthly civil list be increased: 'my body is covered with sores; you can procure the ointment to heal them.' The Foreign Secretary did sanction a small increase in his allowance, but it was hardly sufficient for the state he was expected to maintain, and nothing could soothe his disappointment and sense of betrayal.[14]

Sultan Hamed never forgave the British Government for what he considered had been a piece of sharp practice. He became suspicious and difficult to deal with. He fell under the influence of an Arab advisor named Sheikh Hilal bin Amari, who hated the English and took every opportunity to foster the Sultan's bitterness against them. Hamed surrounded himself with bodyguards and a private army of nearly 1,000 armed men and liked to watch them drill in the square under his balcony. Fights broke out between his personal soldiers and the British-trained regulars of the Zanzibar armed forces. Taking a leaf out of Euan-Smith's book, Hardinge eventually decided that Hilal's influence was becoming a danger to British interests and deported him to Aden. The Sultan was furious but was powerless and during the final year of his reign he turned increasingly to the company of his old friend Peera Dewjee, who was reinstated as his chief steward.

The British Government formally took over the administration in the British sphere on 15 June 1895 and there is a well-known photograph which probably marks this occasion showing a scowling Hamed seated between General Mathews and Arthur Hardinge with four of his Arab officials standing behind.[15] Either the Arab in a splendid Persian robe standing just behind the Sultan to the left or more possibly the fierce looking Arab with a large black beard at his right hand could be Hilal bin Amari. It is interesting to contrast this picture with the one of Barghash taken with his councillors in 1875, just twenty years previously, to see how the role of Sultan had changed. In 1875 Tharia Topan, the Indian merchant, had pushed himself forward amongst the reluctant Arabs in the back row. By 1895 the Sultan was hemmed in by British officials, with Arabs at the back as window dressing and the Indian presence had vanished.

During 1893 Peera Dewjee managed the Sultan's steamship line. In July the Sultan bought SS *Henry Wright*[16] and renamed her *Chueni* after his palace. But his acute shortage of funds meant he couldn't update his ships or make the additions necessary to compete with other shipping lines. In an effort to make a profit Peera Dewjee, who styled himself 'Agent of H H Sultan's line of steamers' placed an announcement in the *Gazette* concerning overweight bags of cloves; double freight would in future be charged on bags weighing more than 40 lbs. Despite enforcing these strict measures, the Sultan's shipping line continued to lose money and sometime in 1894 Peera Dewjee handed over to the House of Keshavji Damodar Jairam, who is reported as being the agent for the Sultan's line of steamers in the *Gazette* for 31 October 1894. In November 1894 the *Nyanza* lost her propeller while the Sultan was on board returning from a visit to Chukwani Palace. Expensive repairs were needed and in December the Sultan suffered further losses when heavy squalls damaged shipping in Zanzibar harbour.

From 1894 Peera Dewjee turned his attention to his own business and his increasingly demanding position as Chief Steward for the Sultan's household and major-domo for public entertainments on feast days. In 1895 a particularly elaborate show was put on to celebrate *Nairuz* or *Siku ya Mwaka*, Swahili New Year, which fell on 21 August that year. Peera Dewjee was chief organiser and the *Zanzibar Gazette* ran a long report about the festivities and its origins. The writer tells us how in former times (30 years previously) there used to be no law on this day – and a debtor could rid himself of his debts by murdering his creditor with no comeback. British Indians would remain closely shut up in their houses in fear and there were stories of Banyans who were drowned while they bathed in the sea by the slaves of someone they had lent money to. The custom was for everyone to go down to the sea and wash themselves and all their possessions to start afresh. Goats, sleeping mats as well as themselves were all washed in the sea. They then put on new clean clothes and paraded about the town looking for old quarrels to be settled. In 1895 this no longer happened; instead it was an excuse for a general party. The Sultan's band played at full blast in the palace square, there was a reception in the Customs House and the town was decorated with palms and hanging lamps.

Peera Dewjee was back in his old role of master of ceremonies, putting on grand banquets at the palace for important guests and organising ceremonial occasions, but he was no longer involved in the political direction and administration of Zanzibar as this had passed completely into British hands. In 1896 he started arranging entertainments for the Sultan's ladies. On 12 February there was a reception for Her Highness the Sultana, on 13 May there was a Grand Banquet for the Sultana's birthday and in July he organised a flower show.[17] The court ladies were beginning to emerge from strict purdah and become more visible in society. Such entertainments for Arab women would have been unheard of a few years previously. Barghash's daughter Nunu, the Sultana, must have known Peera well and appears to have been an outgoing personality, who was well-respected in her own right in Zanzibar. She was more sociable than her husband Sultan Hamed, who by this time had become paranoid about his own security. He had retreated from general view and lived closely guarded by his private bodyguards.

Hamed died suddenly on 25 August 1896 and Zanzibar was immediately thrown into a bitter succession dispute. Khalid, the only surviving son of Barghash, now aged 20, claimed to be the rightful heir and unilaterally declared himself Sultan. He had been plotting behind the scenes for some time and gathering support. His aunt, Bibi Zemzem,[18] one of the daughters of Said, had taken him under her wing after the death of his father and she encouraged him in his bid for the sultanate. The British authorities, however, did not think he would make a suitable sultan. Sir Gerald Portal, when asked to describe his character to the Earl of Rosebery at the Foreign office in 1892, had written that he was a truculent youth with all the temper and cruelty of his father without his intelligence.

> He is of a very sullen and very obstinate temperament, illiterate (in European languages) and inordinately proud. If he were Sultan, he would not only be extremely difficult to control but would very likely give rise to grave scandals by reason of acts of cruelty and oppression.[19]

In 1896 they had not changed their opinion of him. Hamoud bin

Mohammed was their favoured candidate. Hamoud bin Mohammed had little ambition for himself but wanted his son Ali to be educated in England and would do anything to make it happen. As the American consul Mohun pointed out in his consular despatches, Hamoud was a poor man without slaves or property, so would be easier for the British to control.[20]

The Zanzibar Government was at first caught on the back foot. Hamed died unexpectedly when the British Consul, Hardinge, was away on leave and his young assistant, Basil Cave,[21] left in charge. Khalid, with German backing, moved quickly to occupy the palace and declared himself Sultan at 4 pm that same day.

The *Glasgow* fired a royal salute, the palace guns answered and up went the red flag of Zanzibar on all the houses and foreign consulates. The British gave notice that Khalid was not the rightful heir and the flags were lowered again to half-mast (a sign of mourning). Zanzibar waited in suspense. Troops assembled at the Customs House under General Raikes;[22] two warships at anchor in the harbour HMS *Philomel* and *Thrush* ferried marines and bluejackets ashore to join the troops, while others went to guard the British Consulate where the European ladies had taken refuge. HMS *Sparrow* a British gunboat took up a position opposite the palace. By sunset Khalid had assembled 2,500 armed followers and deployed his artillery which consisted of two 12-pounder guns, one Gatling gun and one ancient Portuguese bronze cannon, vintage 1658. He despatched a letter to the American Consul announcing he was Sultan, but Consul Mohun replied in diplomatic speak, that as his accession had not been verified by Her Majesty's Government, it was impossible to reply.

The British Consul sent a message to Khalid asking him to leave the palace. He refused to do so. The Foreign Office, in reply to an urgent telegraph for instructions on what to do in such a situation, gave the consul the not very helpful advice of 'free leave to do as he thought best.'

The following morning two more Royal Navy ships arrived under the command of Rear Admiral Rawson, the gun boat HMS

Racoon and his flagship, the cruiser HMS *St George*. In the evening an ultimatum was sent to Khalid that unless his flag was down by 9 am on Thursday 27 August, the men-of-war would open fire. That evening the American Consul Mohun wrote how 'the silence which hung over Zanzibar was appalling. Usually drums were beating or babies cried but that night there was absolutely not a sound.'

Khalid remained defiant. He did not believe the British would fire their guns and thought it was a bluff. He trained his own guns on the *Glasgow* towards the British ships in retaliation and refused to back down. He had misjudged his opponents. At precisely 9 am *Racoon, Sparrow* and *Thrush* opened fire on the palace and harem. The *Glasgow* fired back but her outdated muzzle loading guns were no match for the breech loaders of the Royal Navy. Every five or ten minutes there was a cessation of fire to allow Khalid to lower his flag and surrender, but nothing happened. The *Glasgow* was holed and rapidly began to sink. Accurate shooting at point blank range brought down the front of the palace exposing the inner rooms. The harem was set alight and the palace square was left in ruins, covered with debris from flying shells and the bodies of dozens of Khalid's supporters, who had been killed or wounded. Khalid, terrified and at last realising all was lost, escaped out of a back door with a few of his followers and ran through the narrow streets to the German Consulate where Baron von Richenburg gave him political asylum. At 9.45 am his flag was shot down and the order to cease fire was given. So-called 'The Shortest War in History,' hostilities had lasted precisely 45 minutes. An hour later Hamoud was proclaimed Sultan. A 21-gun salute was fired from the Royal Navy ships and a large red flag was hung at the corner of the House of Wonders, which, though damaged, still remained mostly intact.[23]

The Sultan's palace (Beit al-Hukm) and the harem lay in ruins. Barghash's clock tower in the square had received a direct hit. Inside the palace, mirrors lay smashed and glass fragments from the chandeliers had fallen amongst the broken furniture and ruined Persian carpets. There was looting especially in the Indian quarter, with twenty people killed, before the Royal Navy was brought in to patrol the streets and restore calm. Khalid was taken to Dar es Salaam in the German warship *Seeadler* and the Germans gave him a large house so he could live in comfort and allowed him to fly the red flag of the Sultanate of Zanzibar. Unlike his father he never became Sultan.[24]

1 [58] Ibeaco, Mackinnon Papers, SOAS PP2

2 Hugh C Robertson went on leave in 1892 for six months but returned to his post later that year and was resident in Zanzibar until 1900. Stephen J North, *Europeans in British Administered East Africa: A Biographical listing 1888-1905*, Wantage, Oxon, Stephen J North, 2005

3 Import duties were abolished and so remained until 1899, when a 5 per cent import duty was re-imposed.

4 Forwood Bros sold its Zanzibar interests to Boustead Ridley & Co on November 15, 1894.

5 Information about the *Zanzibar Gazette* has been taken from an article by A T Matson, 'Early newspapers of East Africa,' *Kenya Weekly News*, July 14 and 21, 1961

6 *Zanzibar Gazette*, August 10, 1892. Abdulhussein's imminent arrival was also announced in the *Chelmsford Chronicle*, September 23, 1892.

7 Information received from the Headmaster's Secretary from the Records of Brentwood School.

8 Lutz J Schwidder, 'Das Hamburger Kolonialshandelshaus Wm O'Swald & Co und die Einfürung von Techniken in die Kolonien 1890-1914,' PhD thesis, University of Hamburg, 2004, p 118

9 See Somerset Playne, comp, and Frank Holderness Gale, ed, '*East Africa its History People, Commerce, Industries and Resources*', London: Foreign and Colonial Compiling and Publishing Co, 1908, p 419-20

10 William Birch junior (1835 - 1900) was both a popular Baptist preacher and a businessman. By all accounts he was a charismatic preacher and exceptionally kind and generous as a man. He set up orphanages and provided aid to poor millworkers and their families. He was born the son of a Wolverhampton builder and may have first met Peera in Manchester in 1875 when he was a prominent Liberal member of the City Council. By 1892 he had withdrawn from business altogether and dissolved his partnership in William Birch Jr & Co Ltd, to devote himself to his religious calling. The firm however continued to trade under his name until 1902 when it was declared bankrupt.

11 On December 21 there was a meeting of the creditors of Rashid Dewjee and on January 3, 1893, 'Rashid Dewjee above named insolvent' applied for his discharge.

12 Hamilton, *Princes of Zinj*, p 231-2

13 Notice in *Zanzibar Gazette*, April 12, 1893

14 Hamilton, *Princes of Zinj*, p 234

15 This photograph is sometimes wrongly attributed as showing Sultan Ali, but the British Consul Arthur Hardinge did not arrive in Zanzibar until in 1894, so it is likely that the occasion recorded is the occasion when the British Government took over from the IBEACo in what is now Kenya.

16 Launched in 1883 for the use of the Church Missionary Society in Zanzibar and named after one of the founders. It was a modest little wooden hulled steamship, 80 feet in length with a single funnel, and had been used as a troop transport in the Witu expedition of 1890.

17 See reports in the *Zanzibar Gazette*.

18 There is a description of Zemzem in Salme's *Memoirs of an Arabian Princess*. Zemzem like Barghash was born to an Abyssinian mother. Salme described her as very practical, not given to extravagance and fond of simplicity and solidity. She owned a plantation close to Salme's and was interested in farming and gave motherly advice to Salme. She married rather late in life a distant cousin called Humud, who according to Salme was an unpopular and stingy individual. The two sisters lost touch once Salme moved to Europe.

19 P J Frankl, 'Exile of Sayyid Khalid b. Barghash al-Busaidi', *British Journal of Middle Eastern Studies*, Vol 33, 2006, p 161-177; Portal to Rosebery, PRO FO/105/57

20 Bennett, *History of the Arab State of Zanzibar*, p 178-9

21 Basil Shillito Cave (1865-1931) arrived in Zanzibar in 1891 as private secretary to General Mathews but was appointed Vice Consul instead. He was made a Companion of the Order of Bath for his part in the Bombardment being the youngest holder of the order at the time.

22 Arthur Edward Harrington Raikes (1867-1915) arrived in Zanzibar in 1894 when he was appointed second in command to General Mathews. A lieutenant in the 62nd Wiltshire Regiment he was promoted to Brigadier General when he took command of the Sultan's forces. He also stood in as First Minister of Zanzibar on a number of occasions.

23 The description of these events has been taken from: Kevin Patience, *Zanzibar and The Shortest War in History*, 1994, p 7-16

24 Zemzem was sad when her nephew left Zanzibar and sent some of her servants to help him. She never saw him again and died in 1900.

Until WWI Khalid lived comfortably under German protection, but in 1917 he was captured by the British during the allied invasion of German East Africa and was exiled first to St Helena and then to the Seychelles. In 1922 he was allowed to reside in Mombasa on condition he gave up the claim to the throne for himself and his children. He died in 1927.

Chapter Sixteen

Major – Domo at the Palace and Religious Dissension

Hamoud's accession ushered in a period of comparative tranquillity for Zanzibar. Slavery ceased to be the burning issue and in 1897 the remaining laws and regulations recognising the status of slavery were abolished.[1] Both German East Africa and British East Africa, which now included Uganda, had been 'pacified' and colonisation gathered pace. The Benadir Coast had been taken by the Italians and the Congo by the Belgians. Only the Coastal Strip and Zanzibar, as a British Protectorate, still flew the red flag of the Sultan alongside the Union Jack. The Sultan appointed his representatives in the coastal towns and he alone had the right to plant his flagstaff in the ground, but he was no longer a power in the land. His role had become entirely ceremonial. British officials carried out his administration. Keeping the Sultan, if only as puppet prince, was deliberate British policy, a part of the tried and tested British system of indirect rule, which they had perfected in India.

Sultan Hamoud bin Mohammed bin Said was formally enthroned in a temporary palace[2] on Sunday, 30 August 1896.

> The usual coffee and sherbet followed, Peera Dewjee in gorgeous raiment acting as Major–domo with his accustomed mastery over the details of the situation. The audience was somewhat short and the perfuming of the handkerchiefs of those received, alas! omitted, for the famous Attar of Roses has gone astray in the general leakage there has been in the stock of Palace effects.[3]

The customary Grand *Baraza* was held the next morning on Monday and several more *barazas* were held during September to give the new Sultan the opportunity to greet his subjects and receive their loyal addresses. One of his first actions was to order scarlet liveries for the *syces* (grooms) and new stables to be built for his horses and carriages, which were put under the professional supervision of the Government vet, Dr Andrade.[4]

A special evening event including fireworks was held on 20 September to escort the Sultan's wife, Khanfora,[5] and his eldest daughter to the palace.[6] Bouquets of fresh roses were presented to them and a new dressing table complete with a set of silver, ivory and cut glass, which the Sultana particularly admired. At the 'Ladies Baraza' the Sultan gave necklaces to all the European ladies present during the bombardment and a pendant star engraved with his name. On 4 November the Sultan, accompanied by General Mathews and Peera Dewjee, was rowed in the state barge to the British Navy flagship *St George* and welcomed on board by Rear-Admiral Rawson[7] with a 21-gun salute. The party were then treated to a display of naval fire power watching a Maxim gun in action and a torpedo explode, before adjourning for a sumptuous lunch. Festivities continued on into November and concluded with a state visit to Chwaka, where Peera Dewjee laid on a huge feast – the table was 120 ft long![8]

Sultan Hamoud accepted the realities of the reduced power and prestige of his position. He adjusted palace protocol and the format of his *barazas* to accommodate the increasing European presence. Peera Dewjee, no longer referred to as 'Chief Steward' but rather as 'Major-domo' of the Palace, helped oversee these changes.[9]

At the Grand Baraza to mark the end of Ramadhan in March 1897,

> Contrary to the custom hitherto in vogue, the various consuls met at the same time at the palace together with their subjects and whilst waiting for their respective audiences were regaled with refreshments from beautifully decorated tables laid here and there in the corridors and anterooms of the Palace.
>
> The various consuls and their subjects were received in turn as before according to the date of establishment of consulates and as each left the Palace the band of HH Sultan played the respective National Anthems.
>
> Never before has the scene within the Palace been more brilliant. The different consuls in their uniforms, the naval officers, the large number of

European laymen present to tone down and give a setting to the former, ecclesiastics in cassock and black and white habits and the officials, combatant and non-combatant of the Zanzibar Government in their black, red and gold uniform worn for the first time on this occasion; - all combined to add colour and life to their surroundings which of themselves were oriental in splendour of colour and sumptuousness of material.

Though the new arrangements seemed somewhat strange at first to those accustomed to the old style of the Baraza, at the end of the proceedings all were however much pleased at the change, which shows up at once the strength of the European community in Zanzibar and ensures the greatest general effect with simplicity of working. The one absent feature generally lamented was the excellent serving of refreshments in the Eastern style which obtained of old, always a conspicuous and admired feature of a Baraza.[10]

Peera Dewjee oversaw the festivities of the *Siku-kuu* and for Eid ul-Fitr, putting on a feast for 3,000 people, and the Sultan was so pleased with the arrangements that he presented Peera with a valuable gold watch and chain. [11]

But this was nothing compared to the celebrations for Eid ul-Adha two months later, when Peera organised a meal for a staggering 8,000 people in the Sultan's palace. The *Gazette* reported that the Sultan ate beneath a canopy at a table in the central courtyard along with his relatives and people of the highest rank. The table's centrepiece was a seven tier cake surmounted by the Sultanate Flag and the Union Jack, 'while below in gold letters were V.R. and H.H.S.Z.' Those next in rank ate in the corridors around the courtyard while 'all the rooms and every available space in the Palace was given over to feasting.'

Accommodation in different parts of the palace was provided for members of the different Muslim sects, yet 'from the Sultan's table to the lowest, the food was of the same quality and nature.' Fifty-five different dishes were placed on the tables all differently tinted and garnished, 'and a new feature was the large number of European preserved vegetables used in their composition,' – perhaps Peera used some of the canned products manufactured by Crosse and Blackwell which were frequently advertised in the *Gazette*.

'The number of plates and dishes bearing food came to close

on ten thousand...Three hundred cooks and assistants furnished this mammoth meal and even the stable accommodation had to be encroached upon to find room for all the fires and pots required for the cooking.'[12]

Following his accession Sultan Hamoud had a special medal struck, called the order of El Hamoudieh, which was awarded to selected officers of the government and the Royal Navy in recognition of their services during the Bombardment. The *Wisam al Hamudieh* (Order of the Praiseworthy) was first conferred in 1897.[13] It was given out in addition to the Brilliant Star of Zanzibar, the most prestigious order of Zanzibar, which had been instituted by Sultan Barghash, after his visit to Europe in 1875. Barghash had been impressed by the medals he had seen worn in Europe and particularly admired the French Legion of Honour, which had been started by Napoleon, and wanted something similar. The Brilliant Star of Zanzibar was a copy of the French medal made of silver gilt, coloured enamel and gold with a five pointed star surrounded by a wreath with a smaller wreath above. The earliest examples were made by jewellers in France and Germany. The Order was originally divided into two classes. The First Class was a sash badge, worn on a red ribbon with white edges draped over the shoulder. It had the crest or *tugra* of the Sultan engraved in gold on red enamel in the medal centre and was reserved for heads of state. The Second Class used an eight-pointed rayed silver star and was awarded to those who had given meritorious service. This was later revised into five grades with medals of various sizes. The third grade was a neck medal in pendant form, while the remainder were worn on the left breast like conventional medals.[14]

There is a photograph taken about this time, showing a number of Zanzibar government and palace staff, which probably records a medal presentation. Seated in the second row are uniformed European personnel wearing sun helmets with General Mathews, First Minister of Zanzibar, in the centre and Brigadier-General Raikes, his second in command, beside him. Both Mathews and Raikes received El Hamoudieh decorations in 1897. The order of El Hamoudieh was made of gold, richly chased and similar in design to the Brilliant Star, but without the colourful enamel work and could be worn either as a sash badge or neck pendant. At the front of the photograph sitting on the ground are members of the Sultan's band and standing behind the seated row are a number of Zanzibari notables including Peera Dewjee who stands in a prominent position behind General Mathews with his second son, Abdulrasul (?) just visible by his shoulder and his eldest son Abdulhussein wearing a boater behind him. Peera Dewjee's beard is now white, but he looks sturdy and determined as he stares out of the picture. Around his neck hangs a medal and the uniformed European possibly Captain Le Page Agnew[15] in front of him has a similar medal round his neck. One of the most treasured possessions of the Peera Dewjee family is a medal, but it is the order of the Brilliant Star of Zanzibar, (neck medal),[16] with the *tugra* of Sultan Hamed.

It is likely Peera Dewjee received various medals, not to mention gold watches, during his long service with the Sultans, although only one known award has survived to be passed down within the family. For instance Dr Pestonji Bhicaji Nariman, the Parsee doctor to Sultans Khalifa, Ali and Hamed, received three medals, the Brilliant Star, third class in 1893, the Order of Hamoudieh in 1897 and the Brilliant Star fourth class in 1901. Medals and decorations were given out with increasing frequency at the end of the nineteenth century. Senior officers and government officials wore them on ceremonial occasions adding colour and sparkle to elaborate dress uniforms and formal wear. The flamboyant Peera, who frequented court circles and liked to impress in gorgeous raiment, may well have had several![17]

Also in 1897, Zanzibar as a British Protectorate put on a series of elaborate festivities to mark the occasion of Queen Victoria's Diamond Jubilee. The celebrations started on 19 June and continued for five days, and Peera's artistic and organisational talents were much in demand. Entertainment on a grand scale had become a family business and we learn that Peera's sons were also involved.[18]

Illuminations were put up in the main streets and houses and shops displayed the Union Jack. The Sultan's palace was profusely decorated.

In addition to the customary palm leaves, red bunting garlanded the whole building with specimens of every fruit and product known in the Island interwoven into it along the frontage, creating, according to the newspaper report, a most unusual effect! Over the doorway two immense red Sultanate flags formed a draped entrance.

The Victoria Gardens was the site chosen for the British Residents Fête, the main event of the Jubilee celebrations and a huge pavilion was specially built, called the *Casino*, raised as if by magic, within a month, under the supervision of Mr Bomanjee Manockjee, Minister of Public Works. At the entrance a triumphal arch had the words *God bless our Empress Queen* with the Royal Arms above. Inside there was a walkway, which followed on from the line of the main promenade of the garden. On one side of the walkway was a huge teak dance floor and on the other side a large reception area. On the night of the Grand Fête the reception area was covered with a carpet and lined with settees and chairs, with a throne set up for the Sultan in the centre. Small tables bearing refreshments and costly glass were placed round the whole area. The *Casino*, large enough to accommodate 1,000 people, was lit by powerful arc lights, glass chandeliers and 'very chaste Wedgwood enamelled pendant lamps in classic design.' Fairy lights hung outside in the gardens. Catering for the guests was a mammoth affair. The salad alone used 200 eggs, while it took 3000 pounds of ice to cool the drinks.

Invitation cards embossed with the Queen's face and gold corners were sent out to the invited guests. The evening programme consisted of music, fireworks, supper and a Grand Masai War Dance. Afterwards the guests danced the night away until well after three in the morning.

The following was the Menu card at the Supper tables – all in French – the height of chic!

MENU

Soupe de queues de bœuf
Poissons bouilli froid, mariné et garni

Poulets froid
Canards froids
Dindes froides
Oies froides
Cuisses de mouton
Aloyaux de Bœuf
Bosses marinées
Bœuf salé
Pâte de Foies gras
Saucisses allemandes
Salade de palmiers à la Zanzibar
Langues de rennes
Langues de Bœufs
Pâte de pigeons
Agneau rôti (chaud)
Jambon froid
Gâteaux au sherry
Olives
Gelées
Blanc-mange
Mince-pies
Tartelettes aux confiture
Glaces
Fruits confits
Fruits
Champagne – George Goulets

Here is the description of the Grand Masai War Dance:

A yell from the entrance and a small boy in Masai war dress rushing along the Promenade to the Casino denoted the party of native dancers had arrived who were to dance the Grand Masai War Dance.

On came closely packed together some sixty blood and red-clay-besmeared horrors, with high feather head-dresses like ruffled turkeys' tails, with beadwork and fringes and red streamers covering their faces and forms. Shackles and leg bells swelled the noise produced by their songs and cries, while spears were held high aloft and some imaginary foe derided at.

A huge ring was formed on the dancing floor and a very Bedlam reigned in the place for some quarter of an hour. To give zest to the proceedings General Sir Lloyd Mathews took a place within the circle and kept their enthusiasm up to fighting pitch. The scene, brightly lit up as it was, was picturesque in the extreme.[19]

The Swahili words to all thirteen of the songs sung by the performers of the Masai War Dance as well as the titles of all the tunes played for the dancing were printed in the *Gazette*, which ran a special supplement for the Diamond Jubilee. Its reporters' coverage of all events was very thorough.

Peera Dewjee took charge of the Grand Arab Banquet held at the British Agency:

The large side-balcony was occupied through its whole length by a table laid for nearly a hundred people and on this placed according to custom, at the one time, were no less than eight hundred dishes in which were forty-five different kinds of food. After many delayed arrivals Mr. Hardinge led in the Sultan's brother together with six Princes of the blood royal, the Cadis, the Walis of the new Districts of the Island of Pemba, followed by the general throng, all of them on entering washed their hands over large silver bowls with water poured on from silver ewers in the Eastern manner.

…The Feast was solemn and slow, the conversation not being racy; East being East, and West being West. After fifty minutes Mr Hardinge and the Sultan's brother were seen to rise and the after-lavations were gone through. The sea front balcony was then adjourned to, where coffee was served and scent sprinkled on the guests, silver censers of fuming ambergris lent for the occasion from the Palace being carried round amongst the guests. Fireworks were then let off and two balloons sent up, both getting successfully away and going due West with some speed till both were lost as distant fading stars.

The *Gazette* went on to report that the guests exchanged farewells with their hosts and then left with 'diminished retinues,'

… for the mob was let loose on the remains of the feast, and retainers and the ubiquitous small boy were to be seen gulping down tit-bits of goat and luscious custard, rice, sweets, and sours, fish, flesh and fowl, all within reach going into young Zanzibar's marvellously capacious maw. Both masters and servants each in their own way evidently enjoyed to the full the evening's proceedings.

A service of thanksgiving was held at the Catholic Cathedral of St Joseph accompanied by music from the Goan band. The British Indian Community gave a special address and there were further receptions at the British Agency. On the final day there was a 60-gun salute and a display of fireworks in the harbour. More balloons were sent up from the Agency pier. There was a four-day public holiday and the townsfolk held a monster *ngoma* at the open space off Mnazi Moja Road.

At the end of it all Consul Hardinge thanked everyone for their efforts and gave special mention to those most responsible for the success of the Jubilee celebrations: 'To Peera Dewjee the Palace Major-Domo who converts gigantic conceptions to actualities the best thanks are due for his labours at the ladies "At Home" and the Arab Banquet at the Agency to name no more.'[20]

The *Casino* pavilion was used again for a *Grand Bal Masque*, which was held in September 1897. The Portuguese Consul General put on the fancy dress party in honour of the birthday of their majesties the King and Queen of Portugal. The description of the event covered a full page in the *Zanzibar Gazette*, which went into rapturous detail of the interior design of the pavilion, which had been transformed into an Aladdin's cave or fairyland. There was also a long list of the different costumes worn – Abdulrasul Peera appeared as 'Divers Samples,' while Bomanjee Manockjee appeared as an Ameer of Cashmere and his wife and daughters as Cashmere ladies. Others came as clowns and shepherdesses and fishermen. A highlight of the evening was a tournament between mounted knights.

> The climax was reached on the arrival of His Highness the Sultan and Son, accompanied by General Sir Lloyd Mathews, and several officials of the Zanzibar Government in uniform, and a retinue of Arabs in their richest dress, Peera Dewjee too being 'beautiful to behold.'[21]

From reading the *Zanzibar Gazette* one might imagine that life in Zanzibar was one long party. Certainly the journalists took great delight in reporting on the grand dinners and receptions held at the palace and by other prominent residents of Zanzibar. These included a Grand Banquet to mark Queen Victoria's 81st birthday, which was given at the British Agency for the leading Arabs of Zanzibar. The Sultan's brother and nephews were among the 50 diners who enjoyed the 'sumptuous feast,' which was followed by a fireworks display. 'The management of the whole was in the hands of Mr Peera Devji.'[22]

Peera Dewjee's mastery as chief caterer and entertainments organiser for Zanzibar continued unabated, although by now he was nearing sixty. In his own family there were weddings and funerals; his second son Abdulrasul married in 1898, but sadly his young wife died in childbirth the following year. One happy occasion was the wedding of his third son Abdulrub, in December 1900. Under 'Local News' the *Gazette* announced:

> WEDDING.– This being the season for weddings amongst the Hindi [i.e. Indian Muslim] population, a number of marriages have been arranged and will take place before the great fast of Ramadan which commences on the 3rd of January 1901.
>
> We are particularly desired to mention the wedding of Abdul Rab, third son of Mr. Peera Deoji, and partner in the firm of Abdool Hossein Bros. & Co., which is to take place on Friday next, with the daughter of Nassur Juma Haimani.
>
> A large number of Europeans are invited to the wedding with a special request by the Bridegroom's father to take part in the procession which will start from his house in Bagani street at 9 p.m. and take the following route to the Bride's house:– Portuguese Street, down by the Custom House and H.H's Palace.[23]

The wedding was reported on at length the following week.

> A good many Indian weddings have been witnessed by us in Zanzibar, but we doubt whether in point of interest shewn by the European residents for, and in the grandeur and pomp which was displayed at the wedding of Mr Abdul Rab, any have been equal to it. It is plain to see that Mr. Peera Dewji has not lost any of his former skill in organising and conducting

such affairs on a huge scale. Practically the entire English community availed themselves of the invitation to the wedding and honoured it with their presence, arriving at Mr. Peera's brilliantly lighted house at 9 p.m. When the guests had taken their seats, Mrs. Peera displayed to them the telegram of congratulation from H. H. the Aga Khan transmitted from Berlin, on a richly embroidered velvet cushion placed on a silver tray – the cushion being the work of Abdul Karim Perbhai jariwala – it was then taken before the Bridegroom who stood and made a profound obeisance to it.

Refreshments were then served, after which Mrs Peera proceeded to decorate all the guests with garlands of jasmine and rose. The guests then moved out to the street which was thronged with spectators and in one blaze of light, to take part in the procession that started as soon as the Bridegroom mounted his white charger. Fireworks were let off at intervals *en route* to the Bride's house and *pan supari* was freely distributed to everyone following in the wake of the procession. In front of the Palace the Bridegroom made a halt, and bowed to H. H. who was standing in the balcony, and who graciously acknowledged the obeisance. The Bride's house was ultimately reached, where the interesting ceremony of receiving the Bridegroom by the Bride's mother was witnessed, amidst deafening sounds of Indian and Swahili music. In spite of the almost overpowering heat which was experienced at this juncture, everybody seemed to be in the best of spirits and one and all responded heartily to the three cheers that were called forth by Mr. Mehta for the Bride and Bridegroom, and which was a fitting termination to the happy proceedings. We wish Mr. and Mrs. Abdul Rab every joy and 'Mubarak' in their married life.

Mr Peera in his great joy has presented a handkerchief each to all the boys of the Euan-Smith Madressa, and has feasted a large number of the poor of the city on *pilau*. After the feast the poor were given a pice each and served with sherbat.[24]

In 1899 the Aga Khan came on a three-month tour of Zanzibar and mainland East Africa. As the date of his arrival approached the *Gazette* reported,

It need scarcely be said that for the past few days the excitement among the Khoja community of Zanzibar has been at fever heat, and their loyalty and devotion to their religious Head has been proved by the extraordinary preparations they have made for his reception and the money that has been lavishly spent for his comfort. From the house which H.H. Aga Khan is to reside as far as the Jamatkhana, the entire route has been canopied in red

cloth and festooned with flags, and several substantial wooden arches have
been erected on which are hung numerous coloured lanterns.[25]

The Aga Khan arrived in Zanzibar on 28 June aboard the SS
Yangtse. He was received with full military honours as he was rowed
ashore in the royal barge. The Sultan's troops and police accompanied
by the band drew up in line at the landing place and General Mathews,
the First Minister, and all the heads of the Ismaili community in
Zanzibar and the German coasts welcomed the Aga Khan. He rode in
the Sultan's coach to his residence and the enthusiastic crowd cheered
along the way.

Peera Dewjee made many arrangements for this visit. He supplied
carriages and personally pulled the Aga Khan in a rickshaw through
the narrow streets of the town, as well as organising several feasts and
receptions.

The pavilion at the Victoria Gardens was renovated for a 'Big
Dinner' given by the Aga Khan to the leading residents of Zanzibar
shortly before he left. During the closing week of his visit he was
entertained at the German Consulate and attended a sports festival,
which included a football match by Khoja boys. He was a guest at
the seaside *shamba* of Mr Jafferbhoy Gangji, where 'he expressed his
greatest pleasure at the beautiful sea-prospect, and discoursed on
the advancement of education amongst the Mahomedan youth of
Zanzibar.'

Followers came from far and wide to meet him.

> RELIGIOUS ZEAL: Four Arabs from Sham (Syria) have been
> deputed by the numerous followers of H. H. the Aga Khan in that country,
> to pay their homage to His Highness, and to hand over a large sum of
> money as their yearly tribute.
>
> These men are now in Zanzibar.
>
> Mr Peera Devji with the permission of His Highness has honourably
> entertained his co-religionists by driving them out and showing them the
> sights of Zanzibar, and also by entertaining them at a grand feast.[26]

Aga Khan III, H H Sir Sultan Mohammed Shah, grandson of

262

Aga Khan I, had inherited the Imamship at the age of eight after the death of his father. He was now aged 21.²⁷ His visit to East Africa had a serious purpose as he came to try and heal a rift that had developed amongst his followers, some of whom questioned his right to be their spiritual leader and disputed his claim to be directly descended from the prophet Mohammed. The dissenters called themselves *Ithna'asheris* or Twelvers as they only recognised the succession of the first twelve Imams.

The movement of dissent had started in Bombay after 1873, when Mulla Qadir Husain, a radical preacher trained in Iraq, began converting the Khoja Ismailis. He taught that the views of the Ithna'asheris represented a truer, purer form of Shi'ism than the Hinduized version practised by the followers of the Aga Khan and called for converts to follow the Koran more closely and worship in mosques. His teachings proved attractive in Zanzibar. In 1877 when Dewji Jamal, a prominent Zanzibar merchant on a visit to Bombay, was expelled from the Jamat for being critical of the Aga Khan's financial dealings and edicts, interest accelerated. Dewji Jamal went on to found the first Ithna'asheri mosque in Zanzibar in 1881.²⁸

Ithna'asheri teachings fell on fertile ground in Zanzibar particularly amongst Ismailis struggling in business. Towards the end of the century, European development of the ports of Mombasa and Dar es Salaam on the mainland was taking much business away from Zanzibar and the Indian traders suffered. They found it hard to bear the tithe demands on their income, which went to the young Aga Khan to spend as he wished, and they became increasingly critical of what they perceived as his lavish lifestyle and Western leanings. They wanted more money to go back into the local community. The seeds of the disillusionment went back to the court case of 1866 when the English judge had ruled that the offerings given to the Aga Khan I belonged to him in his own right as hereditary Imam. A few reformists refused then to accept the ruling but the majority had remained with the Aga Khan. Now resentment smouldered once again.

By 1899 the Ithna'asheris were well entrenched in Zanzibar. The dissenters had their own mosque and a separate burial ground and almost one third of Khoja Ismailis were either converts or waverers. A court case of 1894 involving a matrimonial dispute between husband and wife, one of whom had joined the Ithna'asheris and one of whom remained loyal to the Aga Khan, highlighted the painful divisions amongst the Khojas in Zanzibar. Now Aga Khan III saw how religious dissension was harming the community and leading to fights and arguments within families and decided to take action. He issued a *firman* (edict) which ordered those who wished to follow him to remain and those who would not conform to leave. Henceforth those adhering to the Ithna'asheri creed would no longer be permitted to attend the Ismaili Jamatkhana or participate in any Ismaili function. Furthermore, the disciples of the Aga Khan were told to break off all social and economic ties with the seceders.[29] The Khoja Ithna'asheris were 'outcasted.'

It was a sad time for the Khoja community in Zanzibar as families broke apart and the financial drain of entertaining the Aga Khan for three months caused several to go bankrupt. A British report estimated that about six lakhs of rupees (£40,000) had been taken out of the bazaar as a direct result of the visit.[30]

Peera Dewjee remained loyal to the Aga Khan and to mark the visit he vowed to give a feast every year on 28 June to the Ismaili Khoja community and this was written down in the records of the Jamatkhana of Zanzibar. As promised, until his death Peera provided a feast for the Jamat every year to mark the anniversary of the Aga Khan's visit and reports of the event held at the Ismaili Punjebhai Club regularly appeared in the *Gazette*. The report for 1900 was immediately followed by the following notice:

> By the kindness and influence of His Highness the Aga Khan we hear two trained nurses for the attending of the special needs of the women of Indian Community are coming here, and will it is hoped prove of the greatest benefit to the Indian Community in Zanzibar.[31]

Presumably these nurses were trained midwives, who in future would help to prevent tragedies such as the death of the Abdulrasul's first wife.

Peera Dewjee was by now one of the most prominent and well known Ismaili residents of Zanzibar, but he never took on a religious office. Hatim M Amiji says this was because he was now part of 'the upper establishment' and enjoyed a position in society that transcended caste or community.

Many of the outcasted Ithna'asheris settled in Lamu, where to this day there are few Ismailis. Peera Dewjee's youngest brother, Allaya, was an early convert. In 1902 he was involved in a burial dispute, where the husband was an Ithna'asheri, but the wife was not and had issued on her deathbed a request to be buried as an Ismaili. At the funeral a terrible quarrel broke out and both sides started to fight, attacking each other with sticks and umbrellas. Several were arrested and were brought to court. Allaya Dewji Parpia was convicted but was let off lightly with a 50 rupee fine and a six month probation order.[32]

Peera Dewjee's second son Abdulrasul Peera was also attracted by the new religion. Although he did not openly declare his conversion for some years, Abdulrasul became an influential convert and personally ran Mehfile Muhibbane Husain, a sacred place located in Mtendeni where the Ismailis who had not yet converted could meet in secret to learn about the Ithna'asheri imams and saints and listen to the new teachings. This became known as Mehfile Private as the Khojas feared the wrath of the community leaders in associating with the converts and ousted members.[33] It was a time of great confusion and heartbreak, as families and friendships split apart. Peera Dewjee, as a staunch follower of the Aga Khan, must have suffered great distress to see his close relatives succumb to the new religion.

---

1 In 1907 slavery was abolished entirely in the Sultanate of Zanzibar. In British East Africa (Kenya and Uganda) all slaves were freed by 1904, when compensation ceased and in Tanganyika slavery was abolished in 1927, but in Ethiopia slavery existed until 1942.

2 Presumably the Beit al-Ajaib as the other two waterfront royal palaces had been destroyed in the bombardment. The House of Wonders (Beit al-Ajaib), which had only received slight damage, was repaired and a light unit and signal station were incorporated in a new tower on the roof. A new palace was built on the sight of the harem.

3 *Zanzibar Gazette*, September 2, 1896

4 Dr Luis Antonio Andrade (1865-1933) was born in Goa and arrived in Zanzibar in 1889. He was appointed doctor and veterinary surgeon to Sultan Hamed in December 1895 and was made Master of Horse for Hamoud in 1896. He rose to a senior position in Government service and became Collector of Revenue for Zanzibar Province.

5 Khanfora was the only daughter of Sultan Majid.

6 Hamoud had six sons and four daughters. His eldest daughter Matuka married Khalifa II and became Sultana in her own right. She was the offspring of Khanfora his chief wife, whom he had married c.1882.

7 Rear Admiral Harry Holdsworth Rawson (1843-1910) was commander of British naval forces at the Cape of Good Hope and West Coast of Africa Station. When Sultan Hamed died, Rawson was in Mombasa dealing with the aftermath of the Mazrui Rebellion and had to hurry back to Zanzibar. He was awarded two medals by a grateful Hamoud for his role in the Bombardment.

8 Information from the *Zanzibar Gazette* September and November 1896

9 The word comes from the Latin – major domus - and means an official who has the general management in a large household.

10 *Zanzibar Gazette*, March 10, 1897

11 *Zanzibar Gazette*, March 17 and 24, 1897

12 *Zanzibar Gazette*, May 19, 1897

13 It became obsolete in 1902 after the death of Hamoud.

14 The order became obsolete with the Zanzibar Revolution of 12 January 1964, when the sultanate was abolished.

15 Captain Arthur Le Page Agnew (1861-1941) was appointed Port Officer in 1893. He was forced to retire in 1905 suffering from leprosy. He was awarded the order of Hamoudieh, Second Class on 20 June 1897.

16 According to Kevin Patience.

17 Information about the Brilliant Star of Zanzibar and the El Hamoudieh has been taken from information given by Kevin Patience.

18 Peera Dewjee and his sons received the warmest thanks of the ladies for his laborious efforts on their behalf on the occasion of their "At Home." This was the final entertainment of the four-day celebration and was held at the British Agency.

19 *Zanzibar Gazette*, June 23, 1897
20 *Zanzibar Gazette*, June 23, 1897
21 *Zanzibar Gazette*, September 29, 1897
22 *Zanzibar Gazette*, May 30, 1900
23 *Zanzibar Gazette*, December 19, 1900
24 *Zanzibar Gazette*, December 26, 1900
25 *Zanzibar Gazette*, June 28, 1899
26 *Zanzibar Gazette*, September 6, 1899
27 Sir Sultan Mohammed Shah, His Highness Aga Khan III, was born November 2, 1877 at Karachi.
28 The mosque was named Quwwatul Islam - 'Islam Strength.'
29 A further *firman* in 1905 confirmed the split and made it permanent.
30 Hatim M Amiji: 'Religious dissent in nineteenth-century East Africa,' *African Historical Studies*, IV, 3, 1971
31 *Zanzibar Gazette*, July 4, 1900. This was one of the first of many services in the fields of health and education which the Aga Khans would establish for the welfare of their followers and other communities in East Africa, and which continue up to the present day.
32 *Zanzibar Gazette*, June 11, 1902
33 Information received from Mr Abdulrazak Fazal.

Chapter Seventeen

A Zanzibar Merchant and Grandee: Business to the Bitter End

Peera Dewjee lived and breathed business. It was his driving force throughout life. As both Burton and Christie explained, buying and selling merchandise is what Khoja Ismailis did and were trained to do from childhood. Peera was no different. It is frustrating, therefore, that despite the central role business played in his life, only small snippets of information survive which tell us exactly what this business was.

Peera Dewjee's success as a businessman was improved by his visit to England in 1875 when he made direct contact with exporters in the industrial Northern towns of Manchester, Birmingham and Liverpool. There is evidence he imported English suiting material to Zanzibar, as amongst the accounts for the British Consulate for 5 February 1889 there is an entry for 415 rupees being Peera Dewjee's bill for Broadcloth etc.[1] This is a sizeable sum (approximately £6,000 in today's money) and possibly included the cost of other fabrics for the refurbishment of the British Consulate, being undertaken by Euan-Smith. Broadcloth is usually defined as a fine woollen cloth with a twill weave and smooth finish, but by the end of the nineteenth century it was being made with cotton and other mixtures. It was most commonly used for making uniforms and coats, but a fabric called broadcloth was also used for Arab robes, which came in black and red. There was a considerable demand for European wear in Zanzibar as uniforms and formal black coats were *de rigeur* for palace visits and other ceremonial occasions. European formal dress did not last long in the hot weather before needing replacement.

The chief trade from Kutch had always been cotton and Kutchi traders were renowned as cloth merchants. The traditional cotton trade from India to East Africa took a dip in the nineteenth century due to competition from America, when *Merikani* bleached white cotton cloth became the most popular trade goods item in East Africa, overtaking the blue and patterned cottons of India. Indian cotton manufacture was also badly hit by the protectionist policies of British India, which promoted British factory-made cotton goods coming out of the Northern towns. England imported raw cotton from India as well as America and then produced the finished items, thus ensuring that the main profit and employment remained in England. The superior machinery of the mills made this a most lucrative business, but by the end of the nineteenth century India was catching up and building its own mechanised looms and undercutting the Manchester trade.

Peera Dewjee also imported cotton piece goods from Manchester. These were lengths of brightly coloured and patterned cottons mass-produced in the Manchester mills specifically for the West and East African markets. They were packed in bales for export and each bale bore the location and trade stamp of the buyer so it could be easily identified when shipped. The trade stamps were sometimes very decorative. Although examples can be seen in the Manchester Museum of Science and Industry, the names of the individual traders were not always recorded for posterity, so we don't know which one was Peera Dewjee's personal logo – perhaps it was the sea lion, admired by Sultan Barghash in Paris, or possibly a dancing elephant or a golden flower?

Traditional coastal African dress for women of higher status consisted of one length of cotton cloth tied round the body, with another to cover the head and shoulders. In the early years of the nineteenth century these wraps were usually made from plain lengths of bleached *merikani* cotton or blue-dyed cotton from India called *kaniki*, or sometimes hand-painted Indian cotton known as *barsati*. But in the mid-century a new form of patterned garment known as a *kanga* was introduced, which is still worn today. *Kanga* means guinea fowl in Swahili, and it is suggested the name derives from patterned or spotted handkerchiefs, which were sewn together to make the garment. Missionaries from the 1860s imported a great many machine-printed handkerchiefs into Zanzibar, often with biblical slogans and colourful designs, to hand out along with religious tracts and Bibles to assist in conversion to Christianity. But the local Africans had no use for handkerchiefs.

As the story goes, some stylish Swahili women in Zanzibar had the bright idea of buying up these printed kerchiefs in lengths of six from the bolt of cotton cloth from which the kerchiefs were usually cut off and sold singly. They then cut the six into two lengths of three and sewed them together along one side to make a 3 by 2 sheet, the usual format of their traditional dress. It was an immediate fashion hit and before long enterprising coastal shopkeepers sent away for special designs printed like the six-together kerchiefs, but as a single unit of cloth.[2] The nineteenth century advances in technology meant that the printing could now all be done by machine and patterns and designs likely to appeal to African taste were sent to England and other European countries particularly the Netherlands, and cotton pieces were produced and printed there. The European piece goods trade peaked between c.1870-1890 but then declined as similar Indian printed cotton goods were produced more cheaply.

The *kanga* designs seen nowadays all over East Africa printed with Swahili mottoes and sayings are said to have been first introduced by an Indian cloth merchant called Kaderdina Hajee Issak, who started his business in Zanzibar c. 1880. He was from the Sunni Muslim Memon community, which, like the Khojas, originated in Kutch and Sindh and had converted from Hinduism and were from the merchant class. It was the fashion conscious Swahili women who first came up with the idea, again copied from the missionary handkerchiefs. They chose the content of the sayings and approved the designs, which were then sent away to be printed. Originally sold just as a novelty, the concept became so popular that it became a part of traditional East African *kanga* design. At first the Swahili sayings were printed in Arabic script, and were often proverbs or aphorisms with an erotic or double meaning, but western lettering was introduced in the early twentieth century. Kaderdina Hajee Issak's descendants still sell *kangas* in Mombasa and new designs with fresh sayings come out every year, being in great demand for the main feasts of the Islamic year, when new clothes are traditionally worn.

Hand in hand with the *kanga* went the trade in large brightly-painted shallow bowls, known locally as Zanzibar plates. There is ample evidence that Peera Dewjee was involved in this as many surviving plates have his name stamped on the back. As with the cotton piece goods, the earlier plates were made in England or Europe but were later produced in India and in the twentieth century even in the Far East and Japan. In traditional Swahili, Arab and Indian households, food was served up in these large shallow bowls and eaten without the use of cutlery. On dhows and at the weekly Ismaili feasts people would sit round and eat from communal bowls of rice and curry. The enormous public feasts organised by Peera Dewjee used many hundreds of these bowls, no doubt all supplied by him. Both *kanga* and Zanzibar plates were everyday household items, a must-have for every family.

Decorative plates have a long history on the East African coast as they were used as ornamentation on graves and displayed on the walls and in the niches of Arab and Swahili houses. The oldest plates were blue and white Chinese ware, which came to East Africa from Bombay.[3] But from the late nineteenth century, painted plates from the famous European stoneware centres, copying Majolica ware, became fashionable. European goods came to Zanzibar in increasing quantities after the opening of the Suez Canal in 1869 and these cheap colourful plates were shipped along with the cotton bales, cutlery, clocks and other small manufactured goods to sell in the bazaars and local markets. They came from the Netherlands, Germany, France and England. Names such as Société Ceramique, Maastricht, Villeroy & Bosch, Petrus Regout & Co., Opaque de Sargeminet, Adams, or Frank Beardmore were stamped on the back, showing the origin of the pottery. The designs included clove buds, boldly coloured indeterminate flowers and sometimes an Islamic crescent moon, all deliberately done to appeal to local tastes. There was a booming trade and competition was cutthroat. Sometimes the name of the importer

Pottery Marks

is included. Peera Dewjee was one, who ordered plates made by Frank Beardmore & Company and had his name incorporated in the mark on the back. These must date pre-1904, the date of his death.

His sons' company, Abdool Hoossein Bros, Zanzibar, can also be identified dating before 1911, the year they became insolvent. They had an agreement with the company Ogdens and Madeleys and various plates bear their trademark as well. The lion stamp of the Deutsch Ostafrikanische Gesellschaft was another importer who left his mark.

It is thought that the potential of the African market was first discovered by the Dutch who had been supplying their colonies in

Indonesia with similar plates along with patterned or batiq sarongs for many years. They opened a trading base or 'factory' in Bandar Abbas in the Persian Gulf in the late eighteenth century and noting the success of their wares in Islamic markets started to trade these items in the Indian Ocean area as well. Other European nations followed their example.[4]

The old established German Company, O'Swald & Co,[5] was one of the first to export the stoneware plates into East Africa in large numbers, but faced stiff competition from Indian wholesale merchants such as Peera Dewjee and Adamjee Karimjee, who prospered because they managed to negotiate sole agencies with the potteries. Peera Dewjee had a monopoly agreement with Petrus Regout of Maastricht, whose wares were particularly prized in Zanzibar. His plate business proved so successful that O'Swalds withdrew from the trade as it was no longer profitable.[6] There was a fierce price war, which Peera won, but eventually the price per bowl was fixed at one Maria Theresa dollar. One of Peera Dewjee's great strengths as a businessman lay in his powers of persuasion; he was a natural salesman.

O'Swald faced competition from Peera Dewjee in another area of their business – fez hats. Up until 1903 they had been the chief supplier of red fezzes in Zanzibar. The red fez hat was part of the uniform worn by palace servants, colonial police and the colonial armed forces. Although the locally produced embroidered white caps, *kofia*, remained traditional Swahili head wear, fezzes were in fashion and Peera saw an opening in the market. He began importing cheaper imitation fezzes made in Belgium and India and, according to the disgruntled German report, tried to pass them off as identical to their superior brand. Apparently Peera's fezzes were not good in the rain as the colour tended to run and the material lost its shape! So this was one trade war he did not win.[7] His fezzes were denounced as fakes and withdrawn from the market.

Peera Dewjee also imported luxury items. Sometimes he ordered a product, which he had specially packaged and branded with his own name. Whether this proved a successful sales pitch or not is not known, but it certainly showed imaginative and artistic advertising flair. Abdul Rashid, Peera's great nephew, remembers seeing a one-ply wooden box with a yellow label with Peera Dewjee's photo prominently displayed on top. This contained the finest vermicelli (used in the production of local sweetmeats), which was manufactured in Europe and exported to Zanzibar and all of East Africa for many years.

Sultan Hamoud had a white and gold dinner service made by Wedgwood with his own crest printed on it. This was possibly another of Peera's innovations, furthering the westernising tendencies of the Sultanate. Soon the Sultan would be giving tea parties instead of serving sherbet and coffee.

Peera Dewjee, throughout his life as a general merchant, sought to exploit the market wherever he could and make a profit following on the tradition of the early dhow traders of his boyhood. As he rose up the social ladder and business practices became more sophisticated, he followed the trend. He entered the agency business and acted as a commission agent for several overseas companies, handling their Zanzibar trade for them. In 1902-3 he is reported as being agent for Hintzmann & Co, who exported cement, Swiss cotton goods, and cuckoo clocks to Zanzibar. Forwood Brothers had exported mainly coal and paint to Zanzibar, before selling their agency business to Boustead, Ridley & Co. Peera Dewjee was also the agent for William Birch Jr & Co, the company which gave Peera's eldest son work experience in England. From 1899 they exported cheap beer to Zanzibar, undercutting the more expensive and popular Beck's beer imported by Smith Mackenzie & Co[8] but this ploy failed to save the Birch business as they went bankrupt in 1902. There was a brisk trade in alcoholic beverages in Zanzibar. The large naval contingent as well as the foreign businesses and consulates helped fuel the demand. Africans mainly drank their own local brews, but many Muslims ignored their religious principles and drank alcohol as well. Traditionally it was the Christian Goan shop keepers who dealt in wines and spirits, but it is interesting to see the liberal and westernised Peera Dewjee and his sons importing and distributing beer as one of their core businesses.

Advertisement for Abdool Hoossein Bros. & Co.

Many of the trading ships coming to East Africa from Europe carried fillers as well as their main cargoes – parcels of small high value items such as glassware and ceramics, medicines, lamps, tools and cutlery. These had various names. In England they were known as Manchester or fancy goods, while in Germany this was called the *taka taka* trade. This was the area in which Indian importers specialised and competition was fierce as large profits could be made, if they guessed the market right. Conversely, they faced large losses if the goods did not sell as expected. On at least one occasion Peera left his goods stored in the Smith Mackenzie warehouses and had to be asked to remove them when they had stayed too long.[9] Presumably his delay in collecting his goods meant he was having difficulties selling and he did not want to pay the warehousing fees and duty before he had found customers. Peera's business career appears to have had its share of ups and downs.

He was no stranger to debt and cash flow problems. A low point came in 1890, but with hard work and novel ideas good fortune returned. Unlike Tharia Topan, who became an immensely wealthy wholesale merchant and financier, operating a multi-national business based in Bombay with an army of employees, accountants and English writers, Peera Dewjee's business was local, opportunistic and family orientated.

As a legacy for his five sons, Abdulhussein, Abdulrasul, Abdulrab, Abdulali and Abdulrashid, Peera Dewjee founded the business he called Abdool Hoossein Bros. & Co. It was first established in Zanzibar in 1894 and a branch office opened in Mombasa in 1896. He managed the business on behalf of his sons until they were old enough to take over. Right up until his death he channelled much of his energy into making it a successful venture.

From a government sponsored and prestigious British East Africa business directory for 1908-9 come these descriptions of Abdool Hoosein & Bros & Co: firstly the Mombasa branch:

> Two special points about this Indian firm must be noticed. First they are importers only; and secondly, no stock is carried, as the business is entirely indent...the Mombasa branch is managed by Mr Abdoolali Peera Dewjee. They import from England, the Continent, United States, India, China and Japan, mostly piece goods.

The Zanzibar entry, which starts with a description of the company founder, Peera Dewjee, includes these words:

> The present proprietors of the business…are his sons and there are five brothers in partnership.
> The firm are general merchants and commission agents. They import cotton goods and general merchandise from London, Manchester, and the Continent and export general African produce. They act as agents for Ogdens and Madeleys, Ltd., of London and Manchester, the World Marine Insurance Company, the Reliance Marine Insurance Company and the Bombay-Persia S[team] N[avigation] Company.[10]

From this one gathers they are chiefly cotton merchants and marine insurance brokers, but definitely no longer shopkeepers. The family had moved up in the world away from its humble beginnings in Zanzibar. The family house and business premises were now separate and situated in Shangani, the posh European and Arab quarter of town. Here the roads were wider and the houses larger than the congested old Khoja area of Kiponda behind the market, with its narrow streets and terraces of cramped shop houses.

Even the spelling of Peera Dewjee's name was a deliberately fashionable Anglicisation. Nowadays his name would probably be spelt Pira Devji, but in the Bombay of his youth double ee's were the vogue and showed you had arrived and had been accepted by the international business community. For instance there was Sir Jamsetjee Jeejeebhoy, the leader of the Bombay Parsees, and the first Parsee to receive a baronetcy,[11] Adamjee Jeevanjee[12] and a host of other successful Indian businessmen who liked to use the double ee as a sign of status instead of the more usual short i. The spelling of the sons' company, set up by Peera, also has this feature using a double o in AbdoolHoossein, rather than the more commonplace AbdulHussein. Peera Dewjee personally chose this form of spelling as an expression of how he viewed himself and his family.

Peera's one daughter Fatima, known as Fatupira, who no doubt would have helped with the flower arrangements for his public events and dinners, was later famed for her bridal bouquets and corsages of jasmine and other exotic tropical flowers.[13] She also sold homemade perfumes called *tarbizuna* and cyeliner, *aanjari,* which was made from soot, which was collected and then mixed with ghee. Her granddaughter recalled how the paste was sold in small sea shells which they used to collect from the seashore. 'Normally half a teaspoon was stuffed into a small shell and sold. The application of this paste to the eyes not only enhanced their beauty but also gave a very cooling effect to them.' This recorded memory provides a clear link back to the poor young lamp cleaner, who collected soot to keep his family alive and in business during the hard times of his youth.

In 1902 Peera Dewjee went to England to attend Edward VII's coronation. The old Queen Victoria had finally died and her son, whom Peera remembered fondly from the 1875 trip to Europe, was now King of England and Emperor of India. Edward Prince of Wales had been Sultan Barghash's favourite British Royal. It was he who had broken the ice and made the Sultan feel welcome in England by inviting him into his home to meet his wife and children, a gesture of friendship Barghash never forgot.

Peera travelled together with Ali, Sultan Hamoud's son, and Brigadier-General Raikes as Zanzibar delegates for the coronation ceremony. Upon arrival in Dover they travelled by train to Victoria Station where, according to the newspaper report, the Envoys were met by the King's Master of Ceremonies, The Honorable Sir W J Colville and were taken in the King's carriage to the Westminster Palace Hotel, where they stayed during the London visit.[14] Ali spoke English fluently as he had attended Harrow School for three years, 1898-1901. He had also been to France, Italy and Switzerland and to South Africa and was very much at home in western surroundings. He represented a new breed of Zanzibari Arab, well educated, cosmopolitan and open minded, which his father believed would serve the country well. Sadly his wish was not to be realised as Ali proved too westernised and liberal for his own and Zanzibar's good. He abdicated in 1911 and went to live in Paris and died young. But that was still in the future and his doting father nursed great hopes for his son.

Edward VII's coronation was originally scheduled for 26 June 1902 and was planned as an enormous spectacle of colourful pageantry. Crowned heads of every nation and representatives from all parts of the British Empire gathered in London in eager anticipation of the ceremony. But to the disappointment of many and surely of Peera, that expert arranger of feasts and festivals, the coronation ceremony was suddenly cancelled, just three days beforehand, because the King had been taken ill with appendicitis and required immediate surgery. The postponed coronation eventually took place on 9 August after he had recovered, but in a shortened format. In the early twentieth century an appendectomy was a life-threatening operation and there were real fears that the king would die. On 26 June, instead of a joyful celebration, a solemn service of intercession was held at St Paul's Cathedral, attended by many of the foreign dignitaries who had come to London for the coronation. One unintended effect of the postponement was the departure of some of the foreign delegations. Many of these did not return for the rescheduled ceremony, leaving their countries to be represented only by ambassadors. Those dignitaries who stayed on were accommodated in the homes of the aristocracy.

Initially Ali and his entourage remained and went to stay at Hardenhuish House near Chippenham, Wiltshire with the Clutterbuck family. However, his father's health had been poor for several months and the news from Zanzibar was bad, as his condition had now become critical. Ali, accompanied by Raikes, left London to return to Zanzibar by the French mail in the first week of July, but sadly failed to arrive in time. Sultan Hamoud died on 18 July 1902, just nine days before his son's return. Ali arrived back in Zanzibar on Sunday, 27 July to find he had been proclaimed Sultan at the age of 18.

It is not known whether Peera remained in London to represent Zanzibar at the rescheduled coronation, but he may well have done so. It is known that while he was in London he presented the homage of the faithful to the Aga Khan on behalf of the Ismaili community of Zanzibar and the Aga Khan certainly attended the August ceremony.[15] The homage of the faithful was of course another name for the yearly tithe, and the fact that Peera was entrusted with it, showed how highly he was thought of within the Ismaili community.

In 1903 Peera Dewjee's old friend Sir John Kirk reappeared in Zanzibar, dropping in for a short visit on his way back to England from the grand Durbar at Delhi, which had been organised by Lord Curzon that January to celebrate the accession of Edward VII as Emperor of India. In contrast to the damp squib of the Westminster coronation, this ceremony did not disappoint, as the full panoply and splendour of the Indian Raj went on display. The Aga Khan attended in princely regalia and the occasion we are told remained 'a burning memory, one that seared the idea of Empire ever deeper in his heart.'[16]

On 26 February 1903, 'the members of the Ismaili Jamat held

an "At Home" at their prettily situated Club on the North Road, the object being to welcome Sir John Kirk back to Zanzibar.'[17] Although a number of prominent Ismailis are mentioned amongst the guests, Peera Dewjee's name does not appear, but it is hard to imagine that the two would have missed an opportunity to reminisce about the old days, when Barghash ruled. Perhaps Peera was out of the country or so busy organising the reception that his name failed to get into the paper. We are told the weather was fine and the pretty grounds of the Punjebhai Club were looking at their best and after speeches attended by hundreds of members of the jamat, refreshments were served in the annex. The wording bears all the hallmarks of a Peera style feast!

Peera lived through the reigns of six sultans. It had been a time of momentous upheaval and change. The slave markets had been closed and slavery abolished. Zanzibar was now a British Protectorate and Dar es Salaam under German rule. Steamships, electricity, running water and roads were now commonplace in Zanzibar. There was an English Club, which boasted tennis courts and a croquet lawn. There were hospitals and schools and post offices and banks. Improved communications had transformed the island – maybe the changes had not all been for the better, but the genie could not be put back in its bottle. Peera had seen it all happen, had been there from the beginning and had played his part to the best of his ability. But now he was winding down, his enormous zest for life and boundless energies waning. His health was giving way and, at the age of 63, on 28 August 1904, he suffered a heart attack and died. Reading between the lines of his obituary it seems that business worries and stress, may have contributed to his unexpected death.

His obituary in the Zanzibar Gazette reads:

> We are extremely sorry to have to record the death of one of the most interesting and well known men in Zanzibar – Peera Dewjee, who died quite suddenly of heart disease on Sunday morning while on his way home from his office. Peera Dewjee was born in 1841 and at an early age joined the service of H. H. Seyid Burgash bin Said by whom he was thoroughly trusted for his great zeal and honesty.
>
> He accompanied that Sultan on his visit to England about twenty years

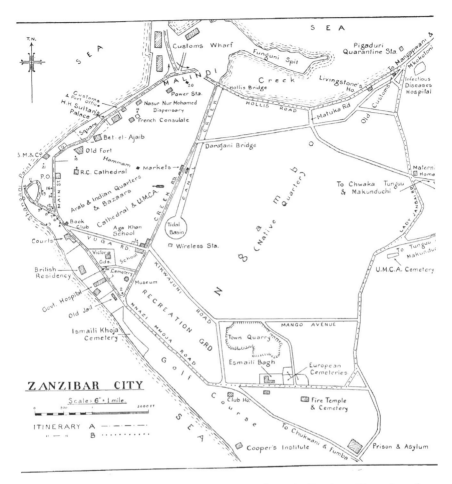

This map dating to the late 1920s comes from A Guide to Zanzibar, by G H Shelswell-White, published by Government Printers. It shows many of the places mentioned in the text. S M & Co (Smith Mackenzie & Co) marks the former site of the old British Consulate on Shangani Point. A new British Residency was built in 1903 overlooking Victoria Gardens, and the Law Courts next door were completed in 1908. The wooden bridge at Darajani had been built as early as 1838, to connect the two parts of the town, but roads came much later. The lower part of the creek was drained and reclaimed as a recreation ground and golf course in 1915.

ago and again went to Europe a few years after to make some considerable purchases on his master's account. After the death of Seyid Burgash he was on and off in the service of the Sultanate until a few years ago, when his affairs not being in a flourishing condition, he retired from business and contented himself with managing his sons' firm, well-known on this coast under the name of Abdool Hussein Brothers. He leaves many friends who will miss the energetic business man so well known and liked by all classes of the community.[18]

No headstone or grave survives for Peera Dewjee as the old Ismaili cemetery in Zanzibar, where Peera was buried, no longer exists. Instead the spirit of this remarkable man lives on in his hundreds of descendants who thrive and prosper, scattered throughout the English speaking countries of the world. It is they who are the living testament to the success of a poor immigrant boy from Kera, who rose from obscurity to make fame and fortune in Zanzibar.

I have left the final words to Sir John Kirk, whose influence left a permanent impression on Peera Dewjee. Kirk was one of the few British officials to publicly acknowledge the central role the Zanzibar Indian merchants played in the ending of slavery and the foundation of British influence in East Africa.

But for the Indians we should not be there now [in East Africa]. It was entirely through gaining possession of these Indian merchants that we were enabled to build up the influence that eventually resulted in our position. (Sir John Kirk giving evidence to the Sanderson Committee, 1910.)[19]

---

1 Zanzibar Archives AA1/68/326

2 Jeanette Hanby and David Bygott, *Kangas: 101 Uses*, 1984

3 Charles Guillain, *Documents sur l'Histoire, la Géographie et le Commerce de l'Afrique Orientale*, vol 3, Paris: A Bertrand, 1856, p 347. 'Most of the porcelain is of Chinese origin and comes almost entirely from Bombay, whose annual export of this commodity to the African coast is worth about 12,000 rupees.' Translation.

4 Judy Aldrick, 'The painted Plates of Zanzibar,' *Kenya Past & Present*, issue 29, 1997, p 26-7

5 O'Swald & Co was first established in Zanzibar in 1848.

6 Lutz J Schwidder, 'Das Hamburger Kolonialhandelshaus Wm O'Swald & Co und die Einfürung von "Techniken" in die Kolonien 1890-1914' PhD thesis, University of Hamburg, 2004, p 324

7 *Ibid.* p 332

8 *Ibid,* p 369, called 'Screw Brand Beer'

9 'In March 1887 the [British] Consul received from Smith Mackenzie a specific request that Messrs Lellanie and Peera Dewjie should immediately collect their goods, as the firm had only two godowns within the Custom House and further accommodation was needed with the approach of the rainy season.' Stephanie Jones, *Two centuries of Overseas Trading: The Origins and Growth of the Inchcape Group*, London: Macmillan in association with Business History Unit, University of London, 1986, p 121

10 Somerset Playne, comp, and Frank Holderness Gale, ed, *East Africa (British): its History, People, Commerce, Industries and Resources*, London: Foreign and Colonial Compiling and Publishing Co, 1908, p 109, 419-20. Only the major businesses are included.

11 Sir Jamsetjee Jeejeebhoy was chosen to represent the City of Bombay at the Coronation of Edward VII and was welcomed to London at a Grand Reception at the Hotel Cecil, possibly attended by Peera Dewjee. The listed guests included the Aga Khan, Sir John Kirk and Sir Charles Euan-Smith. *Zanzibar Gazette*, July 30, 1902.

12 Adamjee Jeevanjee was a famous Bohra merchant of Mombasa, who hosted Winston Churchill on his visit in 1907.

13 Information from Mumtaz Akberali. 'My grandmother was famously known as "Fatupira"…She and my mum were well known for making *kikuba*. A *kikuba* is a small bouquet of intricately designed rosettes which local women wear on their hair as an adornment. They were very popular during the wedding season, but sadly after my granny died the *kikuba* business stopped.' See website, Memories of Zanzibar: http://znzmumtaz.50webs.com/, date last accessed 17.1.15.

14 *Zanzibar Gazette*, July 9, 1902

15 Playne & Gale, *East Africa (British)*, p 419

16 Ann Edwards, *Throne of Gold: The Lives of the Aga Khans*, London: Harper Collins, 1995, p 61-2

17 *Zanzibar Gazette*, March 4, 1903

18 *Zanzibar Gazette*, August 31, 1904

19 As reported in Blanche Rocha D'Souza, *Harnessing the Trade Winds,* Nairobi: Zand Graphics, 2008, p 41

Index